Mastering Data Warehousing with Oracle SQL

Maxwell Vector

Contents

1

Chapter 1

Configuring the PL/SQL Development Environment for Analytics

Acquisition and Installation of Software Components

The initiation of a robust analytic framework necessitates the precise acquisition and installation of critical software components. Foremost among these is the Oracle Database, specifically the 19c release, whose rigorous system prerequisites demand an environment conforming to high availability and performance standards. An evaluation of hardware requirements, operating system compatibility, and network configurations forms the initial phase of this process. In parallel, the procurement of SQL Developer, an integrated development environment tailored for PL/SQL, is executed with careful attention to its alignment with the Oracle suite. The interdependency between these software components underscores the necessity for a meticulous installation procedure that eliminates discrepancies and ensures operational harmony.

Oracle Database Configuration and Optimization

Subsequent to installation, the Oracle Database undergoes a series of configuration steps designed to optimize its performance for analytic operations. This phase emphasizes the calibration of internal memory constructs such as the System Global Area (SGA) and Program Global Area (PGA), which are pivotal in managing intensive data processing tasks. Fine-tuning initialization parameters, along with the adjustment of session management and resource allocation directives, is carried out to facilitate efficient query execution and data retrieval. The configuration process is underscored by a methodical approach that integrates best practices from database performance tuning, thereby configuring a stable cornerstone for advanced PL/SQL analytic routines.

SQL Developer Environment Setup and Customization

The establishment of a proficient development environment is bolstered by the careful configuration of SQL Developer. This integrated tool is refined to interface seamlessly with the Oracle Database, providing a graphical medium for query development, debugging, and performance analysis. The process involves the systematic setup of connection protocols, preference adjustments, and layout customizations tailored to support the nuances of PL/SQL programming. Attention to detail in configuring the user interface and connectivity parameters assures that the dynamics between SQL Developer and the database are optimally synchronized, setting a firm foundation for subsequent analytic program development.

Integration of Supplementary Analytical Tools

In addition to the primary software components, the environment is further enhanced through the integration of auxiliary analytical tools and utilities. The inclusion of performance monitoring applications, version control systems, and data visualization interfaces serves to augment the analytical capabilities of the overall system. These supplementary components are selected based on their ability to integrate with standard Oracle tools and their support for high-volume data processing. Their configuration is conducted in congruence with the established Oracle Database and SQL Developer settings, thereby constructing an ecosystem that is both scalable and resilient.

Verification and Validation of the Configured Environment

A critical aspect of the environment setup is the rigorous verification and validation of all configured systems. This phase involves systematic connectivity tests, performance profiling, and consistency checks to confirm that the Oracle Database and associated tools are operating in unison. Methodical assessments are conducted to verify that key parameters have been correctly applied and that the integrated components maintain a seamless interaction. Such verification is essential to ensure that the environment is poised to support the demands of data analytics applications. The validation process is characterized by quantitative and qualitative analyses that confirm the operational stability and performance efficiency of the configured ecosystem.

Oracle 19c SQL Code Snippet

```
-- Create a table to store expected configuration parameters for
↪    performance tuning
CREATE TABLE DB_CONFIG_EXPECTED (
    PARAMETER_NAME  VARCHAR2(50),
    EXPECTED_VALUE  VARCHAR2(100)
);

-- Insert expected configuration values for key Oracle performance
↪    parameters
INSERT INTO DB_CONFIG_EXPECTED (PARAMETER_NAME, EXPECTED_VALUE)
↪    VALUES ('sga_target', '4G');
INSERT INTO DB_CONFIG_EXPECTED (PARAMETER_NAME, EXPECTED_VALUE)
↪    VALUES ('pga_aggregate_target', '1G');
INSERT INTO DB_CONFIG_EXPECTED (PARAMETER_NAME, EXPECTED_VALUE)
↪    VALUES ('db_cache_size', '2G');
COMMIT;
```

```
-------------------------------------------------------------------------
-- Create a table to capture actual configuration parameters from
↪   the instance
-------------------------------------------------------------------------

CREATE TABLE DB_CONFIG_ACTUAL (
    PARAMETER_NAME   VARCHAR2(50),
    ACTUAL_VALUE     VARCHAR2(100)
);

-- For demonstration, insert sample actual configuration values.
-- In a production environment, these values could be obtained from
↪   V$PARAMETER or V$SGAINFO views.
INSERT INTO DB_CONFIG_ACTUAL (PARAMETER_NAME, ACTUAL_VALUE) VALUES
↪   ('sga_target', '4G');
INSERT INTO DB_CONFIG_ACTUAL (PARAMETER_NAME, ACTUAL_VALUE) VALUES
↪   ('pga_aggregate_target', '900M');
INSERT INTO DB_CONFIG_ACTUAL (PARAMETER_NAME, ACTUAL_VALUE) VALUES
↪   ('db_cache_size', '2G');
COMMIT;


-------------------------------------------------------------------------
-- Function: Convert memory strings (e.g., '4G', '900M') to numeric
↪   values in MB
-------------------------------------------------------------------------

CREATE OR REPLACE FUNCTION convert_to_mb(mem_str VARCHAR2) RETURN
↪   NUMBER IS
    num_val NUMBER;
    unit    VARCHAR2(2);
BEGIN
    -- Extract numeric component
    num_val := TO_NUMBER(REGEXP_SUBSTR(mem_str, '^\d+'));
    -- Extract unit component (assumes format like 'G' or 'M')
    unit := UPPER(REGEXP_SUBSTR(mem_str, '[A-Z]+$'));
    IF unit = 'G' THEN
        RETURN num_val * 1024;
    ELSIF unit = 'M' THEN
        RETURN num_val;
    ELSE
        RETURN num_val; -- default fallback if unit is unrecognized
    END IF;
EXCEPTION
    WHEN OTHERS THEN
        RETURN 0;
END convert_to_mb;
/


-------------------------------------------------------------------------
-- Procedure: Validate DB Configuration by comparing actual vs.
↪   expected values
-------------------------------------------------------------------------
```

13

```
CREATE OR REPLACE PROCEDURE validate_db_configuration IS
    CURSOR c_config IS
        SELECT E.PARAMETER_NAME,
               E.EXPECTED_VALUE,
               A.ACTUAL_VALUE
          FROM DB_CONFIG_EXPECTED E
          LEFT JOIN DB_CONFIG_ACTUAL A
            ON E.PARAMETER_NAME = A.PARAMETER_NAME;
    v_exp_val_mb NUMBER;
    v_act_val_mb NUMBER;
BEGIN
    DBMS_OUTPUT.PUT_LINE('Database Configuration Validation
    ↪ Report:');
    FOR rec IN c_config LOOP
        v_exp_val_mb := convert_to_mb(rec.EXPECTED_VALUE);
        v_act_val_mb := convert_to_mb(rec.ACTUAL_VALUE);
        IF v_act_val_mb >= v_exp_val_mb THEN
            DBMS_OUTPUT.PUT_LINE('Parameter ' || rec.PARAMETER_NAME
                || ' is optimized: Expected ' || rec.EXPECTED_VALUE
                || ', Actual ' || rec.ACTUAL_VALUE);
        ELSE
            DBMS_OUTPUT.PUT_LINE('Parameter ' || rec.PARAMETER_NAME
                || ' is suboptimal: Expected ' || rec.EXPECTED_VALUE
                || ', Actual ' || rec.ACTUAL_VALUE);
        END IF;
    END LOOP;
END validate_db_configuration;
/

-- Execute the configuration validation procedure to check system
↪ settings
BEGIN
    validate_db_configuration;
END;
/

-------------------------------------------------------------------------
-- Algorithm: Calculate the Cache Hit Ratio from simulated buffer
↪ cache statistics
-------------------------------------------------------------------------

-- Create a table to simulate system statistics for buffer cache
CREATE TABLE DB_BUFFER_STATS (
    STAT_NAME    VARCHAR2(50),
    STAT_VALUE   NUMBER
);

-- Insert sample statistics data
INSERT INTO DB_BUFFER_STATS (STAT_NAME, STAT_VALUE) VALUES
↪ ('db_block_gets',   150000);
INSERT INTO DB_BUFFER_STATS (STAT_NAME, STAT_VALUE) VALUES
↪ ('consistent_gets', 500000);
```

14

```sql
INSERT INTO DB_BUFFER_STATS (STAT_NAME, STAT_VALUE) VALUES
↪ ('physical_reads',  20000);
COMMIT;

-- Create a view to compute cache hit ratio based on the formula:
-- Cache Hit Ratio = ((db_block_gets + consistent_gets) -
↪  physical_reads) / (db_block_gets + consistent_gets) * 100
CREATE OR REPLACE VIEW V_CACHE_HIT_RATIO AS
SELECT
    ( ( ( (db_block_gets + consistent_gets) - physical_reads )
      / (db_block_gets + consistent_gets) ) * 100 ) AS
        ↪ cache_hit_ratio
FROM
    (SELECT
        MAX(CASE WHEN STAT_NAME = 'db_block_gets' THEN STAT_VALUE
          ↪ END) AS db_block_gets,
        MAX(CASE WHEN STAT_NAME = 'consistent_gets' THEN STAT_VALUE
          ↪ END) AS consistent_gets,
        MAX(CASE WHEN STAT_NAME = 'physical_reads' THEN STAT_VALUE
          ↪ END) AS physical_reads
    FROM DB_BUFFER_STATS
    );

-- Query the cache hit ratio
SELECT * FROM V_CACHE_HIT_RATIO;

--------------------------------------------------------------------
-- Dynamic SQL: Procedure to compute a weighted total memory
↪  allocation and compare against a threshold
--------------------------------------------------------------------

CREATE OR REPLACE PROCEDURE
↪ calc_weighted_memory_allocation(p_threshold_mb NUMBER) IS
    v_total_memory NUMBER;
BEGIN
    SELECT SUM(convert_to_mb(ACTUAL_VALUE))
      INTO v_total_memory
      FROM DB_CONFIG_ACTUAL;

    IF v_total_memory > p_threshold_mb THEN
        DBMS_OUTPUT.PUT_LINE('Total memory allocated: ' ||
          ↪ v_total_memory
          || ' MB exceeds the threshold of ' || p_threshold_mb || '
          ↪ MB.');
    ELSE
        DBMS_OUTPUT.PUT_LINE('Total memory allocated: ' ||
          ↪ v_total_memory
          || ' MB is within acceptable limits.');
    END IF;
END calc_weighted_memory_allocation;
/
```

```
-- Execute the dynamic memory allocation check procedure with a
↪  specified threshold (e.g., 6000 MB)
BEGIN
    calc_weighted_memory_allocation(6000);
END;
/
```

Multiple Choice Questions

1. In setting up the PL/SQL development environment for analytics, why is it critical to acquire both Oracle Database 19c and SQL Developer together?

   (a) Because each can be installed on entirely different systems without affecting functionality.

   (b) Because SQL Developer provides an independent interface that replaces the Oracle Database.

   (c) Because a synchronized installation ensures the integrated tools communicate seamlessly, thereby providing a robust and unified platform for data analytics.

   (d) Because neither requires any further configuration after installation.

2. What is the primary rationale behind calibrating the System Global Area (SGA) and Program Global Area (PGA) during Oracle Database configuration for analytics?

   (a) To improve the graphical user interface performance in SQL Developer.

   (b) To allocate sufficient memory resources for intensive data processing and optimize query execution.

   (c) To reduce the need for supplementary software tools.

   (d) To ensure that network configurations are bypassed during query execution.

3. Which aspect of SQL Developer customization is most vital for PL/SQL analytics development?

   (a) Adjusting the color scheme and font sizes solely for aesthetic purposes.

(b) Configuring connection protocols, layout settings, and debugging tools to streamline query development and performance analysis.

(c) Installing additional plugins that have no direct integration with Oracle Database.

(d) Disabling all non-essential features to simplify the user interface.

4. The integration of supplementary analytical tools into the PL/SQL environment primarily serves to:

(a) Replace the need for Oracle Database and SQL Developer entirely.

(b) Introduce additional software that functions independently without any need for interoperability.

(c) Augment the core environment by providing enhanced monitoring, version control, and data visualization capabilities, which together improve the overall analytical workflow.

(d) Complicate the system setup by introducing redundant features.

5. Which of the following best describes the purpose of the verification and validation phase after configuring the PL/SQL analytics environment?

(a) To confirm that only the Oracle Database has been installed correctly.

(b) To check that supplementary analytical tools are the only components functioning as expected.

(c) To perform systematic connectivity tests, performance profiling, and consistency checks, ensuring all integrated components operate harmoniously.

(d) To solely verify that SQL Developer is connected to the internet.

6. During the Oracle Database configuration process, which parameter adjustments are most directly related to enhancing data processing efficiency in analytics?

(a) Fine-tuning user interface elements and graphical themes.

(b) Calibrating memory structures such as the SGA and PGA to optimize internal resource allocation.

(c) Modifying the layout of SQL Developer's workspace.

(d) Adjusting the hardware specifications of the host machine.

7. In the context of establishing the PL/SQL development environment, which of the following activities does NOT pertain directly to SQL Developer customization?

(a) Setting up connection protocols to interface with Oracle Database.

(b) Configuring layout, preferences, and debugging features within SQL Developer.

(c) Tuning the Oracle Database's memory parameters like SGA and PGA.

(d) Customizing the SQL Developer interface to support efficient query development.

Answers:

1. **C:** Because a synchronized installation ensures the integrated tools communicate seamlessly, thereby providing a robust and unified platform for data analytics. This answer underlines the importance of cohesive software integration to avoid configuration mismatches and to build a reliable analytic framework.

2. **B:** To allocate sufficient memory resources for intensive data processing and optimize query execution. Adjusting the SGA and PGA is essential to handle the heavy data processing demands typical in analytics applications, ensuring optimal performance and efficient memory utilization.

3. **B:** Configuring connection protocols, layout settings, and debugging tools to streamline query development and performance analysis. Effective customization of SQL Developer enhances the development workflow, making it easier to develop, debug, and analyze PL/SQL code within the analytics environment.

4. **C:** Augment the core environment by providing enhanced monitoring, version control, and data visualization capabilities, which together improve the overall analytical workflow. Supplementary analytical tools enrich the capabilities of the primary environment by adding layers of monitoring, visualization, and source control that aid in comprehensive data analysis.

5. **C:** To perform systematic connectivity tests, performance profiling, and consistency checks, ensuring all integrated components operate harmoniously. Verification and validation are critical to certify that the entire setup—from the Oracle Database to SQL Developer and any supplementary tools—works as intended in a coordinated manner.

6. **B:** Calibrating memory structures such as the SGA and PGA to optimize internal resource allocation. Fine-tuning these memory parameters directly impacts the ability of the Oracle Database to manage large volumes of data and execute complex queries efficiently.

7. **C:** Tuning the Oracle Database's memory parameters like SGA and PGA. Although crucial for overall performance, modifying memory parameters is part of Oracle Database configuration, not SQL Developer customization, which focuses on interface and connectivity settings.

Chapter 2

Fundamentals of PL/SQL Syntax and Structure

PL/SQL Block Structure

The fundamental architecture of PL/SQL is embodied by its block structure. A PL/SQL block is a self-contained unit that encapsulates declarations, execution statements, and exception handling clauses. Each block begins with an optional declarative section, followed by the executable section encapsulated by the *BEGIN* and *END* keywords, and may conclude with an exception-handling section for runtime anomalies. This structured approach promotes localized scope, enabling nested blocks to be embedded within one another for modular design. The design of the block structure adheres to principles of clarity and modularity, thus facilitating rigorous control over variable visibility and execution flow.

Declaration Section: Variables, Constants, and Data Structures

Within the declarative portion of a PL/SQL block, identifiers are introduced and assigned data types that conform to the language's comprehensive type system. Variables, constants, and user-defined data structures are declared to serve as the foundational elements for subsequent computations and logical operations. The declarations are meticulously defined to ensure consistency in type usage and to maintain semantic correctness throughout the program's execution. The explicit declaration of these elements enables the compiler to perform stringent type checking and optimize memory allocation, thereby reinforcing the integrity of the programming environment.

Executable Section and Statement Execution

The executable section of a PL/SQL block, demarcated by the *BEGIN* and *END* delimiters, is the locus of the operational logic. This segment of the block encompasses a sequence of statements that are evaluated and executed in a defined order. The structure supports sequential processing, where each instruction is executed as written, and it also accommodates nested blocks that may independently manage their own execution flows. The explicit separation of the executable section from the declarative and exception-handling sections contributes to a clear delineation between data definition and program logic, thereby enhancing the maintainability and readability of the code.

Control Flow Constructs in PL/SQL

Control flow constructs in PL/SQL enable conditional decision-making and routine iteration within the procedural framework. Conditional constructs, such as the IF-THEN-ELSE and CASE statements, provide mechanisms for evaluating boolean expressions and directing the execution path based on these evaluations. Similarly, iterative constructs—including loops of various forms like the FOR loop, WHILE loop, and unconditional loops—allow for the repetitive execution of code blocks under predetermined conditions. These constructs collectively empower the programmer to implement complex algorithms and handle dynamic data scenarios with precision. The rigorous structure of control flow elements ensures that logical operations are executed reliably within the well-defined boundaries of each block.

Oracle 19c SQL Code Snippet

```sql
-- Create a table to store financial inputs and computed compound
--   interest amounts

CREATE TABLE FINANCIAL_CALCULATIONS (
    CALC_ID    NUMBER GENERATED BY DEFAULT AS IDENTITY,
    PRINCIPAL  NUMBER,
    RATE       NUMBER,
    PERIODS    NUMBER,
    AMOUNT     NUMBER,
    CALC_DATE  DATE DEFAULT SYSDATE,
    CONSTRAINT FINANCIAL_CALC_PK PRIMARY KEY (CALC_ID)
);


-- Insert sample data into FINANCIAL_CALCULATIONS

INSERT ALL
    INTO FINANCIAL_CALCULATIONS (PRINCIPAL, RATE, PERIODS)
        VALUES (1000, 0.05, 10)
    INTO FINANCIAL_CALCULATIONS (PRINCIPAL, RATE, PERIODS)
        VALUES (5000, 0.03, 5)
SELECT * FROM DUAL;
COMMIT;


-- Create a function to calculate compound interest using an
--   iterative method.
-- The compound interest formula: A = P * (1 + r)^n
-- Here, we simulate the exponentiation by multiplying the amount
--   repeatedly.

CREATE OR REPLACE FUNCTION calc_compound_interest(
    p_principal IN NUMBER,
    p_rate      IN NUMBER,
    p_periods   IN NUMBER
) RETURN NUMBER IS
    l_amount   NUMBER := p_principal;
    l_counter  NUMBER := 0;
BEGIN
    IF p_principal < 0 OR p_rate < 0 OR p_periods < 0 THEN
        RAISE_APPLICATION_ERROR(-20001, 'Invalid input. Values must
            be non-negative.');
    END IF;

    WHILE l_counter < p_periods LOOP
        l_amount := l_amount * (1 + p_rate);
        l_counter := l_counter + 1;
    END LOOP;
```

```
        RETURN l_amount;
EXCEPTION
    WHEN OTHERS THEN
        RAISE;
END calc_compound_interest;
/


-----------------------------------------------------------------
-- Create a stored procedure to update the FINANCIAL_CALCULATIONS
↪  table by
-- computing the compound interest for each row and storing the
↪  result.
-----------------------------------------------------------------
CREATE OR REPLACE PROCEDURE update_compound_interest IS
BEGIN
    UPDATE FINANCIAL_CALCULATIONS
    SET AMOUNT = calc_compound_interest(PRINCIPAL, RATE, PERIODS);
    COMMIT;
EXCEPTION
    WHEN OTHERS THEN
        ROLLBACK;
        RAISE;
END update_compound_interest;
/


-----------------------------------------------------------------
-- Execute the procedure to compute compound interest values
-----------------------------------------------------------------
BEGIN
    update_compound_interest;
END;
/


-----------------------------------------------------------------
-- Query the table to view the calculated compound interest results
-----------------------------------------------------------------
SELECT CALC_ID, PRINCIPAL, RATE, PERIODS, AMOUNT, CALC_DATE
FROM FINANCIAL_CALCULATIONS;


-----------------------------------------------------------------
-- Additional Demonstration: Using PL/SQL control flow constructs to
↪  output
-- the compound interest computation for given inputs.
-----------------------------------------------------------------
DECLARE
    v_principal NUMBER := 2000;
    v_rate      NUMBER := 0.04;
    v_periods   NUMBER := 7;
    v_amount    NUMBER;
BEGIN
    v_amount := calc_compound_interest(v_principal, v_rate,
    ↪  v_periods);
```

```
    IF v_amount > 0 THEN
        DBMS_OUTPUT.PUT_LINE('For Principal = ' || v_principal || ',
        ↪  Rate = ' || v_rate ||
                             ', Periods = ' || v_periods ||
                             ', the compounded Amount = ' ||
                             ↪  v_amount);
    ELSE
        DBMS_OUTPUT.PUT_LINE('Calculation resulted in a non-positive
        ↪  amount.');
    END IF;
EXCEPTION
    WHEN OTHERS THEN
        DBMS_OUTPUT.PUT_LINE('Error in compound interest
        ↪  calculation: ' || SQLERRM);
END;
/


-------------------------------------------------------------------------
-- Demonstration of a recursive algorithm: Factorial Calculation
-- This illustrates the use of functions, recursion, and exception
↪  handling.
-------------------------------------------------------------------------
CREATE OR REPLACE FUNCTION factorial(n IN NUMBER) RETURN NUMBER IS
BEGIN
    IF n < 0 THEN
        RAISE_APPLICATION_ERROR(-20002, 'Factorial is not defined
        ↪  for negative numbers.');
    ELSIF n = 0 THEN
        RETURN 1;
    ELSE
        RETURN n * factorial(n - 1);
    END IF;
EXCEPTION
    WHEN OTHERS THEN
        RAISE;
END factorial;
/


-------------------------------------------------------------------------
-- Test the recursive factorial function
-------------------------------------------------------------------------
DECLARE
    v_number NUMBER := 5;
    v_fact   NUMBER;
BEGIN
    v_fact := factorial(v_number);
    DBMS_OUTPUT.PUT_LINE('Factorial of ' || v_number || ' is ' ||
    ↪  v_fact);
EXCEPTION
    WHEN OTHERS THEN
        DBMS_OUTPUT.PUT_LINE('Error calculating factorial: ' ||
        ↪  SQLERRM);
END;
```

24

Multiple Choice Questions

1. Which of the following accurately describes the standard structure of a PL/SQL block?

   (a) An entirely executable script with no declarations.

   (b) Only a declarative section and a control clause.

   (c) A declarative section, an executable section (demarcated by BEGIN and END), and an optional exception-handling section.

   (d) A set of stand-alone SQL commands.

2. What is the primary purpose of the declaration section in a PL/SQL block?

   (a) To execute SQL queries.

   (b) To manage exception handling.

   (c) To declare variables, constants, and user-defined data structures for subsequent use.

   (d) To define iterative control flows.

3. Which keywords are used to delimit the executable portion of a PL/SQL block?

   (a) DECLARE and END.

   (b) BEGIN and END.

   (c) START and FINISH.

   (d) EXECUTE and COMPLETE.

4. Which control flow construct in PL/SQL is specifically designed for iterative operations?

   (a) IF-THEN-ELSE statements.

   (b) CASE expressions.

   (c) LOOP constructs (e.g., FOR, WHILE, or unconditional LOOP).

   (d) RAISE statements.

5. What advantage is provided by the nested block structure within PL/SQL?

    (a) It allows sharing of global variables across different blocks.

    (b) It simplifies the dependency on external SQL queries.

    (c) It enables local scoping of variables, promoting modularity and encapsulation.

    (d) It automatically parallelizes code execution for enhanced performance.

6. How does the separation between declarative and executable sections improve code maintainability in PL/SQL?

    (a) It ensures that all variables are pre-initialized.

    (b) It facilitates compile-time type checking and memory optimization while providing clear demarcation between data definitions and operational logic.

    (c) It combines data declaration with runtime error handling.

    (d) It reduces the need for explicit control flow constructs.

7. Which of the following best characterizes the role of control flow constructs in PL/SQL?

    (a) They are used solely for declaring and initializing variables.

    (b) They provide mechanisms for conditional decision-making and iterative processing, thereby enabling dynamic execution paths.

    (c) They serve only to catch and handle exceptions.

    (d) They act as a front-end interface for database connectivity.

Answers:

1. **C:** A standard PL/SQL block comprises a declarative section where variables and data structures are defined, an executable section delimited by BEGIN and END which contains the operational logic, and optionally an exception-handling section to manage runtime errors. This modular breakdown enforces clear separation of concerns.

2. **C:** The declaration section's primary role is to introduce variables, constants, and user-defined data structures. This not only provides the necessary elements for computation but also allows the compiler to enforce type checking and manage memory allocation efficiently.

3. **B:** The executable portion of a PL/SQL block is clearly defined by the BEGIN and END keywords. This encapsulation distinguishes procedural logic from the declarative definitions and optional exception-handling mechanisms.

4. **C:** Iterative operations in PL/SQL are implemented via loop constructs such as FOR loops, WHILE loops, or unconditional LOOPs. These repeated execution structures are central to processing collections or performing repetitive tasks.

5. **C:** Nesting PL/SQL blocks allows for local scoping of variables, meaning that identifiers declared within an inner block are not visible outside it. This encapsulation enhances modularity, reduces potential naming conflicts, and improves overall code manageability.

6. **B:** The clear separation of declarative and executable sections aids in compiling and maintaining the code by enabling rigorous type checking and memory optimization. It also delineates where data is defined versus where it is manipulated, thereby enhancing readability and maintenance.

7. **B:** Control flow constructs such as IF-THEN-ELSE, CASE statements, and various forms of loops provide the mechanisms for decision-making and repetitive processing. These constructs allow the PL/SQL program to dynamically choose execution paths based on runtime conditions.

Chapter 3

Working with Scalar Data Types and Operators

Scalar Data Types in PL/SQL

PL/SQL, as an extension of the SQL language for procedural operations, relies fundamentally on scalar data types as the atomic units of data representation. These types, which include numeric, character, and date/time categories, serve as the essential building blocks for the formulation and evaluation of analytical expressions. The use of scalar data types in PL/SQL is characterized by an emphasis on precision, flexibility, and adherence to rigorous type constraints. The intrinsic design of these types ensures predictable behavior in mathematical and logical computations, thus underpinning the correctness of complex analytical operations.

1 Numeric Data Types

Numeric data types in PL/SQL are central to performing arithmetic computations and quantitative analyses. The principal numeric data type permits the representation of both integer and floating-point values with a high degree of precision. This flexibility accommodates a broad spectrum of applications ranging from simple additive operations to intricate computations involving exponentiation and division. The underlying representation provides support for scientific notation and variable precision, where the significance of each digit and the position of the decimal point are rigorously maintained. The capacity for explicit declaration of precision and scale serves to guard against the propagation of rounding errors and overflow, thereby ensuring that numerical analyses adhere to stringent computational standards.

2 Character Data Types

Character data types in PL/SQL are devised to handle textual information of varying lengths, offering both fixed-length and variable-length representations. These types support a wide array of operations for manipulation, comparison, and concatenation of character sequences. The design incorporates considerations for character set encoding and collation, which are critical for maintaining the integrity of data in environments where multi-byte characters are prevalent. Character types allow for the precise definition of storage size and format, thereby enabling the accurate modeling of both nominal and descriptive attributes in analytical contexts. Their seamless integration into broader analytical expressions ensures that textual data can be combined with numeric and date/time information in compound expressions without compromising semantic consistency.

3 Date and Time Data Types

Date and time data types within PL/SQL provide specialized facilities for the representation and manipulation of temporal information. These types encapsulate both calendar dates and time components with predefined formats, which facilitate the execution of time-based computations and interval arithmetic. The intrinsic ability to perform operations such as date subtraction and interval addition is pivotal in analytical scenarios where temporal trends and periodic patterns must be quantified. The standardized representation of date and time values ensures that chronological data is stored, retrieved, and compared with high accuracy, thereby supporting a range of statistical and analytical functions that rely on temporal ordering and interval measurements.

Operators in PL/SQL

The operators available in PL/SQL constitute a comprehensive suite of symbols and keywords that enable the formulation of expressions which manipulate scalar data types. These operators can be grouped into several fundamental categories, each designed to perform specific classes of operations such as arithmetic computation, logical decision-making, and data concatenation.

1 Arithmetic Operators

Arithmetic operators in PL/SQL provide the mechanism for performing mathematical calculations on numeric data types. The fundamental symbols, including the addition operator ($+$), subtraction operator ($-$), multiplication operator ($*$), and division operator ($/$), each obey well-defined algebraic properties. These operators are applied in a manner consistent with conventional arithmetic rules, ensuring that expressions are evaluated in a deterministic, left-to-right fashion unless overridden by the use of explicit grouping with parentheses. Particular attention is given to the treatment of division operations, where the possibility of division by zero is mitigated by the language's inbuilt error-handling constructs. The arithmetic operators, when applied to expressions involving numeric operands, yield results that preserve the integrity of the underlying precision and scale attributes defined by the data type declarations.

2 Relational Operators

Relational operators in PL/SQL are employed to compare scalar values, producing boolean outcomes that serve as the basis for conditional logic and control flow decisions. The standard relational operators include equality ($=$), inequality ($\neq$ or $<>$), less-than ($<$), greater-than ($>$), less-than-or-equal-to ($\leq$), and greater-than-or-equal-to ($\geq$). These operators are defined to operate on compatible scalar data types, ensuring that comparisons between numeric, character, or date/time values adhere to a consistent set of semantic rules. The evaluation of relational expressions is integral to the formulation of predicates in conditional statements and loop constructs, thus facilitating precise control over program execution based on the outcome of these comparisons.

3 Logical Operators

Logical operators in PL/SQL are instrumental in the composition of compound conditional expressions that dictate decision-making processes within procedural logic. Operators such as AND, OR, and NOT allow for the combination, inversion, and evaluation of simple relational predicates into more complex boolean expressions. The logical conjunction (AND) operator is used to require the simultaneous satisfaction of multiple conditions, while the disjunction (OR) operator permits flexibility by evaluating to true if any one of a set of conditions is met. The negation operator (NOT) inverts the truth value of a given condition. These operators, when coupled with relational expressions, enable the construction of sophisticated filtering criteria and branching statements that are central to analytical computations.

4 String Concatenation and Date Arithmetic Operators

In addition to the aforementioned categories, PL/SQL supports operators that are specialized for the manipulation of character and date/time data types. The string concatenation operator ($\|$) facilitates the joining of two or more character expressions into a single unified string. This operator is essential in constructing composite textual outputs and is frequently used in the generation of dynamic, human-readable messages or identifiers within analytical routines. Furthermore, date arithmetic in PL/SQL is performed using operators that allow for the direct subtraction and addition of date values. Such operations yield interval measurements or adjusted date values, respectively, thereby enabling temporal calculations that underscore many analytical methodologies inherent to data-centric applications.

Oracle 19c SQL Code Snippet

```
-- Create a sample table to illustrate scalar data types and
↪   operations
CREATE TABLE SCALAR_DATA (
    ID          NUMBER GENERATED BY DEFAULT AS IDENTITY,
    NUM_VALUE   NUMBER(10,2),
    TEXT_VALUE  VARCHAR2(100),
```

```
    EVENT_DATE  DATE,
    CONSTRAINT SCALAR_DATA_PK PRIMARY KEY (ID)
);

-- Insert sample data into SCALAR_DATA
INSERT ALL
    INTO SCALAR_DATA (NUM_VALUE, TEXT_VALUE, EVENT_DATE)
        VALUES (123.45, 'Initial Value', DATE '2023-10-01')
    INTO SCALAR_DATA (NUM_VALUE, TEXT_VALUE, EVENT_DATE)
        VALUES (678.90, 'Second Entry', DATE '2023-10-05')
    INTO SCALAR_DATA (NUM_VALUE, TEXT_VALUE, EVENT_DATE)
        VALUES (101.11, 'Third Data', DATE '2023-10-10')
SELECT * FROM DUAL;
COMMIT;


-------------------------------------------------------------------------
-- Example 1: Function to Compute a Discounted Value
-- Formula: discounted_value = original_value - (original_value *
↪    discount_rate)
-------------------------------------------------------------------------
CREATE OR REPLACE FUNCTION compute_discounted_value (
    p_original_value NUMBER,
    p_discount_rate  NUMBER
) RETURN NUMBER IS
    v_discounted NUMBER;
BEGIN
    v_discounted := p_original_value - (p_original_value *
    ↪  p_discount_rate);
    RETURN v_discounted;
EXCEPTION
    WHEN OTHERS THEN
        RETURN NULL;
END compute_discounted_value;
/


-------------------------------------------------------------------------
-- Example 2: Procedure to Update TEXT_VALUE Based on NUM_VALUE
↪    Conditions
-- Demonstrates the use of relational and logical operators as well
↪    as string concatenation.
-------------------------------------------------------------------------
CREATE OR REPLACE PROCEDURE update_text_based_on_num IS
BEGIN
    UPDATE SCALAR_DATA
       SET TEXT_VALUE = TEXT_VALUE || ' - Updated'
     WHERE NUM_VALUE > 100 AND NUM_VALUE < 700;

    COMMIT;
EXCEPTION
    WHEN OTHERS THEN
        ROLLBACK;
        RAISE;
END update_text_based_on_num;
```

```
/
-------------------------------------------------------------------------
-- Example 3: PL/SQL Block Showcasing Date Arithmetic and Exception
↪  Handling
-- This block adds 15 days to an EVENT_DATE and outputs both the
↪  current and future dates.
-------------------------------------------------------------------------
DECLARE
    v_current_date DATE;
    v_future_date  DATE;
BEGIN
    SELECT EVENT_DATE
      INTO v_current_date
      FROM SCALAR_DATA
     WHERE ID = 1;

    -- Date arithmetic: add 15 days to the current event date
    v_future_date := v_current_date + 15;

    DBMS_OUTPUT.PUT_LINE('Current Date: ' || TO_CHAR(v_current_date,
    ↪  'YYYY-MM-DD'));
    DBMS_OUTPUT.PUT_LINE('Future Date : ' || TO_CHAR(v_future_date,
    ↪  'YYYY-MM-DD'));
EXCEPTION
    WHEN NO_DATA_FOUND THEN
        DBMS_OUTPUT.PUT_LINE('No record found with ID = 1.');
    WHEN OTHERS THEN
        DBMS_OUTPUT.PUT_LINE('Error: ' || SQLERRM);
END;
/


-------------------------------------------------------------------------
-- Example 4: Function to Calculate a Weighted Average of NUM_VALUE
-- Algorithm:
--    1. Use a cursor to iterate over each row in SCALAR_DATA.
--    2. Multiply NUM_VALUE by a weight factor (assumed 1 for
↪  simplicity).
--    3. Compute the weighted average using the formula:
--       weighted_average = (SUM(value * weight)) / (SUM(weights))
-------------------------------------------------------------------------
CREATE OR REPLACE FUNCTION calculate_weighted_average RETURN NUMBER
↪  IS
    CURSOR cur_data IS
        SELECT NUM_VALUE FROM SCALAR_DATA;
    v_total NUMBER := 0;
    v_count NUMBER := 0;
    v_weight NUMBER := 1; -- uniform weight for demonstration
BEGIN
    FOR rec IN cur_data LOOP
        v_total := v_total + (rec.NUM_VALUE * v_weight);
        v_count := v_count + v_weight;
    END LOOP;
```

```
    IF v_count = 0 THEN
        RETURN 0;
    ELSE
        RETURN v_total / v_count;
    END IF;
EXCEPTION
    WHEN OTHERS THEN
        RETURN NULL;
END calculate_weighted_average;
/
```

-- *Execute the update procedure to modify text based on numeric*
↪ *conditions*

```
BEGIN
    update_text_based_on_num;
END;
/
```

-- *Demonstrate the computation of a discounted value using the*
↪ *compute_discounted_value function*

```
DECLARE
    v_original      NUMBER := 500;
    v_discount_rate NUMBER := 0.15;  -- 15% discount
    v_discounted    NUMBER;
BEGIN
    v_discounted := compute_discounted_value(v_original,
    ↪ v_discount_rate);
    DBMS_OUTPUT.PUT_LINE('Original Value  : ' || v_original);
    DBMS_OUTPUT.PUT_LINE('Discounted Value: ' || v_discounted);
END;
/
```

-- *Execute the function to compute and display the weighted average*
↪ *of NUM_VALUE*

```
DECLARE
    v_weighted_avg NUMBER;
BEGIN
    v_weighted_avg := calculate_weighted_average;
    DBMS_OUTPUT.PUT_LINE('Weighted Average of NUM_VALUE: ' ||
    ↪ v_weighted_avg);
END;
/
```

Multiple Choice Questions

1. Which of the following best describes the role of scalar data types in PL/SQL for data analytics?

   (a) They serve as composite structures for aggregating complex data sets.

   (b) They provide the fundamental atomic units of data representation with strict type constraints.

   (c) They facilitate direct manipulation of file system objects.

   (d) They are used solely for dynamic SQL generation.

2. In the context of PL/SQL numeric data types, explicitly declaring precision and scale is most important for:

   (a) Enhancing the visual presentation of numeric output.

   (b) Preventing rounding errors and mitigating the risk of numerical overflow.

   (c) Enabling automated conversion of numbers to text.

   (d) Enforcing locale-specific numeric formatting.

3. Which of the following is an advantage of using PL/SQL's character data types for managing textual data?

   (a) They provide built-in arithmetic capabilities for numeric computations.

   (b) They allow precise definition of storage size and support various character set encodings.

   (c) They automatically convert text to date/time values when necessary.

   (d) They enable direct indexing on binary data.

4. PL/SQL date and time data types primarily support analytic computations by:

   (a) Allowing direct conversion of date values into numeric timestamps.

   (b) Facilitating date arithmetic—such as subtraction—to yield precise interval measurements.

    (c) Automatically synchronizing date values across different time zones.

    (d) Concatenating date values into formatted text strings.

5. Which operator is used in PL/SQL to concatenate string (character) expressions?

    (a) The plus (+) operator.

    (b) The concatenation (||) operator.

    (c) The ampersand () operator.

    (d) The percent (

6. Which set of relational operators is correctly supported in PL/SQL for comparing scalar values?

    (a) ==, !=, <, >

    (b) =, <>, <=, >=, <, >

    (c) =, not=, <, >

    (d) ===, !==, <=, >=

7. Logical operators in PL/SQL, such as AND, OR, and NOT, primarily serve to:

    (a) Perform arithmetic computations on numeric data types.

    (b) Combine simple relational predicates into compound boolean expressions to control the flow of execution.

    (c) Concatenate multiple character strings into a single unified expression.

    (d) Directly index and retrieve data from tables.

Answers:

1. **B: They provide the fundamental atomic units of data representation with strict type constraints.**
Scalar data types in PL/SQL represent the simplest forms of data—numeric, character, and date/time—that ensure precise, predictable behavior in analytic operations, which is central to robust data processing.

2. **B: Preventing rounding errors and mitigating the risk of numerical overflow.**
Explicitly declaring precision and scale ensures that numerical computations maintain the intended accuracy and limits, crucial for high-integrity analytic calculations.

3. **B: They allow precise definition of storage size and support various character set encodings.**
Character data types in PL/SQL enable the accurate modeling of textual data by specifying storage requirements and handling diverse character encodings, which is essential when processing multi-byte and locale-sensitive strings.

4. **B: Facilitating date arithmetic—such as subtraction—to yield precise interval measurements.**
The built-in support for date arithmetic in PL/SQL allows operations such as subtracting two dates to compute intervals, a key functionality for temporal analyses in data analytics.

5. **B: The concatenation (||) operator.**
PL/SQL employs the || operator for string concatenation, seamlessly combining multiple character expressions into a single string, which is invaluable in constructing dynamic textual outputs.

6. **B: =, <>, <=, >=, <, >**
These are the standard relational operators in PL/SQL used for comparing scalar values, forming the basis of conditional expressions and decision-making constructs.

7. **B: Combine simple relational predicates into compound boolean expressions to control the flow of execution.**
Logical operators (AND, OR, NOT) are used to construct complex boolean expressions from basic relational predicates, allowing sophisticated conditional logic essential for controlling program execution.

Chapter 4

Composite Data Types: Records and Collections

Records

Records in PL/SQL embody a composite structure that amalgamates disparate scalar elements into a single, unified data construct. This mechanism permits the definition of a structured type wherein each constituent, called a field, is explicitly associated with a particular scalar data type. The formal specification of record types mandates the explicit declaration of field names and their corresponding data types, thereby yielding a statically typed aggregate that enforces both type safety and semantic coherence. The structural integrity provided by records echoes the theoretical notion of tuples in formal data models, where elements are combined into a single entity for purposes of grouped data manipulation and analytical evaluation. In analytical contexts, the systematic grouping achieved through records enables the representation of complex entities, ensuring that related attributes can be processed collectively with precision and efficiency.

Collections

Collections extend the paradigm of composite data types by serving as aggregators of multiple elements, each drawn from a common data type. The design of collections is predicated on the need to manipulate variable-length data sets, which are integral to comprehensive analysis tasks. Within PL/SQL, the implementation of collections encompasses several distinct constructs that differ primarily in their storage characteristics, indexing strategies, and operational semantics.

1 Arrays

Arrays represent a sequential collection in which the elements are stored in an ordered manner and are accessible via numeric indices. The array construct is characterized by its reliance on contiguous logical positioning, thereby facilitating direct element access with computational complexity approaching $O(1)$ under ideal conditions. The inherent sequential ordering of arrays makes them particularly suitable for scenarios that require iterative traversals and ordered processing of data elements. The explicit declaration of an array's bounds ensures that the size and capacity of the collection are rigorously defined, which in turn assists in the management of memory resources and in the enforcement of boundary constraints during analytical operations.

2 Nested Tables

Nested tables offer an alternative approach to collection management by dispensing with the requirement for contiguous storage. Unlike arrays, nested tables are inherently dynamic and allow for the flexible manipulation of data sets whose cardinality may vary over time. The architecture of nested tables supports operations that are analogous to set-based manipulations, permitting the aggregation, union, and other relational operations to be performed directly on the collection. This dynamic behavior renders nested tables exceptionally adept at modeling one-to-many relationships, where a single element in a parent context is associated with an arbitrarily large collection of subordinate elements. The conceptual framework underpinning nested tables is strongly aligned with mathematical notions of sets and multisets, thereby affording a robust model for the management of complex, variable-sized data sets in analytical procedures.

3 Associative Arrays

Associative arrays, also known as index-by tables, adopt a key-based indexing system that distinguishes them from conventional sequential arrays. In associative arrays, elements are identified not by sequential integer indices but by unique keys that may be drawn from non-numeric domains. This key-value mapping mechanism is analogous to mathematical functions wherein each key is uniquely associated with a corresponding value, thus facilitating efficient lookup, insertion, and deletion operations. The absence of reliance on contiguous storage endows associative arrays with significant flexibility, particularly in contexts where the index set is sparse or non-sequential. The efficiency of associative arrays in performing key-based searches underpins their utility in analytical applications, where the rapid retrieval of specific data points from large and heterogeneous data sets is paramount.

Oracle 19c SQL Code Snippet

```
-- Create an object type to represent a composite record for
↪   analytical metrics.
CREATE OR REPLACE TYPE analytic_record AS OBJECT (
    analysis_id    NUMBER,
    metric_name    VARCHAR2(50),
    metric_value   NUMBER,
    analysis_date  DATE
);
/

-- Create a nested table type based on the analytic_record object.
CREATE OR REPLACE TYPE analytic_record_nt AS TABLE OF
↪   analytic_record;
/

-- Create a table that uses a nested table column to store sets of
↪   analytic_records.
CREATE TABLE analytics_summary (
    summary_id    NUMBER GENERATED BY DEFAULT AS IDENTITY,
    summary_date  DATE,
    records       analytic_record_nt
)
NESTED TABLE records STORE AS analytics_records_nt;
/
```

```
-- Insert sample data into analytics_summary using the nested table
↪  constructor.
INSERT INTO analytics_summary (summary_date, records)
VALUES (
    SYSDATE,
    analytic_record_nt(
        analytic_record(1, 'MetricA', 100, SYSDATE),
        analytic_record(2, 'MetricB', 200, SYSDATE),
        analytic_record(3, 'MetricC', 300, SYSDATE)
    )
);
COMMIT;


-------------------------------------------------------------------------
-- SQL Query: Extract and display individual records from the nested
↪  table column.
-------------------------------------------------------------------------
SELECT a.summary_id,
       a.summary_date,
       r.analysis_id,
       r.metric_name,
       r.metric_value,
       r.analysis_date
FROM analytics_summary a,
     TABLE(a.records) r
WHERE a.summary_id = 1;


-------------------------------------------------------------------------
-- PL/SQL Block: Demonstrate processing of an associative array
↪  (index-by table)
-- for analytic metric aggregation.
-------------------------------------------------------------------------
DECLARE
    -- Define an associative array with VARCHAR2 keys to hold
    ↪  numeric metric values.
    TYPE metrics_assoc_array IS TABLE OF NUMBER INDEX BY
    ↪  VARCHAR2(30);
    v_metrics metrics_assoc_array;
    v_total   NUMBER := 0;
    key       VARCHAR2(30);
BEGIN
    -- Initialize the associative array with sample metric values.
    v_metrics('MetricA') := 100;
    v_metrics('MetricB') := 200;
    v_metrics('MetricC') := 300;

    -- Iterate over the associative array to compute the total
    ↪  metric value.
    key := v_metrics.FIRST;
    WHILE key IS NOT NULL LOOP
        v_total := v_total + v_metrics(key);
        key := v_metrics.NEXT(key);
    END LOOP;
```

41

```
    DBMS_OUTPUT.PUT_LINE('Total Analytical Metric from Associative
    ↪  Array: ' || v_total);
END;
/


-- -----------------------------------------------------------------
-- PL/SQL Block: Use BULK COLLECT to fetch nested table data and
-- ↪  then iterate over it.
-- -----------------------------------------------------------------
DECLARE
    -- Define a local collection type to hold analytic_record
    -- ↪  objects.
    TYPE record_tab IS TABLE OF analytic_record;
    v_records record_tab;
    v_sum     NUMBER := 0;
BEGIN
    -- Retrieve analytic records from the nested table of a specific
    -- ↪  summary.
    SELECT COLUMN_VALUE
    BULK COLLECT INTO v_records
    FROM analytics_summary a, TABLE(a.records)
    WHERE a.summary_id = 1;

    -- Sum up the metric values from the collection.
    FOR i IN 1 .. v_records.COUNT LOOP
        v_sum := v_sum + v_records(i).metric_value;
    END LOOP;

    DBMS_OUTPUT.PUT_LINE('Sum of Metrics from Nested Table: ' ||
    ↪  v_sum);
END;
/


-- -----------------------------------------------------------------
-- Create a function to calculate the average metric value from a
-- ↪  nested table of analytic records.
-- -----------------------------------------------------------------
CREATE OR REPLACE FUNCTION calc_avg_metric(p_records IN
↪  analytic_record_nt)
RETURN NUMBER IS
    v_total NUMBER := 0;
BEGIN
    FOR i IN 1 .. p_records.COUNT LOOP
        v_total := v_total + p_records(i).metric_value;
    END LOOP;
    IF p_records.COUNT > 0 THEN
        RETURN v_total / p_records.COUNT;
    ELSE
        RETURN NULL;
    END IF;
END;
/
```

```
----------------------------------------------------------------
-- PL/SQL Block: Demonstrate the use of the calc_avg_metric function
↪   to compute an average.
----------------------------------------------------------------
DECLARE
    v_avg NUMBER;
BEGIN
    SELECT calc_avg_metric(records)
      INTO v_avg
      FROM analytics_summary
     WHERE summary_id = 1;

    DBMS_OUTPUT.PUT_LINE('Average Metric from Summary ID 1: ' ||
    ↪   v_avg);
END;
/
```

Multiple Choice Questions

1. Which of the following best characterizes a PL/SQL record?

   (a) A dynamic collection of elements accessible by a key.

   (b) A static composite structure that encapsulates multiple scalar elements.

   (c) An unordered set of values used for ad hoc aggregation.

   (d) A sequential array with dynamically allocated memory.

2. What is a primary advantage of using PL/SQL records in analytical applications?

   (a) They support automatic dynamic resizing based on input data volume.

   (b) They enforce semantic coherence via explicit declaration of field names and types.

   (c) They offer key-based indexing for rapid element lookup.

   (d) They perform on-the-fly aggregation of scalar values.

3. Which property best describes PL/SQL arrays?

   (a) They store elements in a contiguous memory block, allowing constant-time access by numeric index.

   (b) They use a key-value mapping system for non-numeric keys.

43

(c) They are dynamically sized collections that adjust bounds during runtime.

(d) They require explicit set-based operations to access individual elements.

4. In contrast to arrays, nested tables in PL/SQL are distinguished by which of the following features?

(a) They require contiguous memory storage with fixed bounds.

(b) They mandate strictly sequential numbering of elements.

(c) They support dynamic sizing and allow non-contiguous storage, facilitating set-like operations.

(d) They enforce immutability once defined.

5. Associative arrays in PL/SQL, also known as index-by tables, are primarily characterized by:

(a) Contiguous sequential storage with fixed index ranges.

(b) The use of unique keys—potentially non-numeric—for indexing elements.

(c) Automatic dynamic resizing with implicit numeric indices.

(d) Built-in support for bulk data transformation without explicit indices.

6. Which of the following is NOT a typical feature of PL/SQL collections in the context of data analytics?

(a) Flexibility in handling variable-length data sets.

(b) Support for both sequential access (arrays, nested tables) and key-based access (associative arrays).

(c) Enforcement of strict type safety via pre-declared contiguous indices.

(d) Provision for modeling complex, dynamic data relationships.

7. How does the integration of records with collections enhance PL/SQL's applicability in analytical scenarios?

(a) It ensures that all information is stored solely as single scalar values.

(b) It enables the grouping of related attributes into composite structures, which can then be managed as dynamic collections.

(c) It automatically converts procedural code into declarative set-based SQL queries.

(d) It enforces object-oriented encapsulation for all types of data.

Answers:

1. **B: A static composite structure that encapsulates multiple scalar elements**
PL/SQL records are deliberately designed as composite data types that consolidate disparate scalar elements. They are statically defined, with each field explicitly declared with a specific data type—this is analogous to tuples in formal data models.

2. **B: They enforce semantic coherence via explicit declaration of field names and types**
By requiring that each constituent field is explicitly declared along with its data type, records ensure both type safety and semantic clarity. This is essential in analytical applications where structured grouping of related attributes is critical.

3. **A: They store elements in a contiguous memory block, allowing constant-time access by numeric index**
Arrays in PL/SQL are characterized by their sequential storage in contiguous memory. This ordering provides efficient element retrieval, typically in $O(1)$ time, making arrays well-suited for iterative processing tasks.

4. **C: They support dynamic sizing and allow non-contiguous storage, facilitating set-like operations**
Unlike arrays, nested tables are flexible in size and do not require contiguous storage. This allows them to manage datasets that vary in size over time and to support operations akin to those performed on mathematical sets.

5. **B: The use of unique keys—potentially non-numeric—for indexing elements**
Associative arrays (index-by tables) differ from standard arrays by employing a key-based indexing mechanism. This

45

design enables the use of non-numeric keys, providing significant flexibility for data retrieval and management.

6. **C: Enforcement of strict type safety via pre-declared contiguous indices**
   While PL/SQL records rigorously enforce type safety through explicit field declarations, collections such as arrays, nested tables, and associative arrays are designed for dynamic index management. They do not require pre-declaration of contiguous indices in the same way, making option C the incorrect feature in this context.

7. **B: It enables the grouping of related attributes into composite structures, which can then be managed as dynamic collections**
   The integration of records with collections leverages the strengths of both constructs. Records provide a statically typed, semantically coherent grouping of related data, while collections offer dynamic and flexible storage. This combination is particularly powerful for managing and processing complex analytic datasets.

Chapter 5

Embedding SQL for Data Retrieval in PL/SQL

The Confluence of Declarative and Procedural Constructs

The design of PL/SQL establishes a synthesis between the declarative semantics of SQL and the procedural control flow of a traditional programming language. In this paradigm, SQL queries are interleaved within procedural blocks in a manner that preserves the declarative intent of data specification while leveraging the iterative and conditional constructs inherent to PL/SQL. The embedded SQL is not relegated to an ancillary role but stands as an integral component of the overall execution model. Through this integration, each SQL statement is subjected to a rigorous process of parsing, semantic verification, and optimization, ensuring that data retrieval operations adhere strictly to the constraints and structures defined by the database schema.

Static SQL Integration and Schema Validation

Within PL/SQL, static SQL statements are incorporated directly into the body of a procedural block, thereby enabling compile-time validation against the database schema. This integration enforces stringent type consistency and structural integrity, as each embedded SQL query must correspond with existing relations, column definitions, and constraints as dictated by the underlying data model. The static nature of these embedded queries allows for early binding, where the SQL compiler examines and optimizes the query based upon the fixed schema context. Consequently, the alignment of declarative SQL with procedural logic ensures that the retrieved data is both accurately specified and efficiently accessible, minimizing the potential for runtime discrepancies.

Data Retrieval and Preprocessing Mechanisms

Embedded SQL facilitates the direct extraction of data from relational tables into PL/SQL data structures, thereby forming a bridge between set-based data manipulation and procedural computation. The process entails the execution of a SQL query within the confines of a PL/SQL block, the results of which are seamlessly mapped onto composite structures such as records or collections. In this framework, retrieval operations obey the rules of relational algebra, where selection, projection, and aggregation are employed to distill raw data into analytically significant attributes. The retrieval mechanism is delineated by the transformation of a relational result set into an in-memory representation, which then becomes accessible for subsequent procedural operations. This tight coupling between data extraction and procedural manipulation supports intricate preprocessing routines that prepare data prior to further analytical evaluation.

Dynamic Query Composition and Parameter Binding

In contrast to static SQL, dynamic query composition within PL/SQL introduces a higher degree of flexibility through the construction of SQL statements at runtime. This approach allows for the formulation of queries that are contingent upon variable parameters and conditional logic determined during program execution. The dynamic construction process involves the systematic binding of runtime values to designated placeholders within the SQL statement, thereby ensuring that the query remains both syntactically correct and semantically aligned with current data requirements. The ability to generate and execute queries dynamically supports the development of adaptive analytical processes, where the precise parameters of data retrieval are not known until execution time. Moreover, the meticulous management of parameter binding serves as a safeguard against inconsistencies and upholds the integrity of the data retrieval operation, even under conditions of non-deterministic input values.

Oracle 19c SQL Code Snippet

```
-- Create a sample EMPLOYEES table for data retrieval demonstration
CREATE TABLE EMPLOYEES (
    EMP_ID        NUMBER GENERATED BY DEFAULT AS IDENTITY,
    FIRST_NAME    VARCHAR2(100),
    LAST_NAME     VARCHAR2(100),
    DEPARTMENT    VARCHAR2(100),
    HIRE_DATE     DATE,
    SALARY        NUMBER,
    CONSTRAINT EMPLOYEES_PK PRIMARY KEY (EMP_ID)
);

-- Insert sample data into the EMPLOYEES table
INSERT ALL
    INTO EMPLOYEES (FIRST_NAME, LAST_NAME, DEPARTMENT, HIRE_DATE,
    ↪ SALARY)
        VALUES ('Alice', 'Smith', 'Analytics', DATE '2021-01-15',
        ↪ 70000)
    INTO EMPLOYEES (FIRST_NAME, LAST_NAME, DEPARTMENT, HIRE_DATE,
    ↪ SALARY)
        VALUES ('Bob', 'Johnson', 'Finance', DATE '2019-06-23',
        ↪ 85000)
    INTO EMPLOYEES (FIRST_NAME, LAST_NAME, DEPARTMENT, HIRE_DATE,
    ↪ SALARY)
```

```
            VALUES ('Charlie', 'Williams', 'Analytics', DATE
            ↪  '2020-11-28', 92000)
SELECT * FROM DUAL;
COMMIT;


---------------------------------------------------------------------
-- Static SQL Integration: Retrieve employee data using embedded SQL
↪   in PL/SQL
---------------------------------------------------------------------


DECLARE
    TYPE EmpRec IS RECORD (
        emp_id        EMPLOYEES.EMP_ID%TYPE,
        first_name    EMPLOYEES.FIRST_NAME%TYPE,
        last_name     EMPLOYEES.LAST_NAME%TYPE,
        department    EMPLOYEES.DEPARTMENT%TYPE,
        salary        EMPLOYEES.SALARY%TYPE
    );
    v_employee EmpRec;
BEGIN
    -- Retrieve a specific employee's details using static SQL
    SELECT EMP_ID, FIRST_NAME, LAST_NAME, DEPARTMENT, SALARY
      INTO v_employee
      FROM EMPLOYEES
     WHERE DEPARTMENT = 'Analytics'
       AND SALARY > 80000;

    -- Output the retrieved details
    DBMS_OUTPUT.PUT_LINE('Employee: ' || v_employee.first_name || '
    ↪   ' || v_employee.last_name ||
                          ', Salary: ' || v_employee.salary);
EXCEPTION
    WHEN NO_DATA_FOUND THEN
        DBMS_OUTPUT.PUT_LINE('No matching employee found.');
END;
/


---------------------------------------------------------------------
-- Dynamic Query Composition: Construct and execute SQL dynamically
↪   with parameter binding
---------------------------------------------------------------------


DECLARE
    v_dept      VARCHAR2(50) := 'Analytics';
    v_min_sal   NUMBER       := 60000;
    v_sql       VARCHAR2(4000);
    TYPE EmpRec IS RECORD (
        emp_id        EMPLOYEES.EMP_ID%TYPE,
        first_name    EMPLOYEES.FIRST_NAME%TYPE,
        last_name     EMPLOYEES.LAST_NAME%TYPE,
        salary        EMPLOYEES.SALARY%TYPE
    );
    TYPE EmpTable IS TABLE OF EmpRec;
```

```plsql
    v_emps      EmpTable;
BEGIN
    -- Build dynamic SQL query with bind variables
    v_sql := 'SELECT EMP_ID, FIRST_NAME, LAST_NAME, SALARY
              FROM EMPLOYEES
              WHERE DEPARTMENT = :dept
                AND SALARY >= :min_sal';

    -- Execute dynamic SQL and collect results into a PL/SQL
    ↪ collection
    EXECUTE IMMEDIATE v_sql BULK COLLECT INTO v_emps USING v_dept,
    ↪ v_min_sal;

    -- Loop through the collection and display employee details
    FOR i IN 1..v_emps.COUNT LOOP
        DBMS_OUTPUT.PUT_LINE('Employee ID: ' || v_emps(i).emp_id ||
                             ', Name: ' || v_emps(i).first_name || '
                             ↪ ' || v_emps(i).last_name ||
                             ', Salary: ' || v_emps(i).salary);
    END LOOP;
EXCEPTION
    WHEN OTHERS THEN
        DBMS_OUTPUT.PUT_LINE('Dynamic SQL Error: ' || SQLERRM);
END;
/


-------------------------------------------------------------------------
-- Data Preprocessing Mechanism: Bulk Collect to efficiently
↪ retrieve data into a collection
-------------------------------------------------------------------------


DECLARE
    TYPE EmpIDTable IS TABLE OF EMPLOYEES.EMP_ID%TYPE INDEX BY
    ↪ PLS_INTEGER;
    v_emp_ids EmpIDTable;
BEGIN
    -- Bulk retrieve employee IDs for the Analytics department
    SELECT EMP_ID BULK COLLECT INTO v_emp_ids
      FROM EMPLOYEES
     WHERE DEPARTMENT = 'Analytics';

    FOR i IN 1..v_emp_ids.COUNT LOOP
        DBMS_OUTPUT.PUT_LINE('Analytics Employee ID: ' ||
        ↪ v_emp_ids(i));
    END LOOP;
EXCEPTION
    WHEN NO_DATA_FOUND THEN
        DBMS_OUTPUT.PUT_LINE('No Analytics employees found.');
END;
/


-------------------------------------------------------------------------
```

```
-- Algorithmic Transformation: Normalizing salary and aggregating
↪    normalized values
---------------------------------------------------------------------

CREATE OR REPLACE PROCEDURE normalize_and_aggregate IS
    v_total_normalized NUMBER;
BEGIN
    -- Normalize salaries relative to the maximum salary in each
    ↪   department (for Analytics)
    UPDATE EMPLOYEES e
       SET e.SALARY = e.SALARY / (
                          SELECT MAX(SALARY)
                            FROM EMPLOYEES
                           WHERE DEPARTMENT = e.DEPARTMENT
                       )
     WHERE e.DEPARTMENT = 'Analytics';

    COMMIT;

    -- Aggregate the normalized salaries for the Analytics
    ↪   department
    SELECT SUM(SALARY) INTO v_total_normalized
      FROM EMPLOYEES
     WHERE DEPARTMENT = 'Analytics';

    DBMS_OUTPUT.PUT_LINE('Total normalized salary for Analytics: '
    ↪   || v_total_normalized);
EXCEPTION
    WHEN OTHERS THEN
         ROLLBACK;
         DBMS_OUTPUT.PUT_LINE('Error in normalization: ' || SQLERRM);
END normalize_and_aggregate;
/

-- Execute the normalization and aggregation procedure
BEGIN
    normalize_and_aggregate;
END;
/
```

Multiple Choice Questions

1. Which of the following best describes the integration of SQL within PL/SQL as discussed in the chapter?

    (a) SQL statements are processed completely separately from PL/SQL procedural logic.

    (b) Embedded SQL in PL/SQL leverages compile-time validation and optimization while integrating declarative data specification with procedural control flow.

(c) SQL is only used for data definition and, once embedded, is not subject to runtime parameter binding.

(d) PL/SQL converts all SQL statements into procedural loops before execution.

2. What is the primary advantage of static SQL integration within PL/SQL as outlined in the chapter?

(a) It allows for runtime generation of SQL queries using dynamic parameters.

(b) It enforces early binding and compile-time schema verification to ensure type consistency.

(c) It bypasses the need for semantic verification during query execution.

(d) It integrates SQL queries without any relation to the underlying database schema.

3. How does embedded SQL facilitate data retrieval and subsequent processing in PL/SQL?

(a) By mapping the results of SQL queries directly into PL/SQL data structures such as records and collections.

(b) By executing SQL queries in a separate process and importing the results afterward.

(c) By restricting data retrieval to static tables without any procedural logic.

(d) By loading all relevant data into temporary variables at the start of the PL/SQL block.

4. Dynamic query composition in PL/SQL is characterized by which mechanism?

(a) Embedding completely fixed SQL queries that remain unchanged at runtime.

(b) Constructing SQL statements at runtime and binding parameters to placeholders to ensure syntactical correctness.

(c) Pre-compiling all possible query variations during development.

(d) Using hardcoded literal values directly in all dynamic SQL statements.

5. In the context of dynamic SQL, what is the primary role of parameter binding?

   (a) To delay query parsing until after the PL/SQL block has executed.

   (b) To substitute runtime values safely into dynamically generated SQL statements, ensuring integrity and compliance with the schema.

   (c) To avoid the need for any SQL optimization at runtime.

   (d) To convert SQL queries into static SQL before execution.

6. The chapter highlights a synthesis between the declarative aspect of SQL and the procedural nature of PL/SQL. Which statement best captures this synthesis?

   (a) It separates the SQL query layer entirely from PL/SQL logic to avoid any integration issues.

   (b) It merges SQL's declarative data specification with PL/SQL's control flow constructs, thereby enabling complex, pre-processed data retrieval.

   (c) It replaces declarative SQL constructs with procedural loops to handle data manipulation.

   (d) It enforces that all SQL validations occur only at run-time, independent of procedural logic.

7. How do SQL parsing, semantic verification, and optimization contribute to the functionality of embedded SQL in PL/SQL, as presented in the chapter?

   (a) They allow SQL statements to bypass schema constraints for faster execution.

   (b) They ensure that each SQL statement adheres to the underlying database schema and is efficiently executed within the procedural block.

   (c) They primarily focus on optimizing the procedural logic rather than the SQL queries.

   (d) They enable the conversion of all SQL commands into non-declarative procedural code.

Answers:

1. **B:** Embedded SQL in PL/SQL leverages compile-time validation and optimization while integrating declarative data specification with procedural control flow.
   Explanation: The chapter emphasizes how SQL statements, when embedded in PL/SQL, retain their declarative nature and are subjected to rigorous parsing, verification, and optimization, thus blending with the procedural logic.

2. **B:** It enforces early binding and compile-time schema verification to ensure type consistency.
   Explanation: Static SQL integration benefits from early binding, where queries are checked against the database schema at compile-time, ensuring that type and structure constraints are met.

3. **A:** By mapping the results of SQL queries directly into PL/SQL data structures such as records and collections.
   Explanation: The chapter describes how embedded SQL allows direct extraction of relational data into PL/SQL constructs, facilitating immediate subsequent processing.

4. **B:** Constructing SQL statements at runtime and binding parameters to placeholders to ensure syntactical correctness.
   Explanation: Dynamic SQL composition involves building queries at runtime where parameters are bound to placeholders, allowing flexible query generation in response to runtime conditions.

5. **B:** To substitute runtime values safely into dynamically generated SQL statements, ensuring integrity and compliance with the schema.
   Explanation: Parameter binding is crucial in dynamic SQL to integrate user or system variables into the SQL command, maintaining both syntactic and semantic integrity.

6. **B:** It merges SQL's declarative data specification with PL/SQL's control flow constructs, thereby enabling complex, preprocessed data retrieval.
   Explanation: This synthesis is central to PL/SQL's design, allowing developers to harness the strengths of SQL's set-based operations alongside PL/SQL's rich procedural constructs.

7. **B:** They ensure that each SQL statement adheres to the underlying database schema and is efficiently executed within the procedural block.

   Explanation: The processes of parsing, semantic verification, and optimization confirm that embedded SQL statements obey schema constraints and are optimized for performance, reinforcing the reliability of data operations.

Chapter 6

Constructing SQL Joins and Subqueries in PL/SQL

Conceptual Foundations of SQL Joins

The operation of joining tables is a fundamental aspect of relational databases, derived from principles in set theory and formalized through relational algebra. In this paradigm, a join constitutes an operation that fuses data from two or more relations based on the satisfaction of a specified predicate. The theoretical basis of the join is often symbolized by the ⋈ operator, which provides a concise notation for the natural integration of tuples sharing equivalent attribute values. This operation not only underpins the mechanism for data amalgamation but also establishes the conceptual framework for deriving multidimensional insights from partitioned data sources. The precision of a join condition is essential to the soundness of the resultant relation, ensuring that each tuple in the output is semantically coherent with respect to the underlying schema.

A range of join types exists to address assorted analytical needs. Inner joins, outer joins (left, right, and full), self-joins, and cross joins each offer a nuanced approach to data correlation. In the context of PL/SQL, these join paradigms are utilized to maintain data integrity and to facilitate a robust analytical environment. Detailed comprehension of these joins, along with the resultant effect on the cardinality of the dataset, is crucial for enabling multi-dimensional analysis. This section therefore establishes an elaborate theoretical foundation, wherein the mathematically rigorous definition of joins is linked directly with their practical implications in data aggregation and transformation.

Subqueries as Instruments of Data Integration

Subqueries serve as a sophisticated mechanism to embed one query within another, thus enabling a layered approach to data retrieval. These nested queries, which can operate in both correlated and uncorrelated forms, are pivotal in constructing conditional boundaries that govern the behavior of join operations. The encapsulation of independent query logic within an outer query permits the delegation of preliminary data filtering and aggregation tasks to a subordinate process. Through this method, the overall query structure benefits from enhanced modularity and logical clarity.

In PL/SQL, subqueries are seamlessly integrated with the surrounding procedural code, allowing for the intersection of declarative SQL expressions and structured control flow. The internal execution order, which allows subqueries to compute a transient set of results, fosters the generation of criteria that may then be deployed as dynamic thresholds in join conditions. The elegance of subqueries lies in their ability to isolate complex selection logic within a self-contained query, thereby supporting both granular data analysis and broad-spectrum data correlation. This compartmentalization is essential for managing the intricacies inherent in multi-source data integration.

Synergistic Combination for Multi-Dimensional Data Analysis

The interplay between join operations and subqueries in PL/SQL embodies the synthesis of flat data retrieval methods with the dynamic execution of nested queries. The strategic combination of these constructs elevates the analytical capabilities of the system, allowing for the synthesis of data across heterogeneous sources to reveal patterns, trends, and anomalies that might otherwise remain obscured. In environments where data is distributed across multiple tables, the harnessing of join operations ensures that data elements are consolidated in a manner that preserves both referential integrity and semantic accuracy.

Subqueries contribute an additional layer of analytical depth by delineating complex conditions and facilitating the computation of intermediate results. The resultant union of these construct types transforms a standard data retrieval operation into a multi-dimensional exploration tool. This synergy is particularly crucial when the analytical task requires contextual determination, such as when aggregating data across temporal or categorical dimensions. The resultant query structure, enriched by subqueries and judicious join conditions, lays the groundwork for computations that span across diverse analytical axes, thereby enabling the derivation of insights from datasets that are both structured and semi-structured.

The detailed integration of these mechanisms in PL/SQL is indicative of the inherent versatility and robustness of the language in addressing the complexities of modern data analysis. The deliberate construction of queries via relational joins, augmented by the conditional precision of subqueries, provides a methodology that is both comprehensive and adaptable. Each component, whether addressing the nuances of table interrelation or the subtleties of predicate evaluation, contributes significantly to the overarching goal of synthesizing a coherent and analytically rich view of disparate datasets.

Oracle 19c SQL Code Snippet

```
-- Create DEPARTMENTS table to simulate organizational divisions
CREATE TABLE DEPARTMENTS (
    DEPT_ID    NUMBER GENERATED BY DEFAULT AS IDENTITY,
    DEPT_NAME VARCHAR2(100),
    LOCATION   VARCHAR2(100),
    CONSTRAINT DEPARTMENTS_PK PRIMARY KEY (DEPT_ID)
);

-- Create EMPLOYEES table to store employee data linked to
↪ departments
CREATE TABLE EMPLOYEES (
    EMP_ID    NUMBER GENERATED BY DEFAULT AS IDENTITY,
    EMP_NAME  VARCHAR2(100),
    SALARY    NUMBER,
    DEPT_ID   NUMBER,
```

```
    HIRE_DATE DATE,
    CONSTRAINT EMPLOYEES_PK PRIMARY KEY (EMP_ID),
    CONSTRAINT EMP_DEPT_FK FOREIGN KEY (DEPT_ID) REFERENCES
    ↪    DEPARTMENTS(DEPT_ID)
);

-- Insert sample data into DEPARTMENTS
INSERT ALL
    INTO DEPARTMENTS (DEPT_NAME, LOCATION) VALUES ('Sales', 'New
    ↪    York')
    INTO DEPARTMENTS (DEPT_NAME, LOCATION) VALUES ('Engineering',
    ↪    'San Francisco')
    INTO DEPARTMENTS (DEPT_NAME, LOCATION) VALUES ('Human
    ↪    Resources', 'Chicago')
SELECT * FROM DUAL;
COMMIT;

-- Insert sample data into EMPLOYEES
INSERT ALL
    INTO EMPLOYEES (EMP_NAME, SALARY, DEPT_ID, HIRE_DATE)
        VALUES ('Alice', 75000, 1, DATE '2020-01-15')
    INTO EMPLOYEES (EMP_NAME, SALARY, DEPT_ID, HIRE_DATE)
        VALUES ('Bob', 85000, 2, DATE '2019-03-22')
    INTO EMPLOYEES (EMP_NAME, SALARY, DEPT_ID, HIRE_DATE)
        VALUES ('Charlie', 50000, 3, DATE '2021-07-01')
    INTO EMPLOYEES (EMP_NAME, SALARY, DEPT_ID, HIRE_DATE)
        VALUES ('Diana', 95000, 2, DATE '2018-11-30')
    INTO EMPLOYEES (EMP_NAME, SALARY, DEPT_ID, HIRE_DATE)
        VALUES ('Evan', 60000, 1, DATE '2022-06-10')
SELECT * FROM DUAL;
COMMIT;

-------------------------------------------------------------------
-- Demonstrate an INNER JOIN between EMPLOYEES and DEPARTMENTS
-- Combines rows where the department IDs match, providing a
↪    complete view.
-------------------------------------------------------------------
SELECT
    E.EMP_NAME,
    E.SALARY,
    D.DEPT_NAME,
    D.LOCATION
FROM
    EMPLOYEES E
INNER JOIN
    DEPARTMENTS D
ON
    E.DEPT_ID = D.DEPT_ID;

-------------------------------------------------------------------
-- Demonstrate a LEFT OUTER JOIN to retrieve all employee records,
-- including those that might not have a matching department.
-------------------------------------------------------------------
```

```sql
SELECT
    E.EMP_NAME,
    E.SALARY,
    D.DEPT_NAME
FROM
    EMPLOYEES E
LEFT OUTER JOIN
    DEPARTMENTS D
ON
    E.DEPT_ID = D.DEPT_ID;


-------------------------------------------------------------------------
-- Demonstrate a SELF JOIN to compare employees within the same
↪   department
-------------------------------------------------------------------------
SELECT
    A.EMP_NAME AS EMPLOYEE_1,
    B.EMP_NAME AS EMPLOYEE_2,
    D.DEPT_NAME
FROM
    EMPLOYEES A
INNER JOIN
    EMPLOYEES B
        ON A.DEPT_ID = B.DEPT_ID
        AND A.EMP_ID <> B.EMP_ID
INNER JOIN
    DEPARTMENTS D
        ON A.DEPT_ID = D.DEPT_ID
ORDER BY
    D.DEPT_NAME, A.EMP_NAME;


-------------------------------------------------------------------------
-- Use a subquery in the WHERE clause to filter employees earning
↪   above the
-- average salary for their own department.
-------------------------------------------------------------------------
SELECT
    E.EMP_NAME,
    E.SALARY,
    D.DEPT_NAME
FROM
    EMPLOYEES E
INNER JOIN
    DEPARTMENTS D
ON
    E.DEPT_ID = D.DEPT_ID
WHERE
    E.SALARY > (
        SELECT AVG(SALARY)
        FROM EMPLOYEES
        WHERE DEPT_ID = E.DEPT_ID
    );
```

61

```
-------------------------------------------------------------------
-- Use a correlated subquery in the SELECT clause to rank employees
↪  by salary
-- within each department.
-------------------------------------------------------------------
SELECT
    E.EMP_NAME,
    E.SALARY,
    D.DEPT_NAME,
    (SELECT COUNT(*)
       FROM EMPLOYEES E2
      WHERE E2.DEPT_ID = E.DEPT_ID
        AND E2.SALARY >= E.SALARY) AS SALARY_RANK
FROM
    EMPLOYEES E
INNER JOIN
    DEPARTMENTS D
ON
    E.DEPT_ID = D.DEPT_ID
ORDER BY
    D.DEPT_NAME, SALARY_RANK;


-------------------------------------------------------------------
-- Use dynamic SQL via PL/SQL to execute a join with a subquery
↪  under runtime conditions
-------------------------------------------------------------------
DECLARE
    v_query VARCHAR2(1000);
    v_dept  VARCHAR2(100) := 'Engineering';
BEGIN
    v_query := 'SELECT E.EMP_NAME, E.SALARY, D.DEPT_NAME
                FROM EMPLOYEES E
                JOIN DEPARTMENTS D ON E.DEPT_ID = D.DEPT_ID
                WHERE D.DEPT_NAME = :dept';
    EXECUTE IMMEDIATE v_query USING v_dept;
END;
/


-------------------------------------------------------------------
-- Create SALES table to simulate transactional data linked to
↪  employees
-------------------------------------------------------------------
CREATE TABLE SALES (
    SALE_ID     NUMBER GENERATED BY DEFAULT AS IDENTITY,
    EMP_ID      NUMBER,
    SALE_DATE   DATE,
    SALE_AMOUNT NUMBER,
    CONSTRAINT SALES_PK PRIMARY KEY (SALE_ID),
    CONSTRAINT SALE_EMP_FK FOREIGN KEY (EMP_ID) REFERENCES
    ↪  EMPLOYEES(EMP_ID)
);

-- Insert sample sales data
```

62

```
INSERT ALL
    INTO SALES (EMP_ID, SALE_DATE, SALE_AMOUNT)
        VALUES (1, DATE '2023-09-01', 1000)
    INTO SALES (EMP_ID, SALE_DATE, SALE_AMOUNT)
        VALUES (2, DATE '2023-09-02', 1500)
    INTO SALES (EMP_ID, SALE_DATE, SALE_AMOUNT)
        VALUES (1, DATE '2023-09-03', 2000)
    INTO SALES (EMP_ID, SALE_DATE, SALE_AMOUNT)
        VALUES (4, DATE '2023-09-04', 2500)
    INTO SALES (EMP_ID, SALE_DATE, SALE_AMOUNT)
        VALUES (2, DATE '2023-09-05', 3000)
SELECT * FROM DUAL;
COMMIT;

-------------------------------------------------------------------------
-- Retrieve a running total of sales per employee using an analytic
↪   function,
-- while joining SALES with EMPLOYEES for multi-dimensional trend
↪   analysis
-------------------------------------------------------------------------
SELECT
    E.EMP_NAME,
    S.SALE_DATE,
    S.SALE_AMOUNT,
    SUM(S.SALE_AMOUNT) OVER (PARTITION BY E.EMP_ID ORDER BY
    ↪   S.SALE_DATE) AS RUNNING_TOTAL
FROM
    SALES S
JOIN
    EMPLOYEES E ON S.EMP_ID = E.EMP_ID
ORDER BY
    E.EMP_NAME, S.SALE_DATE;
```

Multiple Choice Questions

1. Which symbol is conventionally used in relational algebra to denote the natural join operation?

    (a) ∪

    (b) ⋈

    (c) ×

    (d) ∩

2. Which type of join in SQL returns only those rows that have matching values in both participating tables?

    (a) Outer Join

(b) Cross Join

(c) Inner Join

(d) Self Join

3. What is the defining characteristic of a correlated subquery in PL/SQL?

    (a) It can be executed independently of the outer query.

    (b) It depends on values provided by the outer query for its evaluation.

    (c) It always returns a single scalar value.

    (d) It is used exclusively in aggregation functions.

4. How do subqueries contribute to data integration in a multi-dimensional analysis context?

    (a) They flatten multi-dimensional data into a single column.

    (b) They encapsulate complex filtering logic in a modular and reusable unit.

    (c) They eliminate the need for join operations entirely.

    (d) They only perform data aggregation without any filtering.

5. Why is precision in the join predicate condition crucial when constructing SQL joins in PL/SQL?

    (a) It simplifies the SQL syntax by removing explicit conditions.

    (b) It ensures semantic coherence and prevents erroneous data merging.

    (c) It significantly reduces the query execution time in all cases.

    (d) It allows for the automatic generation of table relationships.

6. In the context of PL/SQL, how are subqueries typically integrated with procedural code?

    (a) They are executed independently and their results stored in temporary tables.

(b) They are embedded within declarative SQL expressions and interact seamlessly with control structures.

(c) They replace traditional block-structured programming constructs.

(d) They only function in standalone SQL scripts.

7. What is the primary benefit of combining SQL joins with subqueries in PL/SQL for analytical tasks?

(a) It restricts analysis to a single-table scenario.

(b) It decouples data retrieval from any conditional processing.

(c) It enables the layered synthesis of complex conditions and aggregations across disparate datasets.

(d) It minimizes the need for dynamic SQL.

Answers:

1. **B:** ⋈
In relational algebra, the ⋈ operator is conventionally used to represent the natural join, which fuses tuples from different relations based on shared attribute values.

2. **C: Inner Join**
An inner join returns only those rows with matching values in both tables, ensuring the results contain related data from each relation.

3. **B: It depends on values provided by the outer query for its evaluation.**
A correlated subquery references columns from its outer query, meaning it must be re-evaluated for each row of the outer query, which distinguishes it from an uncorrelated subquery.

4. **B: They encapsulate complex filtering logic in a modular and reusable unit.**
By isolating intricate conditional logic within a subquery, developers can create modular queries that enhance readability and maintainability while facilitating sophisticated data integration.

5. **B: It ensures semantic coherence and prevents erroneous data merging.**

Precisely defined join predicates are essential as they guarantee that only semantically matching data is merged, thereby preserving data integrity and avoiding the inclusion of irrelevant or misleading tuples.

6. **B: They are embedded within declarative SQL expressions and interact seamlessly with control structures.**
In PL/SQL, subqueries are integrated directly into SQL statements and can work in conjunction with procedural control structures, allowing for dynamic data retrieval that complements the procedural logic.

7. **C: It enables the layered synthesis of complex conditions and aggregations across disparate datasets.**
The combination of SQL joins and subqueries allows developers to construct queries that not only merge data from multiple sources but also incorporate complex, conditional logic, thus facilitating comprehensive multi-dimensional analysis.

Chapter 7

Control Structures: Conditional Logic and Looping

Conditional Constructs

1 IF Statements

The IF statement constitutes a fundamental control mechanism grounded in the principles of Boolean logic and structured programming. In a formalized setting, an IF construct evaluates a Boolean condition, denoted as C, and facilitates the execution of a specific block of operations when C holds true. The underlying semantics are rooted in the binary nature of truth values, where the expression C is evaluated to either *true* or *false*. This evaluative process permits the formulation of decision-making pathways within an algorithmic framework.

Within the theoretical model of conditional constructs, the IF statement is extended through the use of multiple branches, commonly structured as an initial IF followed by zero or more ELSIF clauses and, optionally, an ELSE clause. The ELSIF variant introduces the concept of sequential condition testing, wherein each predicate is examined in order and the first instance of a true evaluation determines the operational branch executed. The ELSE clause, serving as the default alternative, is activated when none of the preceding conditions return true. The rigorous control flow enforced by IF statements guarantees that the decision-making process remains transparent and logically coherent, ensuring that the transition from one computational state to another is mathematically well-defined.

2 CASE Expressions

CASE expressions offer an alternative paradigm for implementing multi-branch selection logic within a single, cohesive construct. The construct is reminiscent of piecewise functions in mathematical analysis, where distinct cases are delineated by explicit conditions and their corresponding results. CASE expressions are often categorized into two principal forms: the simple CASE, which compares a singular expression against a set of discrete values, and the searched CASE, in which each branch is determined by its own condition, akin to individual propositions in Boolean algebra.

In this framework, the CASE expression evaluates a sequence of conditions sequentially until the first condition that evaluates to *true* is encountered. The inherent design objective is to replace deeply nested IF statements with a more concise and structurally uniform alternative. This not only improves readability but also aligns the decision-making mechanism with the theoretical underpinnings of conditional evaluation in a formal system. The semantic integrity of the CASE construct is maintained by ensuring that each conditional branch is mutually exclusive, thereby precluding ambiguous outcomes during execution.

Looping Constructs

1 Iterative Paradigms and Fundamental Looping Mechanisms

Iterative control structures are central to algorithmic operations, serving as mechanisms to repeatedly execute a predetermined block of instructions. These constructs are often formalized by declaring a loop variable that iterates over a defined range or by specifying a termination condition based on a Boolean predicate. The mathematical essence of iteration is captured in the notion of a sequence, where each successive iteration corresponds to a discrete step in a well-ordered process.

In one elementary form, the unconditional loop offers a perpetual cycle that necessitates an explicit exit condition encapsulated within the loop body. In contrast, condition-controlled loops, characterized by constructs such as the WHILE loop, initiate the iterative process only when a given condition P is satisfied, and continue as long as the predicate P maintains a truth value of *true*. The controlled evaluation of the termination condition ensures that the computation is both finite and predictable, thereby facilitating rigorous analysis of time complexity and resource utilization.

2 Parameterized and Multi-Dimensional Iteration

More complex iterative paradigms extend beyond simple repetition to encompass parameterized loops and multi-dimensional iterations, which are essential for the processing of structured data and the execution of nested algorithmic routines. Parameterized loops, often implemented via bounded iteration constructs, employ a designated iterator variable that assumes values from a specific domain, typically represented as a finite set $\{a_1, a_2, \ldots, a_n\}$. This systematic progression through a series of predetermined states allows for the efficient traversal of arrays, collections, or any sequentially ordered data structures.

Further intricacy is introduced through the nesting of loops, wherein an inner loop is executed for each iteration of an outer loop. This hierarchical structuring is instrumental in determining the computational complexity of algorithms, especially in scenarios where the number of iterations is multiplicative across dimensions. In such a schema, the total number of iterations can be expressed as the product $\prod_{i=1}^{k} n_i$, where n_i denotes the number of iterations in the ith loop. The rigorous definition of these relationships permits a formal analysis of scalability and performance in systems that require multi-dimensional data processing.

The interplay between conditional logic and iterative mechanisms provides a robust framework for complex decision-making and systematic data traversal. Each control construct, whether facilitating a discrete decision through IF and CASE or enabling repetitive execution via loops, underpins the structural integrity of algorithmic design. The precision with which these constructs are defined ensures that iterative data processing and conditional branching are executed with mathematical rigor and consistency.

Oracle 19c SQL Code Snippet

```
----------------------------------------------------------------------
-- Create a sample table to store numeric values for analytical
↪   processing
----------------------------------------------------------------------
CREATE TABLE NUMERIC_EXAMPLE (
    ID    NUMBER GENERATED BY DEFAULT AS IDENTITY,
    VALUE NUMBER,
    CONSTRAINT NUMERIC_EXAMPLE_PK PRIMARY KEY (ID)
);

-- Insert sample data into NUMERIC_EXAMPLE table (values from 0 to
↪   5)
INSERT ALL
    INTO NUMERIC_EXAMPLE (VALUE) VALUES (0)
    INTO NUMERIC_EXAMPLE (VALUE) VALUES (1)
    INTO NUMERIC_EXAMPLE (VALUE) VALUES (2)
    INTO NUMERIC_EXAMPLE (VALUE) VALUES (3)
    INTO NUMERIC_EXAMPLE (VALUE) VALUES (4)
    INTO NUMERIC_EXAMPLE (VALUE) VALUES (5)
SELECT * FROM DUAL;
COMMIT;


----------------------------------------------------------------------
-- Query demonstrating the use of CASE expression for conditional
↪   logic
-- This query classifies each numeric value as 'Even' or 'Odd'
----------------------------------------------------------------------
SELECT
    VALUE,
    CASE
        WHEN MOD(VALUE, 2) = 0 THEN 'Even'
        ELSE 'Odd'
    END AS PARITY
FROM NUMERIC_EXAMPLE;


----------------------------------------------------------------------
-- Create a PL/SQL function to compute the factorial of a number
-- Demonstrates usage of IF statements and FOR loops as discussed in
↪   the chapter
----------------------------------------------------------------------
CREATE OR REPLACE FUNCTION factorial(n IN NUMBER) RETURN NUMBER IS
    result NUMBER := 1;
BEGIN
    -- Validate input: factorial is not defined for negative numbers
    IF n < 0 THEN
        RAISE_APPLICATION_ERROR(-20001, 'Factorial is not defined
        ↪   for negative numbers');
    ELSIF n = 0 THEN
        RETURN 1;
    ELSE
```

70

```
        -- Iteratively compute factorial using a FOR loop
        FOR i IN 1 .. n LOOP
            result := result * i;
        END LOOP;
    END IF;
    RETURN result;
END factorial;
/


-------------------------------------------------------------------------
-- Create a PL/SQL procedure to compute and display factorials
-- It uses conditional IF statements and iterative looping
↪  constructs
-------------------------------------------------------------------------
CREATE OR REPLACE PROCEDURE compute_factorials IS
    v_factorial NUMBER;
BEGIN
    -- Loop through each record in NUMERIC_EXAMPLE and compute
    ↪  factorial using the function
    FOR rec IN (SELECT VALUE FROM NUMERIC_EXAMPLE) LOOP
        IF rec.VALUE < 0 THEN
            DBMS_OUTPUT.PUT_LINE('Factorial not defined for negative
            ↪  number: ' || rec.VALUE);
        ELSE
            v_factorial := factorial(rec.VALUE);
            DBMS_OUTPUT.PUT_LINE('Factorial of ' || rec.VALUE || '
            ↪  is: ' || v_factorial);
        END IF;
    END LOOP;
EXCEPTION
    WHEN OTHERS THEN
        DBMS_OUTPUT.PUT_LINE('Error encountered: ' || SQLERRM);
END compute_factorials;
/

-- Execute the compute_factorials procedure to display results
BEGIN
    compute_factorials;
END;
/


-------------------------------------------------------------------------
-- Demonstrate nested loops for multi-dimensional iteration
-- This example prints out a simple 3x3 multiplication table
-------------------------------------------------------------------------
DECLARE
    v_product NUMBER;
BEGIN
    FOR i IN 1..3 LOOP
        FOR j IN 1..3 LOOP
            v_product := i * j;
            DBMS_OUTPUT.PUT_LINE('Multiplication: ' || i || ' x ' ||
            ↪  j || ' = ' || v_product);
```

71

```
        END LOOP;
    END LOOP;
END;
/

----------------------------------------------------------------
-- Use a WHILE loop to compute a cumulative sum until reaching a
↪   threshold
-- Illustrates the use of condition-controlled iteration as outlined
↪   in the chapter
----------------------------------------------------------------
DECLARE
    v_sum     NUMBER := 0;
    v_counter NUMBER := 1;
BEGIN
    WHILE v_sum < 15 LOOP
        v_sum := v_sum + v_counter;
        DBMS_OUTPUT.PUT_LINE('After adding ' || v_counter || ',
        ↪   cumulative sum is: ' || v_sum);
        v_counter := v_counter + 1;
    END LOOP;
END;
/
```

Multiple Choice Questions

1. Which of the following best describes the execution flow in an IF-ELSIF-ELSE construct in PL/SQL?

   (a) All branches (IF, ELSIF, ELSE) are executed sequentially regardless of condition evaluation.

   (b) Only the branch corresponding to the first true condition is executed, with all subsequent branches bypassed.

   (c) Every condition is evaluated in parallel, and all true branches execute concurrently.

   (d) The ELSE branch is executed first, followed by evaluation of IF and ELSIF conditions.

2. In a simple CASE expression, what is its defining characteristic compared to a searched CASE expression?

   (a) It compares multiple expressions against a single constant.

   (b) It compares a single expression to a list of specific constant values.

(c) It operates on Boolean conditions for each branch individually.

(d) It supports iterative evaluation over a range of values.

3. Which of the following statements accurately describes the operation of a WHILE loop in PL/SQL?

   (a) It executes the loop body a fixed number of times without any condition check.

   (b) It evaluates the condition after executing the loop body at least once.

   (c) It repeatedly evaluates a Boolean condition before each iteration; the loop continues as long as the condition is true.

   (d) It automatically iterates over a predefined collection without a condition.

4. What is a primary advantage of using a parameterized (FOR) loop over an unconditional loop in PL/SQL?

   (a) It automatically manages the loop counter and boundaries, reducing the possibility of infinite loops.

   (b) It allows for dynamic alteration of loop boundaries during execution.

   (c) It enables parallel execution of loop iterations.

   (d) It bypasses the need for a termination condition by evaluating the loop variable externally.

5. When evaluating the computational complexity of nested loops, if an outer loop iterates n times and an inner loop iterates m times, the total number of iterations is best represented by:

   (a) $n + m$

   (b) $n * m$

   (c) n^m

   (d) m^n

6. What role does the ELSE clause have in a conditional IF construct?

   (a) It is executed alongside each IF and ELSIF branch simultaneously.

(b) It provides a default block that is executed only when none of the preceding conditions evaluates to true.

(c) It allows for re-evaluation of the IF conditions after initial execution.

(d) It serves as a secondary conditional check when the primary IF condition is false.

7. How do nested loops facilitate multi-dimensional data processing in PL/SQL?

(a) By executing several independent loops concurrently without interaction.

(b) By allowing the inner loop to run continuously until manually terminated.

(c) By enabling hierarchical iteration in which the inner loop executes completely for each iteration of the outer loop, effectively forming a Cartesian product.

(d) By dynamically adjusting loop conditions based on previous iteration results.

Answers:

1. **B: Only the branch corresponding to the first true condition is executed, with all subsequent branches bypassed.**
Explanation: In an IF-ELSIF-ELSE construct, conditions are evaluated sequentially. Once a condition evaluates to true, its corresponding code block is executed and the rest of the branches are skipped, ensuring deterministic control flow.

2. **B: It compares a single expression to a list of specific constant values.**
Explanation: A simple CASE expression takes one expression and matches it against a set of constant values. This differentiates it from the searched CASE expression, which evaluates independent Boolean conditions for each branch.

3. **C: It repeatedly evaluates a Boolean condition before each iteration; the loop continues as long as the condition is true.**
Explanation: A WHILE loop checks its condition before executing its body. The loop runs only so long as the condition remains true, ensuring controlled and finite iterations.

4. **A: It automatically manages the loop counter and boundaries, reducing the possibility of infinite loops.**
   Explanation: Parameterized (FOR) loops inherently define their start and end points, automatically incrementing the counter. This built-in management eliminates the risk inherent in unconditional loops that rely on manual exit conditions.

5. **B: n * m**
   Explanation: With nested loops, the inner loop executes entirely for each execution of the outer loop. Therefore, if the outer loop runs n times and the inner loop runs m times, the total iterations amount to n multiplied by m.

6. **B: It provides a default block that is executed only when none of the preceding conditions evaluates to true.**
   Explanation: The ELSE clause in an IF construct serves as a catch-all mechanism, ensuring that if all previous conditions (IF and any ELSIFs) fail, a predetermined block of code is executed.

7. **C: By enabling hierarchical iteration in which the inner loop executes completely for each iteration of the outer loop, effectively forming a Cartesian product.**
   Explanation: Nested loops allow for multi-dimensional traversal by having the inner loop execute for every single iteration of the outer loop. This results in a total number of iterations that is the product of their respective counts, which is particularly useful for processing matrices or multi-dimensional datasets.

Chapter 8

Cursors: Iterative Data Processing Techniques

Fundamentals of Row-by-Row Iterative Processing

In the domain of advanced data processing, a cursor embodies a mechanism for sequentially traversing a finite set of tuples obtained from a relational query. The procedural paradigm that leverages cursors is analogous to a state transition system, where each fetch operation represents a transition from one discrete state to another, denoted as $s_i \rightarrow s_{i+1}$. This iterative model is central to operations where the granularity of processing necessitates the evaluation and manipulation of individual rows, particularly in contexts that demand a high degree of analytical precision.

1 Theoretical Concepts and Operational Semantics

The theoretical framework underlying cursor-based processing rests on the principles of discrete mathematics and automata theory. Each cursor operation—whether an initial open, iterative fetch, or final closure—corresponds to a well-defined state, ensuring that the processing sequence remains both finite and predictable. The semantics of these operations are rigorously defined, such that a cursor, once opened, iterates over a result set in a controlled manner until a terminal condition is met. The stateful nature of cursors permits the encapsulation of both the current context and auxiliary parameters that may influence subsequent evaluations, thereby providing a robust foundation for row-by-row data analysis.

Implicit Cursors

Implicit cursors are automatically instantiated and managed by the execution environment when a SQL statement is executed within a procedural context. They provide a high-level abstraction for handling query results without requiring explicit declaration or manual resource management. The automated nature of implicit cursors ensures that each row is processed in a sequential manner, thus simplifying the paradigm of iterative data manipulation. Their integration within the procedural engine alleviates the need to explicitly demarcate the lifecycle of the iteration, which is particularly advantageous in scenarios where the emphasis is on the analytical transformation applied to each row rather than on the mechanics of data traversal.

1 Automated Cursor Invocation and Resource Management

Within the implicit cursor framework, the initiation, execution, and termination phases are entirely governed by the underlying system. Upon execution of a SQL query that returns one or multiple rows, the procedural environment instantiates an internal cursor that encapsulates the entire result set. The management of this cursor—including the allocation of memory and the tracking of the current row—is performed without manual intervention. This automated approach minimizes potential sources of error and streamlines the processing pipeline, ensuring that each tuple is fetched and processed in a consistent and deterministic fashion.

2 Contextual Role in Detailed Analytical Operations

The employment of implicit cursors in data analytics is particularly beneficial when the primary objective is the transformation or aggregation of data rather than the manipulation of individual cursor states. Their design favors scenarios in which the row-by-row processing model is applied to standardized transformations or computations, enabling the efficient and reliable execution of analytical routines. The abstraction provided by implicit cursors allows analytical operations to focus on the logical aspects of data evaluation, leaving the mechanical intricacies of iterative control to the procedural engine.

Explicit Cursors

Explicit cursors, by contrast, offer a paradigm in which the iteration over a query result is managed with complete programmer control. Their explicit declaration permits detailed specification of the query parameters, and the subsequent open, fetch, and close operations allow for a highly granular management of the cursor lifecycle. This fine-tuned approach is indispensable in contexts where the processing of each row must be accompanied by conditional checks, parameter adjustments, or sophisticated error handling routines. The explicit cursor model is thus aligned with scenarios that demand meticulous control over data processing details and when the iterative logic must be interwoven with complex analytical computations.

1 Initialization, Fetch Operation, and Termination

The lifecycle of an explicit cursor is characterized by discrete, sequential stages. Initially, the cursor is declared and subsequently opened with a predefined query that may include parameterization. Each row is then fetched in a controlled loop, wherein explicit commands govern the transition from one row to the next. The explicit management of the fetch phase permits tailored operations—such as conditional evaluations or incremental aggregations—to be performed on each row. Finally, the explicit closure of the cursor ensures that all resources allocated during its lifecycle are properly released, thereby preserving the integrity of the overall data processing environment.

2 Enhanced Granularity and Robust Error Handling

The principal advantage of explicit cursors lies in the enhanced granularity they afford to iterative processing. By managing cursor state explicitly, it becomes possible to incorporate detailed error handling mechanisms and context-aware control structures within the iterative loop. Each fetch operation serves not only as an iteration trigger but also as a checkpoint at which the current state of data processing can be scrutinized and adjusted in response to runtime anomalies. This fine-grained control is particularly valuable in complex analytical operations where precision is paramount and where the conditions affecting data validity may vary dynamically over the course of the iteration.

Analytical Relevance in Iterative Data Processing

The iterative processing paradigm enabled by cursors is of substantial analytical significance. Both implicit and explicit cursor techniques facilitate the decomposition of comprehensive data sets into discrete, manageable units, allowing for detailed analysis at the row level. The sequential evaluation inherent in cursor-based processing supports the systematic application of advanced analytical operations, such as conditional aggregations, incremental transformations, and state-dependent computations. In contexts that demand a high degree of analytical rigor, the capability to process rows individually—while maintaining awareness of the underlying context and control state—proves indispensable. The deployment of cursors thus embodies a convergence of algorithmic precision and operational efficiency that is central to the construction of robust, data-intensive analytical applications.

Oracle 19c SQL Code Snippet

```
-- Create DATA_POINTS table to simulate data for state transitions
↪   in iterative processing
CREATE TABLE DATA_POINTS (
    POINT_ID        NUMBER GENERATED BY DEFAULT AS IDENTITY,
    VALUE           NUMBER,
    WEIGHT          NUMBER,
    TRANSITION_DATE DATE,
    CONSTRAINT DATA_POINTS_PK PRIMARY KEY (POINT_ID)
);

-- Insert sample data into DATA_POINTS to represent successive
↪   processing states
```

```
INSERT ALL
    INTO DATA_POINTS (VALUE, WEIGHT, TRANSITION_DATE)
        VALUES (100, 0.05, DATE '2023-10-01')
    INTO DATA_POINTS (VALUE, WEIGHT, TRANSITION_DATE)
        VALUES (200, 0.03, DATE '2023-10-02')
    INTO DATA_POINTS (VALUE, WEIGHT, TRANSITION_DATE)
        VALUES (150, 0.04, DATE '2023-10-03')
    INTO DATA_POINTS (VALUE, WEIGHT, TRANSITION_DATE)
        VALUES (250, 0.02, DATE '2023-10-04')
SELECT * FROM DUAL;
COMMIT;

------------------------------------------------------------------------
-- Procedure to compute state transitions using an explicit cursor.
-- The state transition formula used is defined as:
--     S(i+1) = S(i) + (VALUE * (1 + WEIGHT))
-- where each fetch represents a transition from the current state
↪   S(i) to S(i+1).
------------------------------------------------------------------------

CREATE OR REPLACE PROCEDURE compute_state_transitions IS
    current_state NUMBER := 0;  -- Initialize state at 0

    -- Explicit cursor to fetch iterative data ordered by
    ↪   TRANSITION_DATE
    CURSOR data_cursor IS
        SELECT VALUE, WEIGHT
          FROM DATA_POINTS
          ORDER BY TRANSITION_DATE;

    -- Variables to store fetched values
    v_value  DATA_POINTS.VALUE%TYPE;
    v_weight DATA_POINTS.WEIGHT%TYPE;
BEGIN
    DBMS_OUTPUT.PUT_LINE('Initial State: ' || current_state);

    OPEN data_cursor;
    LOOP
        FETCH data_cursor INTO v_value, v_weight;
        EXIT WHEN data_cursor%NOTFOUND;

        -- Apply the state transition formula:
        -- New state = previous state + (VALUE * (1 + WEIGHT))
        current_state := current_state + (v_value * (1 + v_weight));
        DBMS_OUTPUT.PUT_LINE('After processing VALUE = ' || v_value
        ↪   ||
                            ' and WEIGHT = ' || v_weight ||
                            ', New State: ' || current_state);
    END LOOP;
    CLOSE data_cursor;

    DBMS_OUTPUT.PUT_LINE('Final State: ' || current_state);
EXCEPTION
```

```
    WHEN OTHERS THEN
        IF data_cursor%ISOPEN THEN
            CLOSE data_cursor;
        END IF;
        RAISE;
END compute_state_transitions;
/

-- Execute the compute_state_transitions procedure to process each
↪  row explicitly.
BEGIN
    compute_state_transitions;
END;
/


------------------------------------------------------------------------
-- Demonstrate iterative processing using an implicit cursor with a
↪  FOR loop.
-- This block performs the same computation using automatic cursor
↪  management.
------------------------------------------------------------------------


DECLARE
    current_state NUMBER := 0;
BEGIN
    DBMS_OUTPUT.PUT_LINE('Implicit Cursor - Initial State: ' ||
    ↪  current_state);

    FOR rec IN (SELECT VALUE, WEIGHT FROM DATA_POINTS ORDER BY
    ↪  TRANSITION_DATE) LOOP
        -- Apply the state transition formula in the implicit cursor
        ↪  loop:
        -- New state = previous state + (VALUE * (1 + WEIGHT))
        current_state := current_state + (rec.VALUE * (1 +
        ↪  rec.WEIGHT));
        DBMS_OUTPUT.PUT_LINE('After processing VALUE = ' ||
        ↪  rec.VALUE ||
                            ' and WEIGHT = ' || rec.WEIGHT ||
                            ', New State: ' || current_state);
    END LOOP;

    DBMS_OUTPUT.PUT_LINE('Implicit Cursor - Final State: ' ||
    ↪  current_state);
END;
/


------------------------------------------------------------------------
-- Create a materialized view to precompute cumulative state
↪  transitions.
-- This view uses a window function to compute a running state based
↪  on the formula:
```

```
--    running_state = SUM(VALUE * (1 + WEIGHT)) OVER (ORDER BY
↪    TRANSITION_DATE ROWS BETWEEN UNBOUNDED PRECEDING AND CURRENT
↪    ROW)
--------------------------------------------------------------------

CREATE MATERIALIZED VIEW MV_FINAL_STATE
BUILD IMMEDIATE
REFRESH COMPLETE ON DEMAND
AS
SELECT MAX(running_state) AS FINAL_STATE
  FROM (
        SELECT SUM(VALUE * (1 + WEIGHT)) OVER (ORDER BY
          ↪   TRANSITION_DATE
                                          ROWS BETWEEN
                                      ↪      UNBOUNDED
                                      ↪      PRECEDING AND
                                      ↪      CURRENT ROW) AS
                                      ↪      running_state
           FROM DATA_POINTS
  );

-- Query the materialized view to retrieve the precomputed final
↪   state.
SELECT * FROM MV_FINAL_STATE;
```

Multiple Choice Questions

1. The theoretical framework underlying the stateful, row-by-row iteration in cursor-based processing is primarily derived from which of the following?

   (a) Graph theory and combinatorics

   (b) Discrete mathematics and automata theory

   (c) Computational complexity and algorithm analysis

   (d) Formal language theory and semantics

2. Which of the following best describes the resource management mechanism inherent in implicit cursors?

   (a) They require explicit declaration and manual closure by the programmer.

   (b) They are automatically instantiated, managed, and terminated by the PL/SQL engine.

   (c) They incorporate dynamic memory allocation that must be explicitly freed.

(d) They allow selective fetching of rows with programmer intervention at each step.

3. What sequence of operations characterizes the complete life-cycle of an explicit cursor in PL/SQL?

(a) Declaration, dynamic SQL execution, and commit.

(b) Declaration, open, iterative fetches, and close.

(c) Open, fetch, process, and rollback.

(d) Declaration, execution, logging, and purge.

4. The notation $s_i \rightarrow s_{i+1}$ used in the chapter primarily emphasizes:

(a) The concurrent processing of multiple result sets.

(b) The sequential state transition from one row to the next.

(c) The recursive nature of nested queries.

(d) The probabilistic evaluation of result rows.

5. One of the key advantages of explicit cursors in complex data analytics is:

(a) Their ability to operate without programmer intervention.

(b) Enhanced control over each iteration, allowing for conditional processing and error handling.

(c) Automatic optimization of SQL queries during each fetch.

(d) The elimination of row-by-row processing in favor of bulk methods.

6. In contrast to explicit cursors, implicit cursors contribute to iterative processing by:

(a) Mandating manual handling of the cursor lifecycle.

(b) Abstracting away the details of resource allocation, allowing automatic sequential processing.

(c) Providing built-in parallel processing capabilities.

(d) Requiring the programmer to explicitly interweave error handling with each fetch.

7. In the context of data analytics applications, why is row-by-row iterative processing via cursors essential?

(a) It allows developers to easily parallelize complex queries by default.

(b) It enables targeted transformation, aggregation, and state-dependent computations necessary for high analytical precision.

(c) It automates the normalization of large datasets with minimal code.

(d) It bypasses the need for any conditional logic during data transformation.

Answers:

1. **B: Discrete mathematics and automata theory**
   This answer is correct because the chapter clearly explains that the operational semantics of cursors are rooted in discrete mathematics and automata theory, which formalize the concept of state transitions in iterative processing.

2. **B: They are automatically instantiated, managed, and terminated by the PL/SQL engine**
   Implicit cursors are handled entirely by the execution environment, which opens, processes, and closes the cursor without requiring explicit programmer intervention for resource management.

3. **B: Declaration, open, iterative fetches, and close**
   The lifecycle of an explicit cursor is characterized by its explicit declaration, opening with a predetermined query, iterative fetching of rows (which allows detailed operations), and finally closing the cursor to release resources.

4. **B: The sequential state transition from one row to the next**
   The notation $s_i \rightarrow s_{i+1}$ emphasizes the idea that processing each row involves moving from one well-defined state to the next in a sequential manner, mirroring finite state transitions.

5. **B: Enhanced control over each iteration, allowing for conditional processing and error handling**
   Explicit cursors give the programmer fine-tuned control over the iteration process, which is particularly useful for incorporating conditional logic and robust error handling during row-by-row data manipulation.

6. **B: Abstracting away the details of resource allocation, allowing automatic sequential processing**
Implicit cursors simplify iterative processing by letting the PL/SQL engine manage the details of the cursor's lifecycle, so programmers can focus on the data transformation aspects rather than on manual resource management.

7. **B: It enables targeted transformation, aggregation, and state-dependent computations necessary for high analytical precision**
The ability to process data one row at a time is crucial in complex analytical operations where each specific data point may require precise evaluation, transformation, and conditional processing to achieve accurate results.

Chapter 9

Bulk Processing with FORALL and BULK COLLECT Techniques

Conceptual Foundations of Bulk Processing

Traditional row-by-row processing methods incur significant performance penalties when handling extensive datasets. The inherent overhead associated with per-row operations manifests as numerous context switches between the procedural engine and the SQL engine. Mathematically, if the processing of each row involves a fixed overhead, then the total cost scales on the order of $O(n)$ for n rows. In contrast, bulk processing consolidates these operations into fewer, larger transactions. Such consolidation minimizes the cumulative communication overhead and realizes substantial performance improvements. The theoretical framework for bulk operations draws upon principles of collective data manipulation and efficient resource utilization.

1 Limitations of Traditional Iterative Techniques

Processing individual rows sequentially introduces inefficiencies that become pronounced with growing data volumes. Each iteration triggers a discrete call to the underlying SQL processing layer, thereby contributing to incremental latency. The additive nature of these delays is exacerbated when operating on datasets where n is large, leading to suboptimal overall system throughput. This paradigm, while straightforward in concept, fails to scale effectively in environments where high-throughput data analytics is a critical requirement.

2 Theoretical Efficiency of Aggregated Operations

The transition from iterative processing to batch-based operations is undergirded by rigorous efficiency gains. By aggregating a collection of rows into a single operation, the number of context switches is significantly curtailed. Consider a scenario where an entire collection C of n elements is processed within a single statement execution cycle; the effective processing cost then approaches a constant factor independent of n, subject to the constraints imposed by resource management. This theoretical efficiency is a core motivating factor behind the adoption of bulk processing techniques in data analytics systems.

The FORALL Construct

The FORALL construct introduces a mechanism for batch processing of DML operations that is both efficient and scalable. It operates by iterating over a collection of indexed elements and applying a uniform DML statement to each element, thereby consolidating multiple operations into a singular execution context. This approach significantly reduces the interaction frequency between the procedural logic and the SQL engine.

1 Execution Model and Batch DML Processing

FORALL facilitates the application of a DML statement to an entire array or collection in one processing step. The operational model underpinning FORALL transforms what would traditionally be multiple discrete DML executions into a single, bulk operation. The consolidation achieved through this construct not only decreases the number of round trips between layers but also allows for internal optimizations that can leverage the database engine's capacity for handling batch updates. The formulation inherently reduces the runtime complexity associated with repetitive DML calls.

2 Error Handling and Exception Robustness

In addition to its efficiency benefits, the FORALL construct is designed with robust error handling capabilities. When processing a batch of operations, individual errors do not necessarily compromise the integrity of the entire batch. Instead, mechanisms exist to capture exceptions on a per-batch basis. This granular control over error management ensures that anomalies in specific operations can be handled without necessitating a complete rollback of all operations, thereby maintaining overall transactional integrity.

The BULK COLLECT Construct

BULK COLLECT offers an alternative avenue for improving data retrieval efficiency by enabling the simultaneous fetching of multiple rows into PL/SQL collections. This method reduces the number of context switches necessary for retrieving large result sets, as it transfers data in bulk rather than on a per-row basis.

1 Mechanism for Aggregating Query Results

The BULK COLLECT mechanism is predicated on the simultaneous aggregation of multiple result-set rows into in-memory collections. By invoking a single operation to fill these collections, the overhead associated with individual fetch operations is dramatically reduced. This aggregated retrieval aligns with the broader goal of minimizing the interface overhead between the SQL and procedural engines, leveraging the capacity to handle large volumes of data in a single, streamlined operation.

2 Memory Management Considerations

While BULK COLLECT offers substantial performance benefits, it necessitates careful attention to memory management. The aggregation of rows into PL/SQL collections carries with it an increased memory footprint, and it is essential to balance the desire for efficiency with the constraints of available system resources. The optimal size of the bulk collection is often determined through empirical evaluation, taking into account the trade-off between reduced processing time and the potential for memory saturation. This balance is critical in environments where resource allocation is as important as processing speed.

Performance Considerations in Bulk Operations

The salient benefit of both FORALL and BULK COLLECT techniques is the dramatic reduction in context switching overhead, a major performance bottleneck in traditional iterative processing. By minimizing the number of transitions required between procedural and SQL environments, these bulk operations substantially improve throughput.

1   Reducing Context Switching Overhead

The consolidation of operations into bulk transactions decreases the frequency with which control is transferred between the procedural and SQL engines. In conventional loops, each row processed induces a distinct context switch, resulting in a cumulative delay. In bulk processing, the number of context switches is reduced to a few aggregate operations, often described as a constant or sublinear factor relative to the number of rows processed. This reduction is pivotal in achieving lower overall latency in data-intensive analytical tasks.

2   Empirical Evaluation and Analytical Metrics

Empirical analysis of bulk processing performance typically focuses on metrics such as throughput, latency, and resource utilization. Quantitative measurements consistently validate that bulk processing techniques yield significant efficiency gains. Analytical models incorporate parameters such as collection size, batch execution time, and memory consumption to elucidate the relationship between these variables. By formulating performance as a function of these metrics, it becomes feasible to optimize bulk operations to achieve the desired balance between speed and resource constraints. The resulting improvements in processing efficiency are particularly relevant in high-volume, data-centric environments where scalability and speed are of paramount importance.

Oracle 19c SQL Code Snippet

```
-------------------------------------------------------------------------
-- Create BULK_DATA table for simulating bulk processing operations
-------------------------------------------------------------------------
CREATE TABLE BULK_DATA (
    ID              NUMBER GENERATED BY DEFAULT AS IDENTITY,
    VALUE_NUMBER  NUMBER,
    CREATED_AT    DATE DEFAULT SYSDATE,
    CONSTRAINT BULK_DATA_PK PRIMARY KEY (ID)
);


-------------------------------------------------------------------------
-- Insert sample data into BULK_DATA to simulate operations on large
↪  datasets
-------------------------------------------------------------------------
INSERT ALL
    INTO BULK_DATA (VALUE_NUMBER) VALUES (10)
    INTO BULK_DATA (VALUE_NUMBER) VALUES (25)
    INTO BULK_DATA (VALUE_NUMBER) VALUES (35)
    INTO BULK_DATA (VALUE_NUMBER) VALUES (45)
    INTO BULK_DATA (VALUE_NUMBER) VALUES (55)
    INTO BULK_DATA (VALUE_NUMBER) VALUES (65)
SELECT * FROM DUAL;
COMMIT;


-------------------------------------------------------------------------
-- PL/SQL Block: Demonstrate BULK COLLECT and FORALL for Efficient
↪  Bulk Processing
-------------------------------------------------------------------------
DECLARE
    -- Define collections to hold table data fetched in bulk
    TYPE t_ids IS TABLE OF BULK_DATA.ID%TYPE;
    TYPE t_values IS TABLE OF BULK_DATA.VALUE_NUMBER%TYPE;
    l_ids     t_ids;
    l_values  t_values;

    -- Variables for performance measurement of bulk operations
    l_start TIMESTAMP;
    l_end   TIMESTAMP;

    -- Exception index table for capturing FORALL errors (if any)
    TYPE t_errors IS TABLE OF INTEGER INDEX BY PLS_INTEGER;
    l_errors t_errors;
BEGIN
    l_start := SYSTIMESTAMP;

    -- Bulk retrieve rows into collections using BULK COLLECT to
    ↪  minimize context switches.
    SELECT ID, VALUE_NUMBER
      BULK COLLECT INTO l_ids, l_values
      FROM BULK_DATA;
```

```
l_end := SYSTIMESTAMP;
DBMS_OUTPUT.PUT_LINE('Time taken for BULK COLLECT: ' ||
↪  TO_CHAR(l_end - l_start));

-- Output the fetched data details
FOR idx IN 1..l_values.COUNT LOOP
    DBMS_OUTPUT.PUT_LINE('Row ' || idx || ': ID=' || l_ids(idx)
    ↪  || ', Value=' || l_values(idx));
END LOOP;

-- Demonstrate the FORALL construct for batch updates.
-- This updates VALUE_NUMBER by adding 100 to demonstrate the
↪  algorithmic improvement
-- over traditional row-by-row processing (reducing theoretical
↪  O(n) operations to an aggregated update).
FORALL i IN INDICES OF l_values SAVE EXCEPTIONS
    UPDATE BULK_DATA
        SET VALUE_NUMBER = l_values(i) + 100
      WHERE ID = l_ids(i);

COMMIT;

DBMS_OUTPUT.PUT_LINE('Bulk update using FORALL completed
↪  successfully.');
EXCEPTION
WHEN OTHERS THEN
        -- Handle any exceptions during bulk processing without
        ↪  compromising transaction integrity
        DBMS_OUTPUT.PUT_LINE('Error during bulk operations: ' ||
        ↪  SQLERRM);
        ROLLBACK;
END;
/

---------------------------------------------------------------------
-- Verify the bulk update by selecting updated records from
↪  BULK_DATA
---------------------------------------------------------------------
SELECT * FROM BULK_DATA;
```

Multiple Choice Questions

1. Which of the following best describes the primary performance bottleneck in traditional row-by-row PL/SQL processing?

   (a) Excessive memory allocation

   (b) Numerous context switches between the procedural and

SQL engines

(c) High disk I/O operations

(d) Complex SQL parsing overhead

2. Which PL/SQL construct is specifically designed to perform bulk DML operations, thereby reducing the frequency of context switches?

   (a) BULK COLLECT

   (b) FORALL

   (c) CURSOR FOR LOOP

   (d) EXECUTE IMMEDIATE

3. In the context of BULK COLLECT, what critical system resource must be carefully managed to prevent performance degradation?

   (a) CPU cycles

   (b) Memory usage

   (c) Disk space

   (d) Network bandwidth

4. Mathematically, individual row processing in a loop results in an $O(n)$ overhead due to repeated context switches. How does bulk processing, by aggregating operations, affect this overhead?

   (a) It increases the overhead to $O(n^2)$

   (b) It reduces the effective overhead to a nearly constant factor, approximating $O(1)$

   (c) It maintains the $O(n)$ overhead without any improvements

   (d) It reduces the overhead to $O(\log n)$

5. What advantage does the error handling mechanism within the FORALL construct provide during bulk DML operations?

   (a) It aborts all processing immediately upon encountering the first error.

   (b) It captures exceptions on a per-batch basis, allowing successful operations to commit despite individual errors.

(c) It logs errors without providing a means to handle them, requiring manual correction.

(d) It forces a complete rollback of all operations irrespective of where the error occurs.

6. Which of the following best describes the mechanism by which BULK COLLECT minimizes context switching overhead?

    (a) It iteratively retrieves each row from the result set.

    (b) It aggregates multiple rows into a single in-memory collection through one bulk fetch operation.

    (c) It replaces SQL queries with dynamic PL/SQL block executions.

    (d) It processes DML operations one-by-one with enhanced caching.

7. In empirical evaluations of bulk processing performance, which metrics are most critical?

    (a) Throughput, latency, and resource utilization

    (b) Disk I/O rates and network latency exclusively

    (c) CPU clock speed and memory bus throughput

    (d) User interface responsiveness and transaction simplicity

Answers:

1. **B: Numerous context switches between the procedural and SQL engines**
   Traditional row-by-row processing entails a separate context switch for each iteration, which accumulates significant overhead when dealing with large datasets.

2. **B: FORALL**
   The FORALL construct is engineered to perform bulk DML operations by iterating over an entire collection in a single execution context, reducing the number of transitions between PL/SQL and SQL engines.

3. **B: Memory usage**
   BULK COLLECT retrieves multiple rows into an in-memory collection. Without careful memory management, the increased memory footprint can lead to performance issues or system saturation.

4. **B: It reduces the effective overhead to a nearly constant factor, approximating O(1)**
By aggregating operations, bulk processing minimizes the individual cost of context switches. Although the total work remains proportional to the data volume, the number of costly context switches is largely independent of n, effectively approaching O(1).

5. **B: It captures exceptions on a per-batch basis, allowing successful operations to commit despite individual errors**
FORALL's error handling mechanism allows the capture of exceptions at the batch level. This granular error management enables the continuation of processing for non-erroneous records, thereby preserving transactional integrity.

6. **B: It aggregates multiple rows into a single in-memory collection through one bulk fetch operation**
BULK COLLECT drastically reduces context switching by fetching many rows at once, rather than issuing a separate fetch command for every row, thereby reducing computational overhead.

7. **A: Throughput, latency, and resource utilization**
Empirical performance evaluations of bulk processing techniques focus on these metrics to assess how effectively the reduction in context switching improves overall data processing efficiency.

Chapter 10

Data Filtering Techniques and Conditional Querying

Fundamental Constructs for Data Filtering

Data filtering in relational database systems is predicated on the meticulous specification of conditions that delimit the set of tuples retrieved from one or more relations. At its core, the filtering process harnesses the power of the WHERE clause, which encodes logical predicates to determine the membership of each row in the resultant dataset. The semantics of these predicates are grounded in Boolean logic, where each logical expression is evaluated as either true or false. An expression such as $a = b$ or $c > d$ forms the basis of these predicates, and the combination of such elementary comparisons via logical operators enables the construction of intricate filtering criteria.

1 Predicate Evaluation and Boolean Algebra

The formulation of predicates employs a set of relational operators, including $=$, $<$, $>$, $\leq$, and $\geq$, to compare column values against literal constants or other attributes. The integration of these operators within Boolean expressions utilizes the axioms of Boolean algebra, thereby ensuring a coherent and consistent evaluation process. When multiple conditions are required, they are joined through logical connectives such as AND, OR, and NOT. The conjunction (AND) operator requires that all joined conditions evaluate to true, while the disjunction (OR) operator stipulates that the truth of any single condition suffices for overall validation. The application of these operators adheres to a defined order of precedence, which is often made explicit through the use of parentheses. This formalism guarantees that complex expressions involving nested logical conditions are evaluated with precision and that the filtering process remains both predictable and understandable.

2 The Role of the WHERE Clause in Query Syntax

Within the context of query formulation, the WHERE clause serves as the primary conduit for embedding conditional logic directly into the syntax of a SQL statement. This clause is not merely an adjunct to the query; it constitutes the essential mechanism by which records are selectively extracted based on a predefined predicate. The declarative nature of the WHERE clause allows for the expression of criteria without necessitating an explicit procedural control structure, thus aligning with the set-oriented philosophy of relational databases. The design of the WHERE clause affords significant expressive power, permitting query authors to stipulate both rudimentary and composite conditions that precisely encapsulate the required data subset. Such declarative expressions ensure that the process of data retrieval is intrinsically linked to the logical specifications inherent in the query, thereby promoting clarity and analytical rigor.

Advanced Strategies in Conditional Querying

Beyond the elementary application of predicates, advanced conditional querying techniques further refine the ability to isolate relevant data segments. The strategic assembly of multiple logical conditions and the employment of conditional expressions serve to augment the precision and flexibility of data filtering methods.

1 Compound Conditions and Logical Connectives

Compound conditions are constructed by the deliberate combination of several predicates, enabling the filtering mechanism to address scenarios characterized by multi-dimensional criteria. The logical connectives, predominantly AND and OR, facilitate the formulation of composite expressions that capture the complexity of real-world data requirements. In cases with layered conditions, the careful use of parentheses is essential to override the inherent operator precedence, ensuring that the evaluation order mirrors the intended logical structure. Intermediate results obtained from the evaluation of sub-expressions contribute to the overall decision process, rendering the expanded expression an effective instrument for the isolation of highly specific data subsets. This systematic approach, rooted in the formal properties of Boolean algebra, renders the process of conditional querying both scalable and adaptable to varied analytical contexts.

2 Conditional Expressions for Targeted Data Isolation

Conditional expressions introduce an additional layer of sophistication to the process of data filtering by embedding decision-making constructs directly into query expressions. Such expressions enable the query to dynamically adjust its filtering logic based on varying criteria, thus accommodating irregularities and fluctuations within the dataset. These expressions function in a manner analogous to conditional operators found in programming languages, wherein the selection of a particular outcome is contingent upon the evaluation of a preceding condition. For example, a conditional construct may determine the inclusion of a row based on whether a specified attribute exceeds a given threshold. The elegance of this method lies in its ability to condense multiple evaluative steps into a singular declarative statement, thereby enhancing both the readability and the performance of the filtering operation. Through the judicious use of conditional logic, queries gain an increased capacity to isolate data with both precision and efficiency, thereby advancing the analytical capabilities inherent in data filtering practices.

Oracle 19c SQL Code Snippet

```sql
-- Create the ANALYTICS_DATA table to store data for filtering
-- demonstration
CREATE TABLE ANALYTICS_DATA (
    DATA_ID        NUMBER GENERATED BY DEFAULT AS IDENTITY,
    ATTRIBUTE      VARCHAR2(50),
    NUMERIC_VALUE  NUMBER,
    TEXT_VALUE     VARCHAR2(10),
    RECORD_DATE    DATE,
    CONSTRAINT ANALYTICS_DATA_PK PRIMARY KEY (DATA_ID)
);

-- Insert sample data into ANALYTICS_DATA
INSERT ALL
    INTO ANALYTICS_DATA (ATTRIBUTE, NUMERIC_VALUE, TEXT_VALUE,
    -- RECORD_DATE)
        VALUES ('ACTIVE', 120, 'A', DATE '2023-01-15')
    INTO ANALYTICS_DATA (ATTRIBUTE, NUMERIC_VALUE, TEXT_VALUE,
    -- RECORD_DATE)
        VALUES ('INACTIVE', 80, 'B', DATE '2023-02-20')
    INTO ANALYTICS_DATA (ATTRIBUTE, NUMERIC_VALUE, TEXT_VALUE,
    -- RECORD_DATE)
        VALUES ('ACTIVE', 45, 'C', DATE '2023-03-10')
    INTO ANALYTICS_DATA (ATTRIBUTE, NUMERIC_VALUE, TEXT_VALUE,
    -- RECORD_DATE)
        VALUES ('ACTIVE', 95, 'B', DATE '2023-04-05')
SELECT * FROM DUAL;
COMMIT;

-- Basic Filtering Query using simple predicates and Boolean logic
SELECT
    DATA_ID,
    ATTRIBUTE,
    NUMERIC_VALUE,
    TEXT_VALUE,
    RECORD_DATE,
    -- Use CASE for conditional categorization based on
    -- NUMERIC_VALUE
    CASE
        WHEN NUMERIC_VALUE > 100 THEN 'High'
        WHEN NUMERIC_VALUE BETWEEN 50 AND 100 THEN 'Medium'
        ELSE 'Low'
    END AS VALUE_CATEGORY
FROM
    ANALYTICS_DATA
WHERE
    ATTRIBUTE = 'ACTIVE'              -- Equality predicate (a = b)
    AND (NUMERIC_VALUE > 80           -- Comparison predicate (c > d)
        OR TEXT_VALUE IN ('A','B')) -- Compound condition using OR
        -- operator
    AND RECORD_DATE BETWEEN DATE '2023-01-01' AND SYSDATE;
```

```
-----------------------------------------------------------------
-- Stored Procedure demonstrating dynamic data filtering based on an
↪  input threshold
-----------------------------------------------------------------


CREATE OR REPLACE PROCEDURE get_filtered_data (p_threshold IN
↪  NUMBER) IS
BEGIN
    FOR rec IN (
        SELECT DATA_ID, ATTRIBUTE, NUMERIC_VALUE, TEXT_VALUE,
        ↪  RECORD_DATE
        FROM ANALYTICS_DATA
        WHERE NUMERIC_VALUE > p_threshold
          AND ATTRIBUTE = 'ACTIVE'
    ) LOOP
        DBMS_OUTPUT.PUT_LINE('Data ID: ' || rec.DATA_ID || ', Value:
        ↪  ' || rec.NUMERIC_VALUE);
    END LOOP;
EXCEPTION
    WHEN OTHERS THEN
        DBMS_OUTPUT.PUT_LINE('Error in get_filtered_data: ' ||
        ↪  SQLERRM);
END get_filtered_data;
/


-----------------------------------------------------------------
-- PL/SQL Block demonstrating algorithmic conditional filtering and
↪  updates
-----------------------------------------------------------------


DECLARE
    v_count NUMBER;
BEGIN
    -- Count rows that meet advanced filtering criteria using
    ↪  compound conditions and Boolean logic
    SELECT COUNT(*)
      INTO v_count
      FROM ANALYTICS_DATA
     WHERE (NUMERIC_VALUE > 100 AND TEXT_VALUE = 'A')
        OR (NUMERIC_VALUE < 50 AND TEXT_VALUE = 'C');

    DBMS_OUTPUT.PUT_LINE('Number of filtered rows: ' || v_count);

    -- Update NUMERIC_VALUE based on conditions using a CASE
    ↪  expression for targeted transformation
    UPDATE ANALYTICS_DATA
       SET NUMERIC_VALUE = CASE
                              WHEN NUMERIC_VALUE < 50 THEN
                              ↪  NUMERIC_VALUE * 1.10
                              WHEN NUMERIC_VALUE BETWEEN 50 AND
                              ↪  100 THEN NUMERIC_VALUE * 1.05
                              ELSE NUMERIC_VALUE
```

99

```
                              END
        WHERE ATTRIBUTE = 'ACTIVE';

        COMMIT;
EXCEPTION
        WHEN OTHERS THEN
             ROLLBACK;
             DBMS_OUTPUT.PUT_LINE('Error in PL/SQL block: ' || SQLERRM);
END;
/

----------------------------------------------------------------
-- Query using nested subqueries to demonstrate layered filtering
↪   logic with subfiltering
----------------------------------------------------------------

SELECT *
FROM ANALYTICS_DATA
WHERE DATA_ID IN (
      SELECT DATA_ID
         FROM ANALYTICS_DATA
      WHERE NUMERIC_VALUE > 90
);
```

Multiple Choice Questions

1. Which clause in SQL is primarily responsible for filtering rows based on Boolean predicates?

    (a) FROM Clause
    (b) WHERE Clause
    (c) GROUP BY Clause
    (d) ORDER BY Clause

2. In the context of data filtering in SQL, which operator is used to test equality between a column and a literal constant or another column?

    (a) <>
    (b) =
    (c) >
    (d) !=

3. Which logical operator ensures that a composite condition in a SQL WHERE clause evaluates to true only when all individual predicates are true?

(a) OR

(b) AND

(c) NOT

(d) XOR

4. What is the primary purpose of using parentheses in compound logical expressions within a WHERE clause?

(a) They improve the aesthetics of the SQL query.

(b) They force the SQL parser to ignore default operator precedence.

(c) They explicitly define the intended evaluation order of nested predicates.

(d) They enable the execution of procedural logic within a query.

5. Which SQL construct allows embedding conditional logic within a SELECT statement to dynamically return values based on specified criteria?

(a) CASE expression

(b) Subquery

(c) JOIN clause

(d) Aggregate function

6. How do compound conditions enhance data filtering in SQL queries?

(a) By running multiple queries simultaneously.

(b) By allowing combinations of multiple predicates using logical operators and nesting.

(c) By automatically optimizing query execution.

(d) By eliminating the need for explicit predicate definitions.

7. What distinct advantage do dynamic conditional expressions provide in the context of data filtering?

(a) They simplify query syntax by replacing all WHERE clauses.

(b) They enable embedding decision-making logic within single declarative statements, improving readability and maintainability.

(c) They automatically generate indexes for faster query performance.

(d) They minimize the need for security auditing in database queries.

Answers:

1. **B: WHERE Clause**
   The WHERE clause is used to restrict the rows returned by a query based on specified Boolean predicates. Its role is essential for filtering data in relational databases.

2. **B: =**
   The equality operator "=" is fundamental in SQL for comparing column values with either literal constants or other columns, thus serving as a cornerstone for constructing predicates in data filtering.

3. **B: AND**
   The AND operator stipulates that all combined conditions must evaluate to true for the overall expression to be true, ensuring that only rows meeting every predicate are selected.

4. **C: They explicitly define the intended evaluation order of nested predicates**
   Parentheses are crucial in compound logical expressions because they override the default operator precedence, thereby clarifying the evaluation order and ensuring that the logic is executed as intended.

5. **A: CASE expression**
   The CASE expression allows a SQL query to include inline conditional logic. This construct dynamically returns values based on specified conditions, which is ideal for situations where output needs to adapt according to data values.

6. **B: By allowing combinations of multiple predicates using logical operators and nesting**
   Compound conditions enhance the expressiveness of SQL queries by enabling the combination of several predicates. The logical operators (AND, OR) and the use of parentheses for nesting

empower developers to construct sophisticated filtering criteria.

7. **B: They enable embedding decision-making logic within single declarative statements, improving readability and maintainability**

   Dynamic conditional expressions, exemplified by constructs like CASE, encapsulate complex logic directly within the query. This encapsulation not only streamlines the query but also makes the logic clearer and easier to maintain compared to procedural implementations.

Chapter 11

Aggregation Functions and Grouping in PL/SQL

Conceptual Foundations of Aggregation in PL/SQL

Aggregation functions constitute a class of operators that transform a collection of values into a singular representative metric. Within PL/SQL, these functions play an integral role by bridging the procedural constructs of the language with the declarative strengths of SQL. Fundamental functions such as SUM, AVG, $COUNT$, MIN, and MAX are designed to encapsulate the arithmetic and statistical properties of data sets, thereby enabling the consolidation of disparate data records into meaningful summaries. The process of aggregation is not performed arbitrarily; rather, it is grounded in well-established mathematical principles that ensure the operations are both stable and predictable. By incorporating these functions directly into PL/SQL queries, the language offers a robust mechanism for translating a large volume of detailed, row-level data into concise analytic insights.

Mathematical Formulation and Properties of Aggregate Functions

Mathematically, each aggregate function in PL/SQL can be viewed as a mapping from a set of numeric or ordered values to a single value that characterizes some aspect of the distribution. For example, the SUM function is formally defined as

$$SUM(X) = \sum_{x \in X} x,$$

where X is a finite set of values. Similarly, the AVG function is expressed as

$$AVG(X) = \frac{\sum_{x \in X} x}{|X|},$$

with $|X|$ representing the cardinality of the set X. The $COUNT$ function, in its dual capacity, may quantify the total number of elements in X or exclude null entries depending on the context of application. These functions inherently rely on properties such as commutativity and associativity, which are crucial for ensuring that parallel computations and incremental updates yield consistent results. Such properties underscore the theoretical rigor behind the deployment of aggregate functions in data analytics and highlight the careful balance between computational efficiency and mathematical precision.

The Role of the GROUP BY Clause

The GROUP BY clause serves as the structural foundation for organizing data into distinct partitions prior to the evaluation of aggregate functions. This clause systematically divides an entire dataset into disjoint subsets based on one or more specified attributes. Formally, if D denotes the dataset and an equivalence relation is defined over a subset of its attributes, then the GROUP BY clause partitions D into groups $\{G_1, G_2, \ldots, G_k\}$ such that any two elements a and b in D belong to the same group if and only if they satisfy the equivalence condition. This methodical partitioning enables each aggregate function to operate within the localized context of a group, thereby producing a set of summary records that reflect the inherent structure of the original data. The precise evaluation of groups is facilitated by the underlying Boolean logic that governs predicate evaluation, ensuring that each record is accurately assigned to a corresponding subset based on its attribute values.

Applications in Analytic Data Consolidation

The integration of aggregate functions with the GROUP BY clause provides a potent framework for synthesizing analytic insights from large and complex datasets. When applied to grouped data, aggregate functions yield essential descriptive statistics such as total sums, averages, counts, and extreme values, each offering a different perspective on the data's distribution. This process of consolidation is pivotal in transforming raw, granular data into high-level summaries that can reveal critical trends and anomalies. In many analytic contexts, such as the evaluation of temporal trends or the segmentation of categorical data, the conjoint application of these techniques helps in isolating the salient features of the data. By summarizing data along the lines of natural groupings, PL/SQL enables the derivation of insights that are both precise and computationally efficient, thereby expediting the overall process of data analysis and decision-making.

Oracle 19c SQL Code Snippet

```
-- Create a table to simulate sales data demonstrating aggregation
↪   functions and grouping
CREATE TABLE SALES_REPORT (
    SALE_ID      NUMBER GENERATED BY DEFAULT AS IDENTITY,
    SALE_DATE    DATE,
    REGION       VARCHAR2(30),
    PRODUCT      VARCHAR2(50),
    QUANTITY     NUMBER,
    UNIT_PRICE   NUMBER,
    CONSTRAINT SALES_REPORT_PK PRIMARY KEY (SALE_ID)
);

-- Insert sample data into SALES_REPORT
INSERT ALL
    INTO SALES_REPORT (SALE_DATE, REGION, PRODUCT, QUANTITY,
    ↪   UNIT_PRICE)
        VALUES (DATE '2023-10-01', 'North', 'ProductA', 10, 15.5)
    INTO SALES_REPORT (SALE_DATE, REGION, PRODUCT, QUANTITY,
    ↪   UNIT_PRICE)
```

```
            VALUES (DATE '2023-10-01', 'South', 'ProductB', 8, 22.0)
    INTO SALES_REPORT (SALE_DATE, REGION, PRODUCT, QUANTITY,
    ↪  UNIT_PRICE)
            VALUES (DATE '2023-10-02', 'North', 'ProductA', 5, 15.5)
    INTO SALES_REPORT (SALE_DATE, REGION, PRODUCT, QUANTITY,
    ↪  UNIT_PRICE)
            VALUES (DATE '2023-10-02', 'East', 'ProductC', 12, 18.0)
    INTO SALES_REPORT (SALE_DATE, REGION, PRODUCT, QUANTITY,
    ↪  UNIT_PRICE)
            VALUES (DATE '2023-10-03', 'South', 'ProductB', 7, 22.0)
    INTO SALES_REPORT (SALE_DATE, REGION, PRODUCT, QUANTITY,
    ↪  UNIT_PRICE)
            VALUES (DATE '2023-10-03', 'East', 'ProductC', 9, 18.0)
SELECT * FROM DUAL;
COMMIT;


-------------------------------------------------------------------------
-- Demonstrate aggregate functions: SUM, AVG, COUNT, MIN, MAX and
↪  the use of GROUP BY
--
-- Note: The total sale per transaction is calculated as:
--      SALE_VALUE = QUANTITY * UNIT_PRICE.
--
-- The aggregate equations in mathematical terms are:
--      SUM(X) = SUM(QUANTITY * UNIT_PRICE) for a set X of
↪  transactions.
--      AVG(X) = (SUM(QUANTITY * UNIT_PRICE)) / (COUNT(*))
-------------------------------------------------------------------------


SELECT
    REGION,
    COUNT(*) AS TOTAL_TRANSACTIONS,
    SUM(QUANTITY) AS TOTAL_QUANTITY,
    SUM(QUANTITY * UNIT_PRICE) AS TOTAL_SALES,
    AVG(QUANTITY * UNIT_PRICE) AS AVG_SALE_VALUE,
    MIN(UNIT_PRICE) AS MIN_UNIT_PRICE,
    MAX(UNIT_PRICE) AS MAX_UNIT_PRICE
FROM SALES_REPORT
GROUP BY REGION;


-------------------------------------------------------------------------
-- Grouping by multiple dimensions (SALE_DATE and REGION) to analyze
↪  daily figures per region
-------------------------------------------------------------------------


SELECT
    SALE_DATE,
    REGION,
    SUM(QUANTITY) AS DAILY_QUANTITY,
    SUM(QUANTITY * UNIT_PRICE) AS DAILY_SALES
FROM SALES_REPORT
GROUP BY SALE_DATE, REGION
ORDER BY SALE_DATE, REGION;
```

```
--------------------------------------------------------------
-- Using the HAVING clause to filter groups: show regions with
↪   TOTAL_SALES greater than 200
--------------------------------------------------------------

SELECT
    REGION,
    SUM(QUANTITY * UNIT_PRICE) AS TOTAL_SALES
FROM SALES_REPORT
GROUP BY REGION
HAVING SUM(QUANTITY * UNIT_PRICE) > 200;


--------------------------------------------------------------
-- Demonstrate the use of window functions for computing a running
↪   total of sales per region
--------------------------------------------------------------

SELECT
    SALE_DATE,
    REGION,
    SUM(QUANTITY * UNIT_PRICE) AS DAILY_SALES,
    SUM(SUM(QUANTITY * UNIT_PRICE)) OVER (PARTITION BY REGION ORDER
    ↪   BY SALE_DATE) AS RUNNING_TOTAL
FROM SALES_REPORT
GROUP BY SALE_DATE, REGION
ORDER BY REGION, SALE_DATE;


--------------------------------------------------------------
-- Cleanup: Optionally drop the SALES_REPORT table after
↪   demonstration
-- DROP TABLE SALES_REPORT PURGE;
--------------------------------------------------------------
```

Multiple Choice Questions

1. Which of the following best captures the role of aggregate functions in PL/SQL?

    (a) They serve merely as arithmetic operators applied individually to each row.

    (b) They bridge the procedural constructs of PL/SQL with SQL's declarative power by summarizing large datasets.

    (c) They exclusively perform data transformations without enabling statistical analysis.

    (d) They eliminate the need for data filtering by replacing the WHERE clause.

2. Which of the following formulas correctly defines the AVG function in PL/SQL?

   (a) AVG(X) = (X x) / |X|

   (b) AVG(X) = (X x) - |X|

   (c) AVG(X) = |X| / (X x)

   (d) AVG(X) = MAX(X)

3. Which mathematical properties are essential for aggregate functions to ensure consistent outcomes in parallel or incremental computation?

   (a) Commutativity and Distributivity

   (b) Commutativity and Associativity

   (c) Associativity and Idempotence

   (d) Distributivity and Identity

4. What is the primary purpose of the GROUP BY clause in the context of PL/SQL aggregation?

   (a) To sort query results in a specific order.

   (b) To partition a dataset into disjoint subsets so that each group can be aggregated independently.

   (c) To join multiple tables using common columns.

   (d) To filter out rows that do not meet specified conditions.

5. In the framework of set theory, how does the GROUP BY clause partition a dataset D?

   (a) It randomly segments D into a fixed number of groups.

   (b) It sorts D in ascending or descending order, implicitly grouping similar records.

   (c) It establishes an equivalence relation on selected attributes, partitioning D into groups where any two records are equivalent based on those attributes.

   (d) It duplicates records so that each appears in every possible subset.

6. Which scenario best illustrates the analytical consolidation achieved by using aggregate functions in conjunction with the GROUP BY clause?

(a) Computing a running total across ungrouped transactional data.

(b) Calculating the average, sum, and count of sales figures segmented by geographical region.

(c) Inserting individual rows into a table without performing any summary operations.

(d) Updating individual records on a row-by-row basis.

7. Why is the integration of aggregation functions with the GROUP BY clause critical in analytic data processing within PL/SQL?

(a) It allows for encrypting each row's data at a granular level.

(b) It transforms granular row-level data into concise, group-specific summaries that reveal underlying trends and patterns.

(c) It replaces the need for traditional SQL queries entirely.

(d) It speeds up the processing of individual records without any summarization.

Answers:

1. **B: They bridge the procedural constructs of PL/SQL with SQL's declarative power by summarizing large datasets.**
This option correctly reflects that aggregate functions in PL/SQL integrate set-based SQL operations with procedural logic to transform detailed data into meaningful summaries.

2. **A: $AVG(X) = (X x) / |X|$**
The average function is mathematically defined as the sum of the elements divided by the number of elements. This formula directly captures the definition used in PL/SQL aggregations.

3. **B: Commutativity and Associativity**
These properties ensure that the order of operations does not affect the final aggregated result, which is critical in parallel computations and when updating data incrementally.

4. **B: To partition a dataset into disjoint subsets so that each group can be aggregated independently.**

The GROUP BY clause is designed to segregate data into distinct groups based on specified attributes, enabling aggregate functions to compute summaries per group.

5. **C: It establishes an equivalence relation on selected attributes, partitioning D into groups where any two records are equivalent based on those attributes.**
This option explains how, from a set-theoretical perspective, GROUP BY uses an equivalence relation to divide data into subsets where records share common attribute values.

6. **B: Calculating the average, sum, and count of sales figures segmented by geographical region.**
Grouping sales data by region and then applying aggregate functions is a canonical example of how detailed data is consolidated into high-level summaries, enabling effective trend analysis.

7. **B: It transforms granular row-level data into concise, group-specific summaries that reveal underlying trends and patterns.**
By combining aggregation with grouping, PL/SQL facilitates the derivation of insightful summaries from detailed records, which is a cornerstone of analytical data processing.

Chapter 12

Sorting and Ranking Data with Analytic Functions

Ordering Concepts in Analytic Queries

Within the realm of analytic queries, the notion of ordering is foundational for the subsequent evaluation of ranking functions. The ordering of data is achieved by imposing a total ordering on one or more attributes, thereby creating a sequence in which each element is comparable using relational operators such as $<$ and $>$. This structured sequence enables the classification of elements within a dataset according to their relative magnitude or precedence. In analytic functions, the ordering is defined within the analytical context by specifying an order within each partition of data. The existence of a well-defined ordering facilitates the correct and meaningful application of ranking functions by ensuring that the analytical operations are applied to a cohesive, sorted set of values derived from the larger dataset.

Conceptual Examination of the RANK Function

The $RANK$ function is an analytic tool designed to assign a rank to each row within an ordered partition. Conceptually, the rank of a row is determined by the number of rows that precede it in the specified order. More formally, let T be a finite set of tuples and let an ordering function $g : T \to \mathbb{R}$ be defined such that for any two tuples t_i and t_j, the comparison $g(t_i) < g(t_j)$ is meaningful. In this context, the $RANK$ of a tuple t_i is defined as

$$\text{RANK}(t_i) = 1 + |\{t \in T : g(t) < g(t_i)\}|,$$

where the cardinality operator $|\cdot|$ counts the number of elements that possess a strictly lower ordering value than t_i. An important characteristic of the $RANK$ function is that when multiple tuples share an identical ordering value, they are assigned the same rank. Consequently, this mechanism produces gaps in the sequence of ranking numbers, as the subsequent rank is incremented by the total number of tied records rather than by a single unit. The mathematical formulation emphasizes the role of the underlying order and the set cardinality in defining the rank, ensuring that the assigned values truly represent the ordinal positions within each partition.

Distinct Characteristics of the DENSE_RANK Function

In contrast to the $RANK$ function, the $DENSE\_RANK$ function provides an alternative approach to ranking in which the sequence of ranking numbers is contiguous, even in the presence of tied values. For a dataset partitioned and ordered in a manner analogous to that used in the $RANK$ function, the $DENSE\_RANK$ of a tuple t_i is determined by the number of distinct ordering values that precede or are equal to $g(t_i)$. Formally, if Y represents the set of unique ordering values extracted from the partition, then the assignment is given by

$$\text{DENSE\_RANK}(t_i) = 1 + |\{y \in Y : y < g(t_i)\}|.$$

This formulation ensures that ties do not induce any gaps in the ranking sequence, as each increment corresponds directly to a distinct order value rather than to the multiplicity of tied records. The absence of gaps in the dense ranking sequence allows for a more streamlined interpretation of ordinal positions, which is particularly advantageous in scenarios where data segmentation and prioritization require an uninterrupted sequence of rank values. The dense ranking approach maintains close adherence to the conceptual model of ranking by normalizing the treatment of tied entries and delivering a refined ranking that mirrors the uniqueness of the underlying data distribution.

Implications for Data Prioritization and Segmentation

Analytic functions that perform sorting and ranking serve as powerful mechanisms for data prioritization and segmentation within large-scale analytical environments. By applying functions such as $RANK$ and $DENSE\_RANK$, it is possible to partition a dataset into carefully ordered subsets, each reflecting a specific order of significance as determined by the chosen attributes. The process begins with the establishment of a well-defined ordering criterion, which systematically arranges the data. Following this, the ranking functions calculate the ordinal positions of each element within the partition, thereby enabling the identification of top entries, median positions, or other segments of interest.

This methodology affords the capability to prioritize records based on their relative standing, ensuring that analytical results are not only descriptive but also inferential in nature. In settings where resource allocation, performance measurement, or competitive analysis is paramount, the ability to assign ranks to data entries facilitates the isolation of key elements that merit further consideration. The contrast between the $RANK$ and $DENSE\_RANK$ functions offers versatility in addressing varying analytical requirements. The introduction of gaps in the ranking sequence under the $RANK$ function can highlight the concentration of identical values, while the contiguous sequencing of the $DENSE\_RANK$ function provides a simplified and cohesive ranking structure.

By rigorously defining ordering and ranking mechanisms through formal mathematical expressions and leveraging analytic functions to apply these definitions, data segmentation and prioritization are executed with both precision and clarity. Such techniques underscore the integral role of analytic functions in transforming raw, unstructured data into meaningful ordered representations that facilitate advanced analytical operations.

Oracle 19c SQL Code Snippet

```
-- Drop the EMP_SALARY table if it already exists (using an
↪ anonymous PL/SQL block)
BEGIN
    EXECUTE IMMEDIATE 'DROP TABLE EMP_SALARY';
EXCEPTION
    WHEN OTHERS THEN
        IF SQLCODE != -942 THEN
            RAISE;
        END IF;
END;
/

-- Create the EMP_SALARY table to store employee records with salary
↪ details.
CREATE TABLE EMP_SALARY (
    EMP_ID        NUMBER GENERATED BY DEFAULT AS IDENTITY,
    EMP_NAME      VARCHAR2(50),
    DEPARTMENT    VARCHAR2(50),
    SALARY        NUMBER,
    CONSTRAINT EMP_SALARY_PK PRIMARY KEY (EMP_ID)
);

-- Insert sample employee records into EMP_SALARY.
-- Some employees have identical SALARY values to demonstrate
↪ ranking with ties.
INSERT ALL
    INTO EMP_SALARY (EMP_NAME, DEPARTMENT, SALARY) VALUES ('Alice',
    ↪ 'Sales', 9000)
    INTO EMP_SALARY (EMP_NAME, DEPARTMENT, SALARY) VALUES ('Bob',
    ↪ 'Sales', 8000)
    INTO EMP_SALARY (EMP_NAME, DEPARTMENT, SALARY) VALUES
    ↪ ('Charlie', 'Sales', 9000)
    INTO EMP_SALARY (EMP_NAME, DEPARTMENT, SALARY) VALUES ('Dave',
    ↪ 'HR',    7000)
    INTO EMP_SALARY (EMP_NAME, DEPARTMENT, SALARY) VALUES ('Eve',
    ↪ 'HR',    7000)
    INTO EMP_SALARY (EMP_NAME, DEPARTMENT, SALARY) VALUES ('Frank',
    ↪ 'HR',    8500)
    INTO EMP_SALARY (EMP_NAME, DEPARTMENT, SALARY) VALUES ('Grace',
    ↪ 'IT',    9500)
    INTO EMP_SALARY (EMP_NAME, DEPARTMENT, SALARY) VALUES ('Heidi',
    ↪ 'IT',    9500)
    INTO EMP_SALARY (EMP_NAME, DEPARTMENT, SALARY) VALUES ('Ivan',
    ↪ 'IT',    7000)
    INTO EMP_SALARY (EMP_NAME, DEPARTMENT, SALARY) VALUES ('Judy',
    ↪ 'IT',    8200)
SELECT * FROM DUAL;
COMMIT;
```

```
-- Demonstration 1: Overall Ranking using Analytic Functions
--
-- The RANK function assigns a rank to each row ordered by SALARY
↪  (in descending order).
-- It is defined conceptually as:
--    RANK(t) = 1 + (number of rows with SALARY greater than the
↪  current row)
-- In cases of ties, identical SALARY values receive the same rank
↪  which results in gaps.
--
-- The DENSE_RANK function, in contrast, assigns consecutive ranking
↪  numbers without gaps.
-------------------------------------------------------------------------

SELECT
    EMP_ID,
    EMP_NAME,
    DEPARTMENT,
    SALARY,
    RANK() OVER (ORDER BY SALARY DESC) AS OVERALL_RANK,
    DENSE_RANK() OVER (ORDER BY SALARY DESC) AS OVERALL_DENSE_RANK
FROM
    EMP_SALARY
ORDER BY
    OVERALL_RANK;


-------------------------------------------------------------------------
-- Demonstration 2: Partitioned Ranking within Departments
--
-- Here, the dataset is partitioned by DEPARTMENT so that ranking is
↪  computed
-- within each department independently.
--
-- The formulation remains the same:
--    RANK(t) within a partition = 1 + (number of rows in the same
↪  department
--                                   with a higher SALARY)
--    DENSE_RANK uses distinct SALARY values to generate a
↪  continuous sequence.
-------------------------------------------------------------------------

SELECT
    EMP_ID,
    EMP_NAME,
    DEPARTMENT,
    SALARY,
    RANK() OVER (PARTITION BY DEPARTMENT ORDER BY SALARY DESC) AS
    ↪  DEPT_RANK,
    DENSE_RANK() OVER (PARTITION BY DEPARTMENT ORDER BY SALARY DESC)
    ↪  AS DEPT_DENSE_RANK
FROM
    EMP_SALARY
ORDER BY
```

```
DEPARTMENT, DEPT_RANK;
```

```
---------------------------------------------------------------------
-- Demonstration 3: Running Total Computation based on Ordered
↪  Salaries
--
-- This query shows how a running total (cumulative aggregation)
↪  depends
-- on the well-defined ordering of data. The ordering concept is
↪  crucial
-- for computing sequential aggregates.
---------------------------------------------------------------------
```

```
SELECT
    EMP_ID,
    EMP_NAME,
    SALARY,
    SUM(SALARY) OVER (ORDER BY SALARY DESC
                      ROWS BETWEEN UNBOUNDED PRECEDING AND CURRENT
                      ↪  ROW) AS RUNNING_TOTAL
FROM
    EMP_SALARY
ORDER BY
    SALARY DESC;
```

——– – This SQL
code snippet, designed for Oracle 19c, demonstrates the – implementation of key analytic functions relevant to sorting and ranking. – It implements the algorithms and formulas discussed in the
chapter: – – 1. The RANK() function assigns ranks based on the
number of records with – higher values, introducing gaps in the
ranking for tied values. – – 2. The DENSE_RANK() function
computes a contiguous set of rank numbers – independent of the
multiplicity of tied values. – – 3. Partitioning by an attribute,
such as DEPARTMENT, allows localized – ranking within groups,
underscoring the versatility of analytic functions. – – 4. The running total query demonstrates the importance of ordering – when
applying window functions for cumulative analysis. ——————

——————————————————————————————–

Multiple Choice Questions

1. What is the primary role of ordering in analytic queries as
   described in the chapter?

   (a) To perform aggregate computations on grouped data.

(b) To filter data based solely on equality conditions.

(c) To impose a total ordering on one or more attributes, thereby enabling meaningful ranking.

(d) To randomize the dataset for unbiased sampling.

2. How is the RANK function conceptually defined in an ordered partition?

    (a) It assigns a rank based on the natural order of data insertion.

    (b) It assigns a rank as the total number of rows in the partition.

    (c) It assigns a rank equal to 1 plus the number of rows that have a strictly lower ordering value than the current row.

    (d) It assigns a rank based on the sum of all preceding ordering values.

3. Which statement best explains the key difference between the RANK and DENSE_RANK functions?

    (a) RANK produces a continuous sequence while DENSE_RANK creates gaps for tied values.

    (b) RANK fails to handle ties, whereas DENSE_RANK ignores the ordering criteria.

    (c) RANK assigns identical ranks to tied entries with gaps in the subsequent sequence, whereas DENSE_RANK assigns consecutive, uninterrupted rank numbers.

    (d) RANK is used only for numerical data, while DENSE_RANK is applicable to textual data.

4. Which of the following mathematical formulations correctly represents the conceptual definition of the RANK function for a tuple t_i?

    (a) $RANK(t_i) = | t \ T : g(t) > g(t_i) |$

    (b) $RANK(t_i) = 1 + | t \ T : g(t) < g(t_i) |$

    (c) $RANK(t_i) = | t \ T : g(t) = g(t_i) |$

    (d) $RANK(t_i) = 1 + (g(t) < g(t_i))$

5. How does the DENSE_RANK function determine the rank of a tuple within a partition?

(a) By counting all rows with lower ordering values and then adding one.

(b) By counting the number of distinct ordering values that are less than the tuple's ordering value and adding one.

(c) By computing the arithmetic mean of the ordering values.

(d) By assigning the row number based on its physical storage location.

6. What practical advantage do analytic functions like RANK and DENSE_RANK provide in data segmentation and prioritization?

(a) They automatically eliminate duplicate rows from the dataset.

(b) They simplify the process of aggregating text data.

(c) They enable the partitioning of data into ordered subsets that identify relative standings or priorities.

(d) They accelerate join operations by reorganizing data physically.

7. Why is establishing a well-defined ordering criterion crucial when applying analytic ranking functions?

(a) Because it minimizes the storage space required by the database.

(b) Because it ensures that functions operate on a cohesive, sorted set of data, thus yielding meaningful and accurate ranks.

(c) Because it allows functions to bypass the necessity of partitioning data.

(d) Because it enables the direct computation of aggregate functions without additional sorting.

Answers:

1. **C: To impose a total ordering on one or more attributes, thereby enabling meaningful ranking.**
This option correctly reflects the purpose of ordering in analytic queries as described in the chapter, which is to establish a defined sequence that supports subsequent ranking operations.

2. **C: It assigns a rank equal to 1 plus the number of rows that have a strictly lower ordering value than the current row.**
The chapter explains that the rank of a tuple is determined by the number of tuples with a lower ordering value plus one, ensuring an ordinal position is assigned within the partition.

3. **C: RANK assigns identical ranks to tied entries with gaps in the subsequent sequence, whereas DENSE_RANK assigns consecutive, uninterrupted rank numbers.**
This option captures the key distinction detailed in the chapter: RANK results in gaps when there are ties, while DENSE_RANK maintains a contiguous ranking sequence independent of tied values.

4. **B: $RANK(t_i) = 1 + | t \ T : g(t) < g(t_i) |$**
This mathematical formulation is directly taken from the chapter's explanation, accurately representing how the RANK function is conceptually defined.

5. **B: By counting the number of distinct ordering values that are less than the tuple's ordering value and adding one.**
The chapter describes that DENSE_RANK is based on the count of unique ordering values below (or equal to) the current value, ensuring that ties do not create gaps in the rank sequence.

6. **C: They enable the partitioning of data into ordered subsets that identify relative standings or priorities.**
The practical benefit lies in the ability of analytic functions like RANK and DENSE_RANK to segment data based on a well-defined order, which is essential for data prioritization and focused analysis.

7. **B: Because it ensures that functions operate on a cohesive, sorted set of data, thus yielding meaningful and accurate ranks.**
A well-defined ordering is crucial as it establishes the framework under which the ranking functions can compare rows systematically, ensuring that the subsequent ranking reflects the true ordinal relationships within the data.

Chapter 13

Building User-Defined Functions for Analytics

Conceptual Framework of User-Defined Functions

User-defined functions in PL/SQL constitute a formal mechanism for encapsulating analytic computations into discrete, callable entities. In the context of data analytics, these functions are designed to accept one or several parameters, apply a predetermined transformation or aggregation, and return a result that integrates seamlessly into complex queries. Such functions may be mathematically modeled as mappings $f : D \to R$, where D represents a well-defined input domain and R the output range. This abstraction enables a clear separation between the logical specification of an analytical operation and its procedural instantiation, thereby reinforcing principles of software modularity and maintainability.

Design Principles for Reusable Analytical Logic

The construction of robust user-defined functions requires a thorough understanding of design principles that prioritize reusability and clarity. Each function should encapsulate a singular analytical task, ensuring that its interface reflects a one-to-one correspondence with the underlying mathematical operation it represents. By isolating analytical logic within self-contained units, the overall complexity of the data processing workflow is significantly reduced. This design paradigm emphasizes the minimization of side effects, thereby facilitating reliable function composition and enabling the preservation of referential transparency. Indeed, when a function f adheres to the constraint that $f(d)$ is invariant for every $d \in D$, the correctness of the analytic operation is maintained irrespective of its point of invocation within a larger procedural context.

Encapsulation of Complex Analytical Logic

Encapsulation serves as a cornerstone for managing the inherent complexity of advanced data analytics. Custom PL/SQL functions provide an ideal vehicle for isolating intricate computations such as statistical aggregations, conditional transformations, and domain-specific calculations. Such encapsulation not only streamlines the integration of analytical logic into broader application workflows but also simplifies the process of testing and verification. When analytical functionalities are embedded within user-defined functions, each logical unit may be independently validated, thereby reducing the propagation of errors and enhancing the overall reliability of the system. This practice ultimately supports the decomposition of a multifaceted analytical problem into smaller, well-defined computational routines, each of which adheres to rigorous standards of correctness.

Modularity and Maintainability in Extended Analytical Workflows

The modular architecture afforded by user-defined functions underpins both scalability and maintainability within expansive analytical systems. By decoupling analytic logic from the procedural scaffolding of larger applications, these functions enable a cohesive yet flexible framework wherein each component can be updated or replaced in isolation. The employment of clearly defined input and output specifications facilitates a level of abstraction that renders complex operations transparent and manageable. In scenarios involving repeated invocation of similar analytical routines, the reuse of established functions minimizes redundancy and promotes consistency across multiple facets of the analytic workflow. Such a modular approach is instrumental in accommodating both incremental enhancements and comprehensive refactoring, thereby ensuring that the system remains robust in the face of evolving analytical requirements.

Formal Considerations in Function Design

1 Mathematical Formalism and Functional Integrity

The rigorous formulation of user-defined functions is deeply rooted in mathematical function theory. For a function $f : D \rightarrow R$, essential properties such as idempotence, purity, and strictness can be formally defined and analyzed. A function is considered pure if, for any $d \in D$, the evaluation of $f(d)$ produces a consistent result without inducing side effects; this condition is central to achieving referential transparency. Additionally, the composability of functions is of paramount importance. Given two functions $f : A \rightarrow B$ and $g : B \rightarrow C$, their composition, denoted $g \circ f$, yields a new function mapping elements from A to C. Such compositional constructs are critical in aggregating smaller analytic routines into a cohesive, higher-order functionality. The adherence to these formal properties not only undergirds the correctness of individual user-defined functions but also reinforces the reliability of the overall analytical framework when these functions are deployed at scale.

2 Ensuring Consistency Through Defined Interfaces

The establishment of rigorously defined interfaces in user-defined functions serves as a guarantee of consistency across diverse analytic operations. Interfaces should explicitly declare the types and ranges of input parameters, as well as detail the nature of the returned output. This explicit specification plays a crucial role in enforcing domain constraints and verifying that the function behaves as intended within the larger system. By treating each function as a mathematical black box with a well-defined contract, the design process eliminates ambiguity and facilitates methodical unit testing. In complex analytical environments, such defined interfaces are indispensable for maintaining the integrity of data processing, allowing for straightforward substitution and upgrading of individual functions without compromising the overall system dynamics.

Oracle 19c SQL Code Snippet

```
-- Create ANALYTICS_DATA table to store metric values for analytical
↪   functions
CREATE TABLE ANALYTICS_DATA (
    DATA_ID    NUMBER GENERATED BY DEFAULT AS IDENTITY,
    METRIC_A   NUMBER,
    METRIC_B   NUMBER,
    WEIGHT_A   NUMBER,
    WEIGHT_B   NUMBER,
    ENTRY_DATE DATE DEFAULT SYSDATE,
    CONSTRAINT ANALYTICS_DATA_PK PRIMARY KEY (DATA_ID)
);


-- Insert sample data into ANALYTICS_DATA
INSERT INTO ANALYTICS_DATA (METRIC_A, METRIC_B, WEIGHT_A, WEIGHT_B)
VALUES (100, 200, 0.4, 0.6);

INSERT INTO ANALYTICS_DATA (METRIC_A, METRIC_B, WEIGHT_A, WEIGHT_B)
VALUES (150, 250, 0.5, 0.5);

INSERT INTO ANALYTICS_DATA (METRIC_A, METRIC_B, WEIGHT_A, WEIGHT_B)
VALUES (200, 300, 0.3, 0.7);
COMMIT;


-- Create a pure user-defined function to calculate a weighted
↪   average
-- This function models the equation:
--    f(METRIC_A, METRIC_B, WEIGHT_A, WEIGHT_B) = (METRIC_A *
↪   WEIGHT_A + METRIC_B * WEIGHT_B) / (WEIGHT_A + WEIGHT_B)
CREATE OR REPLACE FUNCTION get_weighted_average(
    p_metric_a IN NUMBER,
    p_metric_b IN NUMBER,
    p_weight_a IN NUMBER,
    p_weight_b IN NUMBER
) RETURN NUMBER IS
    v_result NUMBER;
BEGIN
    IF (p_weight_a + p_weight_b) = 0 THEN
        RETURN NULL;  -- Avoid division by zero
```

```
    END IF;
    v_result := (p_metric_a * p_weight_a + p_metric_b * p_weight_b)
    ↪ / (p_weight_a + p_weight_b);
    RETURN v_result;
EXCEPTION
    WHEN OTHERS THEN
        RAISE;
END get_weighted_average;
/


-------------------------------------------------------------------------
-- Create a second function to normalize a metric based on a
↪ specified range
-- This encapsulates the formula:
--   normalize(x, min, max) = (x - min) / (max - min)
-------------------------------------------------------------------------
CREATE OR REPLACE FUNCTION normalize_metric(
    p_value IN NUMBER,
    p_min   IN NUMBER,
    p_max   IN NUMBER
) RETURN NUMBER IS
BEGIN
    IF p_max = p_min THEN
        RETURN 0;  -- Return a default value when range is zero to
        ↪ keep function strict
    END IF;
    RETURN (p_value - p_min) / (p_max - p_min);
EXCEPTION
    WHEN OTHERS THEN
        RAISE;
END normalize_metric;
/


-------------------------------------------------------------------------
-- Create a composite function demonstrating function composition
-- It first computes a weighted average and then normalizes the
↪ result.
-------------------------------------------------------------------------
CREATE OR REPLACE FUNCTION get_composite_metric(
    p_metric_a IN NUMBER,
    p_metric_b IN NUMBER,
    p_weight_a IN NUMBER,
    p_weight_b IN NUMBER,
    p_min      IN NUMBER,
    p_max      IN NUMBER
) RETURN NUMBER IS
    v_weighted_avg NUMBER;
    v_normalized   NUMBER;
BEGIN
    v_weighted_avg := get_weighted_average(p_metric_a, p_metric_b,
    ↪ p_weight_a, p_weight_b);
    v_normalized   := normalize_metric(v_weighted_avg, p_min,
    ↪ p_max);
```

```
        RETURN v_normalized;
EXCEPTION
    WHEN OTHERS THEN
        RAISE;
END get_composite_metric;
/

-------------------------------------------------------------------------
-- Use the user-defined functions in a query to enrich analytical
↪  insight
-------------------------------------------------------------------------
SELECT
    DATA_ID,
    METRIC_A,
    METRIC_B,
    WEIGHT_A,
    WEIGHT_B,
    get_weighted_average(METRIC_A, METRIC_B, WEIGHT_A, WEIGHT_B) AS
    ↪  WEIGHTED_AVERAGE,
    normalize_metric(METRIC_A, 0, 300) AS NORMALIZED_METRIC_A,
    get_composite_metric(METRIC_A, METRIC_B, WEIGHT_A, WEIGHT_B, 0,
    ↪  300) AS COMPOSITE_METRIC
FROM ANALYTICS_DATA;

-------------------------------------------------------------------------
-- PL/SQL block to demonstrate calling the get_weighted_average
↪  function
-- and outputting the computed value using DBMS_OUTPUT.
-------------------------------------------------------------------------
DECLARE
    v_avg NUMBER;
BEGIN
    SELECT get_weighted_average(100, 200, 0.4, 0.6)
        INTO v_avg
        FROM dual;

    DBMS_OUTPUT.PUT_LINE('Computed Weighted Average: ' || v_avg);
END;
/
```

Multiple Choice Questions

1. Which of the following best describes the role of user-defined
   functions in PL/SQL analytics as discussed in this chapter?

   (a) They serve solely as wrappers for direct SQL queries.

   (b) They encapsulate discrete analytic computations into
       callable, modular units.

(c) They are used exclusively for error handling in data processing.

(d) They automatically generate dynamic reports without parameterization.

2. In the provided mathematical model $f : D \rightarrow R$ for user-defined functions, what do D and R represent, respectively?

(a) D is the output domain, and R is the input range.

(b) D represents a set of declarations, and R represents the routine body.

(c) D is the defined input domain, and R is the output range.

(d) D stands for data logs, and R for result sets.

3. Which design principle is emphasized for ensuring reusability of analytical logic in user-defined functions?

(a) Integrating multiple analytic tasks into one function to reduce function calls.

(b) Isolating a singular analytic operation with minimal side effects.

(c) Merging procedural code with business logic for enhanced performance.

(d) Embedding SQL directly into analytic routines to increase flexibility.

4. How does encapsulation in PL/SQL functions contribute to managing complex analytical logic?

(a) It increases dependency on external variables to simplify the code.

(b) It isolates intricate computations into self-contained units, easing testing and verification.

(c) It combines several unrelated analytic operations into a single monolithic block.

(d) It permits uncontrolled side effects to propagate through the analytic process.

5. Which of the following properties is crucial for a function to be considered pure, as highlighted in the formal considerations of this chapter?

(a) Idempotence, ensuring the function can be called multiple times with diminishing returns.

(b) Strictness, causing the function to evaluate all its arguments before execution.

(c) Purity, ensuring that for each input the function produces a consistent output without side effects.

(d) Complexity, implying the function handles multiple analytic operations simultaneously.

6. What is the primary purpose of establishing rigorously defined interfaces in user-defined functions?

(a) To obscure the internal logic and prevent unit testing.

(b) To enforce consistency by explicitly declaring input parameters and output types.

(c) To enable dynamic changes in data types during runtime.

(d) To couple the function tightly with the database schema.

7. How does modularity achieved through user-defined functions enhance maintainability in extended analytical workflows?

(a) By coupling analytic logic with the procedural scaffolding, forcing changes in all parts when one module updates.

(b) By isolating analytic logic into discrete units that can be updated, tested, and reused independently.

(c) By consolidating all analytics into a single monolithic function for simplified debugging.

(d) By embedding all analytic routines directly into the application's main codebase.

Answers:

1. **B: They encapsulate discrete analytic computations into callable, modular units**
This answer is correct because the chapter explains that user-defined functions in PL/SQL are designed to package analytic computations into self-contained, reusable entities, thereby promoting modularity.

2. **C: D is the defined input domain, and R is the output range**
   The mathematical abstraction presented in the chapter models functions as mappings from a well-defined input domain (D) to an output range (R), clearly separating the analytical specification from its procedural implementation.

3. **B: Isolating a singular analytic operation with minimal side effects**
   Emphasis is placed on designing functions that perform one analytic task only, ensuring that they are free of side effects and hence facilitate reusability and maintainability.

4. **B: It isolates intricate computations into self-contained units, easing testing and verification**
   Encapsulation is critical for breaking down complex analytical processes, allowing each function to be independently validated and maintained, which minimizes error propagation.

5. **C: Purity, ensuring that for each input the function produces a consistent output without side effects**
   Purity, as defined in the chapter, ensures that a function's result is solely dependent on its input, making it predictable and easier to reason about, a key property in functional design.

6. **B: To enforce consistency by explicitly declaring input parameters and output types**
   Rigorously defined interfaces guarantee that functions behave as promised by specifying the types and constraints of inputs and outputs, which is essential for reliability and consistency in a larger system.

7. **B: By isolating analytic logic into discrete units that can be updated, tested, and reused independently**
   Modularity decouples analytic operations from the surrounding code, thereby enhancing maintainability, scalability, and reducing redundancy across extended analytical workflows.

Chapter 14

Developing Stored Procedures for Data Transformation

Conceptual Framework for Stored Procedures in Data Transformation

Stored procedures represent an essential construct in relational database systems, functioning as encapsulated sequences of operations dedicated to the transformation of data. In the context of automated analytics, these procedures perform methodical manipulations of raw datasets to produce refined, analysis-ready results. A stored procedure can be formally regarded as a mapping $T : D \rightarrow R$, where D denotes the domain of unprocessed data and R symbolizes the transformed result set. This abstraction emphasizes the dual objectives of precision and reproducibility in complex data transformations, establishing stored procedures as the operational workhorses that enable continuous, automated processing within large-scale analytic environments.

Architectural Principles Underlying Procedure Design

The design of stored procedures for data transformation necessitates a rigorous architectural framework that emphasizes modularity, maintainability, and transactional integrity. Procedures must be architected to uphold the principles of atomicity, consistency, isolation, and durability, ensuring that each discrete transformation operation is executed reliably even in the presence of concurrent data modifications. By decomposing complex transformation tasks into isolated, logically coherent sub-operations, stored procedures facilitate systematic error handling and robust transaction management. This approach not only increases the ease of testing and debugging individual components but also supports the reuse of transformation logic across multiple analytic processes without sacrificing performance or data integrity.

Mechanisms and Patterns for Complex Data Transformation

The execution of intricate data transformations within stored procedures relies on a rich assembly of control structures and design patterns. Conditional branches, recursion, and iterative loops are routinely employed to traverse large datasets and to apply sophisticated decision-making logic at each processing stage. These mechanisms support the precise application of filtering, sorting, aggregating, and pivoting operations. Furthermore, the procedural framework allows for the staged handling of intermediate data representations, thereby enabling complex transformation pipelines that adapt dynamically to varying data conditions. Such patterns in procedural design underscore the importance of a disciplined approach to constructing operations that are both logically sound and optimized for the intensive demands of automated analytics.

Integration and Modularity in Automated Analytics Workflows

Within the broader ecosystem of automated analytics, stored procedures assume a central role due to their inherent modularity and their capacity for seamless integration with other data processing components. The encapsulation of transformation logic into well-defined procedures promotes a clear separation of concerns, which facilitates independent development, rigorous testing, and straightforward maintenance. This decoupled architecture ensures that individual procedures can be deployed, updated, or replaced without necessitating extensive modifications to the surrounding infrastructure. As stored procedures serve as the critical intermediaries between raw data inputs and analytic models, their modular composition is instrumental in constructing scalable and adaptable workflows that can evolve in tandem with changing analytic requirements.

Optimization and Scalability in Data Transformations

The performance characteristics of stored procedures are pivotal, given the extensive data volumes and high throughput demands typical of modern analytic systems. Optimization strategies focus on minimizing computational overhead through the efficient structuring of transformation logic and the judicious management of temporary data states. Careful consideration is given to reducing redundant calculations and leveraging the native efficiencies of the underlying database engine. As a result, stored procedures are designed not only to execute complex data transformations accurately but also to achieve scalability in environments where resource management and processing speed are of paramount importance. This balance between operational intricacy and performance optimization is critical for sustaining the automated, high-volume processing that defines contemporary data analytics workflows.

Oracle 19c SQL Code Snippet

```
------------------------------------------------------------------------
-- Create RAW_DATA table to simulate the domain D (unprocessed data)
------------------------------------------------------------------------
CREATE TABLE RAW_DATA (
    RAW_ID          NUMBER GENERATED BY DEFAULT AS IDENTITY,
    SOURCE_VALUE    VARCHAR2(100),
    NUMERIC_VALUE   NUMBER,
    CREATED_DATE    DATE,
```

```
        STATUS          VARCHAR2(10),
        CONSTRAINT RAW_DATA_PK PRIMARY KEY (RAW_ID)
);


-------------------------------------------------------------------------------
-- Create TRANSFORMED_DATA table to represent the range R
↪  (transformed results)
-------------------------------------------------------------------------------
CREATE TABLE TRANSFORMED_DATA (
    TRANS_ID         NUMBER GENERATED BY DEFAULT AS IDENTITY,
    SOURCE_VALUE     VARCHAR2(100),
    TRANSFORMED_NUM  NUMBER,
    PROCESSED_DATE   DATE,
    TRANSFORM_STATUS VARCHAR2(20),
    CONSTRAINT TRANSFORMED_DATA_PK PRIMARY KEY (TRANS_ID)
);


-------------------------------------------------------------------------------
-- Insert sample raw data into RAW_DATA
-------------------------------------------------------------------------------
INSERT ALL
    INTO RAW_DATA (SOURCE_VALUE, NUMERIC_VALUE, CREATED_DATE,
    ↪  STATUS)
        VALUES ('A', 100, DATE '2023-10-01', 'NEW')
    INTO RAW_DATA (SOURCE_VALUE, NUMERIC_VALUE, CREATED_DATE,
    ↪  STATUS)
        VALUES ('B', 200, DATE '2023-10-02', 'NEW')
    INTO RAW_DATA (SOURCE_VALUE, NUMERIC_VALUE, CREATED_DATE,
    ↪  STATUS)
        VALUES ('C', 300, DATE '2023-10-03', 'ERROR')
SELECT * FROM DUAL;
COMMIT;


-------------------------------------------------------------------------------
-- Create a stored procedure to transform raw data using the mapping
↪  T: D -> R
-- This procedure encapsulates transformation logic, error handling,
↪  bulk processing,
-- and transactional integrity as discussed in the chapter.
-------------------------------------------------------------------------------
CREATE OR REPLACE PROCEDURE transform_raw_data IS

    -- Cursor to collect raw data with status 'NEW'
    CURSOR raw_cursor IS
        SELECT RAW_ID, SOURCE_VALUE, NUMERIC_VALUE, CREATED_DATE,
        ↪  STATUS
          FROM RAW_DATA
          WHERE STATUS = 'NEW';

    -- Collection type for raw data rows
    TYPE raw_data_tab IS TABLE OF raw_cursor%ROWTYPE;
    raw_data raw_data_tab;
```

```
-- Define a record type for transformed data
TYPE transform_rec IS RECORD (
    SOURCE_VALUE      RAW_DATA.SOURCE_VALUE%TYPE,
    TRANSFORMED_NUM   NUMBER,
    PROCESSED_DATE    DATE,
    TRANSFORM_STATUS VARCHAR2(20)
);

-- Collection type for storing transformed records
TYPE transform_tab IS TABLE OF transform_rec;
transformed_data transform_tab := transform_tab();

-- Collection to collect RAW_IDs for status update
TYPE id_tab IS TABLE OF RAW_DATA.RAW_ID%TYPE;
raw_ids id_tab := id_tab();

BEGIN
    -- Bulk collect raw data with status 'NEW'
    OPEN raw_cursor;
    FETCH raw_cursor BULK COLLECT INTO raw_data;
    CLOSE raw_cursor;

    IF raw_data.COUNT = 0 THEN
        DBMS_OUTPUT.PUT_LINE('No new raw data to transform.');
        RETURN;
    END IF;

    -- Process each record: apply transformation logic T, e.g.,
    ↪  multiply NUMERIC_VALUE by 1.1
    FOR i IN 1..raw_data.COUNT LOOP
        transformed_data.EXTEND;
        transformed_data(transformed_data.COUNT).SOURCE_VALUE :=
            raw_data(i).SOURCE_VALUE;
        transformed_data(transformed_data.COUNT).TRANSFORMED_NUM :=
            raw_data(i).NUMERIC_VALUE * 1.1;  -- 10% increase as
            ↪  transformation
        transformed_data(transformed_data.COUNT).PROCESSED_DATE :=
            SYSDATE;
        transformed_data(transformed_data.COUNT).TRANSFORM_STATUS :=
            'COMPLETED';

        -- Collect the RAW_ID for bulk update of status
        raw_ids.EXTEND;
        raw_ids(raw_ids.COUNT) := raw_data(i).RAW_ID;
    END LOOP;

    ↪  --------------------------------------------------------------------
    -- Bulk insert the transformed data into TRANSFORMED_DATA using
    ↪  FORALL

    ↪  --------------------------------------------------------------------
    FORALL idx IN INDICES OF transformed_data
```

134

```
        INSERT INTO TRANSFORMED_DATA (SOURCE_VALUE, TRANSFORMED_NUM,
        ↪  PROCESSED_DATE, TRANSFORM_STATUS)
        VALUES (transformed_data(idx).SOURCE_VALUE,
              transformed_data(idx).TRANSFORMED_NUM,
              transformed_data(idx).PROCESSED_DATE,
              transformed_data(idx).TRANSFORM_STATUS);


    ↪  -------------------------------------------------------------------------
    -- Bulk update the RAW_DATA table to mark the processed records
    ↪  as 'PROCESSED'

    ↪  -------------------------------------------------------------------------
    FORALL idx IN INDICES OF raw_ids
        UPDATE RAW_DATA
           SET STATUS = 'PROCESSED'
         WHERE RAW_ID = raw_ids(idx);

    COMMIT;
    DBMS_OUTPUT.PUT_LINE('Transformation complete for ' ||
    ↪  raw_data.COUNT || ' records.');
EXCEPTION
    WHEN OTHERS THEN
        ROLLBACK;
        DBMS_OUTPUT.PUT_LINE('Error during transformation: ' ||
        ↪  SQLERRM);
        RAISE;
END transform_raw_data;
/


-------------------------------------------------------------------------------
-- Execute the stored procedure to transform raw data
-------------------------------------------------------------------------------
BEGIN
    transform_raw_data;
END;
/


-------------------------------------------------------------------------------
-- Query the TRANSFORMED_DATA table to verify the transformed
↪  results
-------------------------------------------------------------------------------
SELECT *
FROM TRANSFORMED_DATA;


-------------------------------------------------------------------------------
-- Demonstrate the use of dynamic SQL for an optional advanced data
↪  transformation scenario
-- Example: Archive raw data that is older than a specified
↪  threshold
-------------------------------------------------------------------------------
DECLARE
    v_sql VARCHAR2(1000);
```

```
BEGIN
    v_sql := 'UPDATE RAW_DATA SET STATUS = ''ARCHIVED'' WHERE
    ↪   CREATED_DATE < :threshold';
    EXECUTE IMMEDIATE v_sql USING DATE '2023-10-02';
    COMMIT;
    DBMS_OUTPUT.PUT_LINE('Old raw data archived.');
EXCEPTION
    WHEN OTHERS THEN
        ROLLBACK;
        DBMS_OUTPUT.PUT_LINE('Dynamic SQL execution failed: ' ||
        ↪   SQLERRM);
        RAISE;
END;
/
```

Multiple Choice Questions

1. A stored procedure for data transformation is formally modeled as a mapping. Which of the following correctly represents this abstraction?

   (a) $T : R \to D$

   (b) $T : D \to R$

   (c) $T : D \times R$

   (d) $T : R \ D$

2. The design of stored procedures in data transformation is underpinned by ACID principles. Which set of properties correctly defines the ACID model?

   (a) Atomicity, Consistency, Isolation, Durability

   (b) Accuracy, Completeness, Isolation, Data-integrity

   (c) Atomicity, Connectivity, Integration, Durability

   (d) Alignment, Consistency, Isolation, Durability

3. When iterating over large datasets within stored procedures for complex transformations, which control structure is most appropriate?

   (a) Recursive function calls

   (b) Iterative loops such as FOR and WHILE

   (c) Embedded static SQL statements

   (d) Exception handling blocks

4. Decomposing complex data transformation tasks into isolated sub-operations is a key design pattern. What is the primary benefit of this decomposition?

   (a) It allows immediate data commits regardless of errors.

   (b) It simplifies error handling and promotes modularity.

   (c) It eliminates the need for transaction management.

   (d) It accelerates execution by avoiding conditional checks.

5. In complex transformation pipelines, managing intermediate data representations is essential. Which mechanism is most frequently utilized for this purpose?

   (a) Embedding dynamic SQL queries exclusively

   (b) Utilizing temporary variables and transient tables

   (c) Implementing persistent object-relational mappings (ORM)

   (d) Using static stored functions to bypass intermediate states

6. Optimizing stored procedures for high-volume data processing is critical in automated analytics. Which strategy is most effective for enhancing performance?

   (a) Avoiding transaction management to reduce overhead

   (b) Reducing redundant calculations and managing temporary data efficiently

   (c) Processing all data in a single monolithic block to maximize concurrency

   (d) Relying solely on user-defined functions without control structures

7. In integrated automated analytics workflows, how does a modular design of stored procedures contribute to overall system flexibility and maintainability?

   (a) It restricts each procedure to isolated operation, limiting cross-functionality.

   (b) It facilitates independent development, testing, and updates without impacting the entire system.

   (c) It enforces a rigid, monolithic structure ensuring uniformity.

(d) It requires complete system refactoring for any minor procedural change.

Answers:

1. **B: T : D → R**
This abstraction represents the stored procedure as a transformation function that maps unprocessed data (D) to its refined, analysis-ready form (R), emphasizing reproducibility and precision in data transformations.

2. **A: Atomicity, Consistency, Isolation, Durability**
These four properties define the ACID model, which is fundamental in ensuring that each stored procedure executes reliably while maintaining data integrity, even with concurrent data modifications.

3. **B: Iterative loops such as FOR and WHILE**
Iterative loops are most suitable for traversing and processing rows in large datasets within stored procedures, enabling controlled, stepwise data transformation operations.

4. **B: It simplifies error handling and promotes modularity**
Decomposing complex tasks into isolated sub-operations facilitates targeted error detection, easier debugging, and the reuse of transformation logic across different analytic workflows.

5. **B: Utilizing temporary variables and transient tables**
Managing intermediate states with temporary variables or tables allows stored procedures to handle complex transformations in stages, optimizing resource management and ensuring data consistency.

6. **B: Reducing redundant calculations and managing temporary data efficiently**
Optimizing resource use by minimizing redundant processing and smartly handling temporary data helps stored procedures scale to handle high data volumes while maintaining performance.

7. **B: It facilitates independent development, testing, and updates without impacting the entire system**
A modular design allows parts of the system to be modified

or improved independently, significantly enhancing maintainability and flexibility in evolving automated analytics environments.

Chapter 15

Modular Programming with PL/SQL Packages

Theoretical Underpinnings of Modularity in PL/SQL

The concept of modularity in software engineering is rooted in the principle of decomposing a complex system into discrete, self-contained units that interact via well-defined interfaces. In the context of PL/SQL, packages serve as the primary mechanism for achieving this decomposition. These packages are structured to encapsulate both functions and procedures, thereby offering a logical grouping of related operations. The abstraction afforded by packaging promotes a clear separation of concerns in which internal implementation details are hidden from external dependencies. This encapsulation mirrors the formal notion of a module in computer science, where each package implements a mapping $M : I \rightarrow O$ from an internal interface I to an external set of operations O, thereby ensuring that the operations remain insulated from external modifications.

Structural Design of PL/SQL Packages

The architectural layout of a PL/SQL package is constituted by two principal components: the specification and the body. The package specification defines the interface by declaring the functions, procedures, constants, and variables that are accessible to other modules. Concurrently, the package body contains the implementation details of the declared subprograms and any private constructs that are not exposed externally. This bifurcation adheres to the principle of information hiding, facilitating robust modular design. By delineating the interface from the implementation, the design promotes a disciplined approach to software development where modifications to internal logic need not impact external calling environments. The formal separation of interface and implementation in a package is emblematic of the abstraction layers widely adopted in advanced software architectures.

Advantages of Function and Procedure Bundling

Bundling related functions and procedures into packages yields multiple advantages, paramount among which is the enhancement of code reuse. When discrete functionalities are centralized within a single package, they become accessible to multiple analytic processes and applications, thereby reducing duplication and fostering a unified code base. In addition, bundling facilitates systematic testing and debugging. The isolated and cohesive nature of packages allows developers to rigorously verify each module's behavior without interference from unrelated components. This modularization also supports robust transaction control and easier error handling, as the scope of each package is confined to a well-defined set of operations. The aggregate of these benefits contributes to an overall increase in system reliability and maintainability, qualities that are particularly critical in the development of large-scale analytic applications.

Strategies for Effective Package Organization

Effective organization within PL/SQL packages is achieved through careful adherence to design principles and naming conventions that delineate functional boundaries. Logical grouping of related subprograms ensures that external interfaces remain intuitive while promoting internal cohesion. Techniques such as grouping similar functionalities, employing consistent naming schemes, and segregating public interfaces from private implementations are essential to streamline the development process. Moreover, dependency management within packages is critical; by minimizing cross-package interdependencies, one ensures that modifications remain localized. Such strategies not only facilitate easier maintenance but also optimize collaborative development, where multiple developers can work concurrently on distinct packages without interference.

Implications for Large-Scale Analytic Applications

In environments characterized by extensive data processing and high-volume analytics, the modular organization of PL/SQL code through packages proves indispensable. When analytic operations are distributed across several functional units, the system benefits from scalability and enhanced performance management. By encapsulating transformation algorithms and query operations within discrete packages, the updating, testing, and deployment of analytic modules become markedly more efficient. This structured approach supports the construction of pipelines where each package serves as a stable and consistent unit of functionality. The resulting architecture ensures that system modifications can be made without triggering widespread disruptions, thereby fostering an adaptive and resilient environment suitable for the demands of contemporary data analytics.

Oracle 19c SQL Code Snippet

```
-- Create a sample table ANALYTIC_DATA to hold data for analytic
↪    processing
CREATE TABLE ANALYTIC_DATA (
    DATA_ID    NUMBER GENERATED BY DEFAULT AS IDENTITY PRIMARY KEY,
    CATEGORY   VARCHAR2(50),
    VALUE      NUMBER,
    DATA_DATE  DATE
);

-- Insert sample data into ANALYTIC_DATA
INSERT ALL
    INTO ANALYTIC_DATA (CATEGORY, VALUE, DATA_DATE)
        VALUES ('A', 100, DATE '2023-10-01')
    INTO ANALYTIC_DATA (CATEGORY, VALUE, DATA_DATE)
        VALUES ('A', 150, DATE '2023-10-02')
```

```sql
     INTO ANALYTIC_DATA (CATEGORY, VALUE, DATA_DATE)
         VALUES ('B', 200, DATE '2023-10-01')
     INTO ANALYTIC_DATA (CATEGORY, VALUE, DATA_DATE)
         VALUES ('B', 250, DATE '2023-10-02')
SELECT * FROM DUAL;
COMMIT;


-------------------------------------------------------------------------
-- Create a PL/SQL package to encapsulate analytical formulas and
↪  algorithms.
-- This package demonstrates modular design by grouping related
↪  functions and procedures.
-------------------------------------------------------------------------


-- Package specification for analytics_pkg
CREATE OR REPLACE PACKAGE analytics_pkg AS
    -- Function to compute the moving average for a given category.
    -- It calculates the average of the first p_window rows ordered
    ↪  by DATA_DATE.
    FUNCTION compute_moving_average(p_category VARCHAR2, p_window
    ↪  NUMBER)
        RETURN NUMBER;

    -- Procedure to transform data by applying a scaling factor.
    -- This simulates an algorithmic transformation on the VALUE
    ↪  column.
    PROCEDURE transform_data(p_category VARCHAR2, p_scale_factor
    ↪  NUMBER);

    -- Function to calculate a custom analytic metric.
    -- Metric formula: (SUM(VALUE)/COUNT(*)) * (MAX(VALUE) -
    ↪  MIN(VALUE))
    FUNCTION calculate_custom_metric(p_category VARCHAR2)
        RETURN NUMBER;
END analytics_pkg;
/

-- Package body for analytics_pkg with implementations of the
↪  declared subprograms
CREATE OR REPLACE PACKAGE BODY analytics_pkg AS

    -- Function to compute the moving average by selecting the first
    ↪  p_window rows.
    FUNCTION compute_moving_average(p_category VARCHAR2, p_window
    ↪  NUMBER)
        RETURN NUMBER
    IS
        v_moving_avg NUMBER;
    BEGIN
        -- Oracle 19c supports row limiting with the FETCH FIRST
        ↪  clause.
        SELECT AVG(VALUE) INTO v_moving_avg
          FROM (
```

143

```
            SELECT VALUE
              FROM ANALYTIC_DATA
              WHERE CATEGORY = p_category
              ORDER BY DATA_DATE
              FETCH FIRST p_window ROWS ONLY
    );
    RETURN v_moving_avg;
EXCEPTION
    WHEN NO_DATA_FOUND THEN
        RETURN NULL;
    WHEN OTHERS THEN
        RAISE;
END compute_moving_average;

-- Procedure to update the VALUE by a scaling factor,
↪   demonstrating data transformation.
PROCEDURE transform_data(p_category VARCHAR2, p_scale_factor
↪   NUMBER) IS
BEGIN
    UPDATE ANALYTIC_DATA
       SET VALUE = VALUE * p_scale_factor
     WHERE CATEGORY = p_category;
    COMMIT;
EXCEPTION
    WHEN OTHERS THEN
        ROLLBACK;
        RAISE;
END transform_data;

-- Function to calculate a custom analytic metric using the
↪   provided formula.
FUNCTION calculate_custom_metric(p_category VARCHAR2)
    RETURN NUMBER
IS
    v_sum    NUMBER;
    v_count  NUMBER;
    v_max    NUMBER;
    v_min    NUMBER;
BEGIN
    SELECT SUM(VALUE), COUNT(*), MAX(VALUE), MIN(VALUE)
      INTO v_sum, v_count, v_max, v_min
      FROM ANALYTIC_DATA
     WHERE CATEGORY = p_category;

    IF v_count = 0 THEN
        RETURN 0;
    END IF;

    RETURN (v_sum / v_count) * (v_max - v_min);
EXCEPTION
    WHEN NO_DATA_FOUND THEN
        RETURN 0;
    WHEN OTHERS THEN
```

144

```
            RAISE;
        END calculate_custom_metric;

    END analytics_pkg;
    /

    ------------------------------------------------------------------
    -- Demonstrate the usage of the analytics_pkg package in an
    ↪   anonymous PL/SQL block.
    -- This block invokes the functions and procedure defined in the
    ↪   package.
    ------------------------------------------------------------------

    DECLARE
        v_mavg   NUMBER;
        v_metric NUMBER;
    BEGIN
        -- Calculate the moving average for category 'A' using a window
        ↪   of 2 rows.
        v_mavg := analytics_pkg.compute_moving_average('A', 2);
        DBMS_OUTPUT.PUT_LINE('Moving Average for category A: ' ||
        ↪   v_mavg);

        -- Calculate the custom analytic metric for category 'B'
        v_metric := analytics_pkg.calculate_custom_metric('B');
        DBMS_OUTPUT.PUT_LINE('Custom analytic metric for category B: '
        ↪   || v_metric);

        -- Transform the data for category 'A' by scaling the VALUE by a
        ↪   factor of 1.1.
        analytics_pkg.transform_data('A', 1.1);
        COMMIT;
        DBMS_OUTPUT.PUT_LINE('Data transformation applied for category
        ↪   A.');
    EXCEPTION
        WHEN OTHERS THEN
            DBMS_OUTPUT.PUT_LINE('Error encountered: ' || SQLERRM);
    END;
    /
```

Multiple Choice Questions

1. Which of the following best encapsulates the concept of modularity in PL/SQL packages as discussed in this chapter?

   (a) Integrating all analytic logic into a single monolithic block

   (b) Decomposing a complex system into discrete, self-contained units with well-defined interfaces

(c) Relying exclusively on ad hoc stored procedures for data transformation

(d) Dynamically constructing SQL queries at runtime without fixed structure

2. In the formal representation of a package as a mapping $M : I \rightarrow O$, what do the symbols I and O denote?

(a) I: Instruction set; O: Operational codes

(b) I: Internal data; O: Output streams

(c) I: Internal interface (hidden implementation details); O: External set of operations (public API)

(d) I: Initialization routines; O: Organizational logic

3. What are the two principal components that form the architectural layout of a PL/SQL package?

(a) Header and Footer

(b) Declaration and Execution Block

(c) Specification and Body

(d) Interface and Constructor

4. What is the primary role of the package specification within a PL/SQL package?

(a) To implement the core business logic and perform data transformations

(b) To define the external interface by declaring functions, procedures, constants, and variables accessible to other modules

(c) To compile all the internal procedures into a single executable unit

(d) To enforce transaction control and maintenance routines

5. Which advantage is directly associated with bundling related functions and procedures together in PL/SQL packages?

(a) Enhanced code reuse and more systematic testing of cohesive modules

(b) Increased dependence on external libraries for error handling

(c) Improved dynamic SQL performance by reducing query complexity

(d) Automatic memory optimization during runtime execution

6. Which of the following strategies is recommended for effective package organization according to the chapter?

   (a) Mixing public and private subprograms randomly throughout the package to maximize code density

   (b) Grouping similar functionalities, employing consistent naming conventions, and clearly separating public interfaces from private implementations

   (c) Collapsing all subprograms into a single anonymous block to reduce the overhead of multiple procedures

   (d) Eliminating strict dependency management to allow cross-package access without restrictions

7. How does modular packaging in PL/SQL contribute to the development and maintenance of large-scale analytic applications?

   (a) It forces all analytic processes into a single unified module, thereby centralizing updates.

   (b) It allows for isolated updates, rigorous testing, and efficient deployment by encapsulating transformation algorithms and query operations into distinct units.

   (c) It discourages collaboration due to rigid package boundaries and increased interdependencies.

   (d) It eliminates the need for transaction control by automatically handling error propagation.

Answers:

1. **B: Decomposing a complex system into discrete, self-contained units with well-defined interfaces**
   This answer is correct because the chapter emphasizes that modularity in PL/SQL is achieved by decomposing a large system into packages, each encapsulating its own set of functions and procedures with a clearly defined interface.

2. **C: I: Internal interface (hidden implementation details); O: External set of operations (public API)**
   The chapter discusses the mapping $M : I \to O$ to represent how a package hides its internal implementations (I) and exposes a public set of operations (O) to the rest of the system.

3. **C: Specification and Body**
   The architectural layout of a PL/SQL package is clearly divided into two parts: the specification, which declares the external interface, and the body, which contains the actual implementation details.

4. **B: To define the external interface by declaring functions, procedures, constants, and variables accessible to other modules**
   The package specification's main role is to expose what is available outside the package, thereby enforcing the separation of the interface from the implementation details housed in the package body.

5. **A: Enhanced code reuse and more systematic testing of cohesive modules**
   Bundling related subprograms into packages enhances code reuse and facilitates isolated testing, as developers can verify a cohesive set of functionalities without interference from unrelated code.

6. **B: Grouping similar functionalities, employing consistent naming conventions, and clearly separating public interfaces from private implementations**
   Effective package organization is achieved by logically grouping related subprograms, maintaining clear naming conventions, and segregating public and private elements, all of which are highlighted in the chapter.

7. **B: It allows for isolated updates, rigorous testing, and efficient deployment by encapsulating transformation algorithms and query operations into distinct units**
   The modular approach using packages supports scalable, maintainable large-scale analytic applications by enabling localized modifications and systematic deployment without causing widespread disruptions.

Chapter 16

Managing Transactions in PL/SQL

Foundations of Transaction Control in PL/SQL

Transaction control in PL/SQL is predicated on a rigorous framework designed to ensure that multiple data manipulation operations execute as an indivisible unit. At the core of this framework is the notion that the database must transition from one consistent state to another. The transaction paradigm is firmly grounded in the principles of atomicity, consistency, isolation, and durability (collectively known as the ACID properties). Atomicity guarantees that each series of operations is treated as a single logical unit, such that either all changes are effected or none are. Consistency ensures that every transaction transforms the database from one valid state to another, strictly adhering to predefined integrity constraints. Isolation regulates how concurrently executing transactions interact, thereby preventing the interference that could lead to transient inconsistencies. Finally, durability provides the assurance that once a transaction has been committed, its effects are permanently recorded in the persistent storage, regardless of subsequent system failures.

Transactional Operations: The Role of COMMIT

The COMMIT operation serves as the definitive mechanism by which modifications effected during a transaction are rendered permanent. In the transactional model, a COMMIT converts the provisional state of changes—accumulated during the active execution of a transaction—into a durable state visible to all other sessions. This operation is not merely a procedural command but a critical assurance of data persistence and consistency. The model can be succinctly described by considering an initial state S_0 and a final state S_f, where the explicit execution of a COMMIT assures that all transitions from S_0 to S_f adhere strictly to the ACID guarantees. The immediate persistence of data post-COMMIT underscores the commitment to maintaining a stable and predictable database environment, particularly in systems engaged in intensive analytical processing.

Reversibility and the Semantics of ROLL-BACK

In contrast to COMMIT, the ROLLBACK operation is designed to annul the effects of a transaction that has yet to be finalized. ROLLBACK is employed to revert the database to its previous consistent state, thereby discarding any intermediate modifications that have accumulated during the course of the transaction. The operation is essential in scenarios where a breach of consistency is detected or an error precludes the successful completion of the intended operations. Conceptually, if a transaction transitions the database from state S_0 to an unstable state S_t, the invocation of a ROLLBACK restores the system to S_0, eliminating any partial updates. This reversibility is critical in preserving the integrity of the database, ensuring that data anomalies introduced by failed or erroneous operations do not persist.

Maintaining Data Integrity in Analytical Data Processing

In the realm of analytical data processing and transformation, the maintenance of data integrity through controlled state transitions is paramount. Analytical processes often involve complex, multi-stage data transformations that require stringent adherence to transactional guarantees. The deliberate execution of COMMIT commands demarcates the successful culmination of such transformations, thereby ensuring that only complete and verified changes transition into the persistent state of the database. Conversely, the controlled use of ROLLBACK operations provides a mechanism to retract incomplete or inconsistent transformations, preventing the propagation of errors throughout analytical pipelines. By enforcing strict protocols for data modification, the transactional control mechanisms intrinsic to PL/SQL support robust analytical workflows, where data integrity remains uncompromised even under conditions of high computational intensity and concurrent operations.

Transaction Isolation and Concurrency in High-Volume Environments

The execution of concurrent transactions in high-volume analytical environments necessitates a sophisticated approach to transaction isolation. Isolation levels govern the extent to which transactions are insulated from the operations of others, thereby mitigating the risks associated with concurrent data modifications. In scenarios involving substantial data processing, carefully calibrated isolation mechanisms prevent adverse phenomena such as dirty reads, non-repeatable reads, and phantom reads. The design of PL/SQL transaction control incorporates these considerations to ensure that each transaction interacts with a consistent snapshot of the database. This is achieved through a combination of system-level isolation settings and explicit transaction control commands, resulting in a transactional environment that is both scalable and resilient. The rigorous enforcement of isolation further fortifies the reliability of analytical transformations, ensuring that concurrent transactional operations do not compromise the overall integrity and consistency of the data.

ACID Properties and Their Theoretical Implications in PL/SQL

The ACID properties represent the conceptual underpinnings of robust transaction management in PL/SQL. Atomicity is ensured by treating a sequence of operations as a single unit, such that failure in any component of the transaction prompts a complete reversion to the initial state. Consistency is maintained by enforcing the database constraints and business rules integral to the data model. Isolation is achieved by regulating the visibility of transactional updates among concurrent operations, thereby preventing interference that could corrupt the logical sequence of data transformations. Durability guarantees that once a COMMIT operation has been executed, the changes are immutable in the face of subsequent system failures. These properties are not merely abstract concepts but are operationalized through the explicit use of COMMIT and ROLLBACK commands in PL/SQL. The theoretical rigor provided by the ACID framework is indispensable in preserving data integrity during the execution of complex analytical tasks, ensuring that each transaction robustly adheres to the highest standards of data management practice.

Oracle 19c SQL Code Snippet

```
-- Create TRANSACTION_DEMO table to simulate transactional state
↳  changes

CREATE TABLE TRANSACTION_DEMO (
    TRANSACTION_ID NUMBER GENERATED BY DEFAULT AS IDENTITY,
    DESCRIPTION    VARCHAR2(100),
    VALUE_BEFORE   NUMBER,
    VALUE_AFTER    NUMBER,
    ENTRY_DATE     DATE DEFAULT SYSDATE,
    CONSTRAINT TRANSACTION_DEMO_PK PRIMARY KEY (TRANSACTION_ID)
);


-- Insert baseline data to represent the initial state (S0)

INSERT INTO TRANSACTION_DEMO (DESCRIPTION, VALUE_BEFORE,
↳  VALUE_AFTER)
VALUES ('Initial State', 100, 100);
COMMIT;
```

```
-------------------------------------------------------------------
-- Demonstrate a transactional update with COMMIT operation
-- This PL/SQL block retrieves the current state, performs an update
↪   (SO -> S_t),
-- and then commits the changes, ensuring a transition to a final
↪   state (S_f)
-------------------------------------------------------------------
DECLARE
    v_initial NUMBER;
    v_updated NUMBER;
BEGIN
    -- Lock the row for update for transactional consistency
    SELECT VALUE_AFTER
      INTO v_initial
      FROM TRANSACTION_DEMO
     WHERE DESCRIPTION = 'Initial State'
       AND ROWNUM = 1
      FOR UPDATE;

    -- Simulate a transformation: increase the value by 50
    v_updated := v_initial + 50;

    -- Update the initial state with the new value
    UPDATE TRANSACTION_DEMO
       SET VALUE_AFTER = v_updated
     WHERE DESCRIPTION = 'Initial State';

    -- Log the successful committed transaction
    INSERT INTO TRANSACTION_DEMO (DESCRIPTION, VALUE_BEFORE,
    ↪   VALUE_AFTER)
    VALUES ('Committed Transaction', v_initial, v_updated);

    COMMIT;

    DBMS_OUTPUT.PUT_LINE('Transaction committed: ' || v_initial || '
    ↪   -> ' || v_updated);
EXCEPTION
    WHEN OTHERS THEN
        ROLLBACK;
        DBMS_OUTPUT.PUT_LINE('Error during commit transaction: ' ||
        ↪   SQLERRM);
END;
/

-------------------------------------------------------------------
-- Demonstrate transaction reversibility using ROLLBACK
-- This block simulates an error scenario where an update would
↪   violate
-- a consistency rule (e.g., generating a negative value), thus
↪   triggering a rollback.
-------------------------------------------------------------------
DECLARE
```

```
    v_current NUMBER;
BEGIN
    -- Lock the "Committed Transaction" row for update
    SELECT VALUE_AFTER
      INTO v_current
      FROM TRANSACTION_DEMO
     WHERE DESCRIPTION = 'Committed Transaction'
       AND ROWNUM = 1
     FOR UPDATE;

    -- Simulate an erroneous update by subtracting a large number
    UPDATE TRANSACTION_DEMO
       SET VALUE_AFTER = v_current - 9999
     WHERE DESCRIPTION = 'Committed Transaction';

    -- Validate the new state; if negative, rollback to preserve
    ↪    consistency
    IF (v_current - 9999) < 0 THEN
        ROLLBACK;
        DBMS_OUTPUT.PUT_LINE('Rollback executed: Negative state
        ↪    detected.');
    ELSE
        COMMIT;
        DBMS_OUTPUT.PUT_LINE('Transaction committed after
        ↪    subtraction: '
                                || (v_current - 9999));
    END IF;
EXCEPTION
    WHEN OTHERS THEN
        ROLLBACK;
        DBMS_OUTPUT.PUT_LINE('Exception during rollback demo: ' ||
        ↪    SQLERRM);
END;
/


-------------------------------------------------------------------------
-- Advanced transactional control using SAVEPOINT in a multi-step
↪    update
-- This block demonstrates setting a savepoint, performing a partial
↪    update,
-- checking conditions, and rolling back to the savepoint if
↪    necessary.
-------------------------------------------------------------------------
DECLARE
    v_balance NUMBER;
BEGIN
    -- Retrieve the current state from the "Initial State" row
    SELECT VALUE_AFTER
      INTO v_balance
      FROM TRANSACTION_DEMO
     WHERE DESCRIPTION = 'Initial State'
       AND ROWNUM = 1
     FOR UPDATE;
```

154

```
        SAVEPOINT before_increment;

        -- Simulate a deposit operation by adding 200
        UPDATE TRANSACTION_DEMO
           SET VALUE_AFTER = VALUE_AFTER + 200
         WHERE DESCRIPTION = 'Initial State';

        -- Re-read the updated balance
        SELECT VALUE_AFTER
          INTO v_balance
          FROM TRANSACTION_DEMO
         WHERE DESCRIPTION = 'Initial State'
           AND ROWNUM = 1;

        -- If the new balance exceeds a threshold (e.g., 500), revert to
        ↪  the savepoint
        IF v_balance > 500 THEN
            ROLLBACK TO SAVEPOINT before_increment;
            DBMS_OUTPUT.PUT_LINE('Reverted to savepoint: Deposit aborted
            ↪   due to high balance.');
        ELSE
            COMMIT;
            DBMS_OUTPUT.PUT_LINE('Deposit committed: New balance is ' ||
            ↪   v_balance);
        END IF;
EXCEPTION
    WHEN OTHERS THEN
        ROLLBACK;
        DBMS_OUTPUT.PUT_LINE('Error in multi-step transaction: ' ||
        ↪   SQLERRM);
END;
/


-------------------------------------------------------------------------
-- Demonstrate transactional isolation in a high-volume environment
-- The session is set to SERIALIZABLE isolation to ensure a
↪  consistent snapshot is used.
-------------------------------------------------------------------------
ALTER SESSION SET ISOLATION_LEVEL = SERIALIZABLE;

DECLARE
    v_value_before NUMBER;
    v_value_after  NUMBER;
BEGIN
    -- Capture the pre-update state (consistent snapshot of S0)
    SELECT VALUE_AFTER
      INTO v_value_before
      FROM TRANSACTION_DEMO
     WHERE DESCRIPTION = 'Initial State'
       AND ROWNUM = 1;

    -- Perform an update within the transaction
```

```
UPDATE TRANSACTION_DEMO
   SET VALUE_AFTER = VALUE_AFTER + 10
   WHERE DESCRIPTION = 'Initial State';

   -- Capture the post-update state (S_t leading to S_f upon
   ↪  commit)
   SELECT VALUE_AFTER
     INTO v_value_after
     FROM TRANSACTION_DEMO
     WHERE DESCRIPTION = 'Initial State'
       AND ROWNUM = 1;

   COMMIT;
   DBMS_OUTPUT.PUT_LINE('Isolation demo: Value updated from '
                        || v_value_before || ' to ' ||
                        ↪  v_value_after);
EXCEPTION
   WHEN OTHERS THEN
       ROLLBACK;
       DBMS_OUTPUT.PUT_LINE('Error in isolation demonstration: ' ||
       ↪   SQLERRM);
END;
/

-----------------------------------------------------------------------
-- Reset the session isolation level to the default READ COMMITTED
↪  mode
-----------------------------------------------------------------------
ALTER SESSION SET ISOLATION_LEVEL = READ COMMITTED;
```

Multiple Choice Questions

1. Which of the following best describes the principle of atomicity in PL/SQL transaction management?

   (a) Each transaction is executed over several discrete steps, allowing partial commits.

   (b) Each transaction is treated as an indivisible unit that either fully succeeds or completely fails.

   (c) Transactions can be segmented into independent parts with selective rollbacks.

   (d) Atomicity ensures automatic isolation of concurrent transactions.

2. What is the primary purpose of the COMMIT statement in PL/SQL?

(a) To temporarily save changes made during a transaction.

(b) To permanently record all modifications made in the current transaction.

(c) To undo any changes made during the transaction.

(d) To initiate a new transaction immediately after data modification.

3. Which PL/SQL command is used to reverse modifications and restore the database to its previous consistent state?

   (a) SAVEPOINT

   (b) ROLLBACK

   (c) COMMIT

   (d) MERGE

4. How do the ACID properties reinforce data integrity during complex analytical processing in PL/SQL?

   (a) They automatically optimize query performance without manual intervention.

   (b) They provide a theoretical framework ensuring that transactions maintain consistent, accurate, and stable data states.

   (c) They allow for non-deterministic execution paths in transactions to enhance flexibility.

   (d) They enforce dynamic data schema alterations based on workload.

5. In high-volume, concurrent analytical environments, what role does transaction isolation play?

   (a) It enables simultaneous access to all uncommitted data by any session.

   (b) It restricts the visibility of uncommitted changes to prevent interference among concurrent transactions.

   (c) It accelerates transaction execution by bypassing integrity constraints.

   (d) It periodically flushes cached data to improve performance.

6. In a scenario where a multi-stage data transformation encounters an anomaly, which transaction control command should be used to maintain data integrity?

   (a) COMMIT, to finalize valid changes before the error.

   (b) ROLLBACK, to cancel all modifications made during the ongoing transaction.

   (c) SAVEPOINT, to mark the error point but continue later.

   (d) MERGE, to combine error-free segments with previous committed data.

7. Which ACID property ensures that once a transaction is committed, its effects persist regardless of future system failures?

   (a) Atomicity

   (b) Durability

   (c) Consistency

   (d) Isolation

Answers:

1. **B: Each transaction is treated as an indivisible unit that either fully succeeds or completely fails.**
   Atomicity requires that a transaction's set of operations is executed as a single unit; if any part fails, the entire transaction is rolled back, ensuring no partial updates are applied.

2. **B: To permanently record all modifications made in the current transaction.**
   The COMMIT command finalizes the transaction by making all changes permanent and visible to other sessions, thereby ensuring the persistence and consistency of the data.

3. **B: ROLLBACK**
   ROLLBACK undoes all changes in the ongoing transaction, reverting the database to its last committed state. This is crucial when errors or inconsistencies are identified during a transaction.

4. **B: They provide a theoretical framework ensuring that transactions maintain consistent, accurate, and stable data states.**

The ACID properties (Atomicity, Consistency, Isolation, Durability) guarantee that data transformations adhere to strict correctness rules, which is essential for the reliability of complex analytical operations.

5. **B: It restricts the visibility of uncommitted changes to prevent interference among concurrent transactions.**

Isolation ensures that concurrent transactions do not affect each other by limiting the exposure of in-progress modifications, thereby preserving the integrity of each transaction's view of the data.

6. **B: ROLLBACK, to cancel all modifications made during the ongoing transaction.**

When an error is encountered during a multi-stage transformation, invoking ROLLBACK reverts all changes made within that transaction, thereby maintaining overall data integrity.

7. **B: Durability**

Durability guarantees that once a transaction has been committed, its changes are permanently recorded in the system, even in the event of system failures or crashes.

Chapter 17

Utilizing Dynamic SQL for Flexible Analytics

Conceptual Foundations of Dynamic SQL

Dynamic SQL represents a paradigm shift in data manipulation, whereby the structure of a query is not predetermined at compile-time but instead is synthesized at runtime based on contextual parameters and evolving analytic requirements. This approach enables the generation of queries that adapt to variable data schemas, user-defined criteria, and emergent patterns within the dataset. Unlike static SQL statements, which are fixed in their syntax and structure, dynamic SQL permits the formulation of commands where components such as table names, predicates, and even join conditions are constructed and executed on the fly. Such flexibility is essential when addressing complex analytical scenarios, wherein the precise nature of the query may depend upon inputs that are only available during the execution phase. The theoretical framework for dynamic query construction can be formalized by considering a query function $Q(P)$, where P represents a set of runtime parameters. As these parameters vary, the resultant query $Q(P)$ exhibits the dynamism necessary to reflect the true state of evolving analytic needs.

Mechanisms for Runtime Query Construction

The generation of dynamic SQL involves several key stages, beginning with the modular assembly of query components into a composite string. In this mechanism, base clauses such as SELECT, FROM, and WHERE are concatenated with variable conditions that may be dictated by analytic insights gleaned during runtime. The process is akin to the assembly of a mathematical expression, where each segment is parameterized and later reassembled into the final construct. This layered composition allows for granular adjustments within each segment of the query, thereby facilitating the creation of tailored queries that accurately represent the current analytic context. The construction phase must also account for the syntactic and semantic integrity of SQL, ensuring that any dynamically generated statement adheres to the rigorous formatting and operational standards required for successful execution.

Execution Semantics and Runtime Evaluation

Once a dynamic query is constructed, its execution follows a two-fold process. First, the constructed query string is submitted to the underlying SQL engine, where it undergoes parsing and validation. This phase ensures that the expression satisfies both the syntactic rules of SQL and the contextual constraints imposed by the database schema. Subsequently, the validated query is executed against the database, with the results reflecting the latest state of the underlying data. In this context, the dynamics of SQL are harnessed to enable an interplay between compile-time logic and runtime evaluation, providing a mechanism by which analytic queries can be both flexible and robust. The evaluation can be perceived as a mapping from the constructed query space to a result set, formalized by the relation $E : Q(P) \mapsto R$, where R denotes the set of returned data. The performance attributes of the execution phase are critically dependent upon the efficiency of the parsing and optimization algorithms within the database engine, particularly in environments characterized by high data volume and complex analytic demands.

Integration with Analytic Applications

The use of dynamic SQL finds significant utility in analytic applications that require the adaptability to dynamically changing data landscapes. By enabling the on-demand synthesis of queries, dynamic SQL facilitates the real-time generation of tailored analytic reports, ad hoc data explorations, and intricate data mining operations. In scenarios where analytic models must traverse disparate data sources or pivot based on emergent trends, the ability to generate and execute queries dynamically becomes indispensable. This integration is achieved through a systematic approach where analytic parameters are first captured and then transformed into corresponding SQL components, thereby ensuring that the resultant query faithfully mirrors the underlying analytical requirements. The synchronization between dynamic query construction and analytic processing is critical in maintaining accuracy and relevance in the results, particularly when the data environment is subject to frequent updates and schema modifications.

Considerations of Flexibility and Adaptability in Dynamic Queries

Flexibility in dynamic SQL is achieved through a careful balance between query generality and specificity. The methodology mandates an in-depth understanding of both the structural aspects of database schemas and the functional requirements of the analytic model. This dual focus ensures that dynamically generated queries are not only syntactically valid but also semantically aligned with the intended analytical tasks. Adaptability is further enhanced by incorporating conditional logic during the assembly of query strings; such logic permits the inclusion or exclusion of certain query components depending on the runtime context. As analytic needs evolve, the dynamic query framework must be robust enough to accommodate new parameters, additional filters, and alternative join strategies, all while sustaining computational efficiency. This adaptive quality is paramount in advanced analytical settings, where the ability to respond to unforeseen data patterns or emergent business requirements can provide a decisive competitive advantage.

Implications for Analytic Scalability and Performance

In high-volume analytic environments, the scalability of data processing operations is a critical consideration. Dynamic SQL contributes to scalability by reducing the need for precompiled, static queries that may be insufficiently adaptable to diverse and rapidly changing data characteristics. The capability to generate queries that precisely capture the nuances of current analytic contexts allows for more targeted data retrieval and processing. This selective approach minimizes overhead, as queries are optimized based on the immediate state of the dataset rather than a generalized schema. Moreover, the execution of dynamic queries benefits from the optimization routines built into modern SQL engines, which can reoptimize the query plan considering the current data distribution and system workload. As a result, dynamic SQL is not only a tool for enhancing flexibility but also an instrument for achieving improved performance metrics in environments where analytic demands continuously evolve.

Oracle 19c SQL Code Snippet

```
-- Create a sample analytics table to serve as the data source for
↪   dynamic queries.

CREATE TABLE FACT_ANALYTICS (
    ANALYTICS_ID NUMBER GENERATED BY DEFAULT AS IDENTITY,
    METRIC_NAME  VARCHAR2(100),
    METRIC_VALUE NUMBER,
    REPORT_DATE  DATE,
    CATEGORY     VARCHAR2(50),
    CONSTRAINT FACT_ANALYTICS_PK PRIMARY KEY (ANALYTICS_ID)
);

-- Insert sample analytic data into FACT_ANALYTICS.

INSERT ALL
    INTO FACT_ANALYTICS (METRIC_NAME, METRIC_VALUE, REPORT_DATE,
    ↪   CATEGORY)
        VALUES ('Sales', 1500, DATE '2023-10-01', 'Revenue')
    INTO FACT_ANALYTICS (METRIC_NAME, METRIC_VALUE, REPORT_DATE,
    ↪   CATEGORY)
        VALUES ('Sales', 2000, DATE '2023-10-02', 'Revenue')
```

```
    INTO FACT_ANALYTICS (METRIC_NAME, METRIC_VALUE, REPORT_DATE,
    ↪  CATEGORY)
        VALUES ('Expense', 800, DATE '2023-10-01', 'Cost')
    INTO FACT_ANALYTICS (METRIC_NAME, METRIC_VALUE, REPORT_DATE,
    ↪  CATEGORY)
        VALUES ('Expense', 1200, DATE '2023-10-02', 'Cost')
SELECT * FROM DUAL;
COMMIT;


-------------------------------------------------------------------------
-- Procedure: dynamic_query_analytics
-- Description: Constructs and executes a dynamic SQL statement
↪   based on runtime parameters.
-- This procedure embodies the concept of Q(P) where P represents
↪   the runtime parameters
-- and Q(P) dynamically formulates a query to aggregate analytic
↪   metrics.
-------------------------------------------------------------------------
CREATE OR REPLACE PROCEDURE dynamic_query_analytics (
    p_metric      IN VARCHAR2,   -- Filter for the metric name
    p_category    IN VARCHAR2,   -- Filter for the category
    p_start_date  IN DATE,       -- Start date for the report period
    p_end_date    IN DATE        -- End date for the report period
) IS
    v_sql   VARCHAR2(4000);
    v_total NUMBER;
BEGIN
    -- Construct the dynamic SQL query by concatenating fixed
    ↪   clauses with bind variable markers.
    v_sql := 'SELECT SUM(METRIC_VALUE) FROM FACT_ANALYTICS ' ||
            'WHERE METRIC_NAME = :metric ' ||
            'AND CATEGORY = :category ' ||
            'AND REPORT_DATE BETWEEN :start_date AND :end_date';

    DBMS_OUTPUT.PUT_LINE('Constructed Query: ' || v_sql);

    -- Execute the dynamic SQL query using EXECUTE IMMEDIATE.
    EXECUTE IMMEDIATE v_sql INTO v_total
        USING p_metric, p_category, p_start_date, p_end_date;

    DBMS_OUTPUT.PUT_LINE('Total ' || p_metric || ' for category ' ||
    ↪   p_category ||
                        ' between ' || TO_CHAR(p_start_date,
                        ↪   'YYYY-MM-DD') ||
                        ' and ' || TO_CHAR(p_end_date,
                        ↪   'YYYY-MM-DD') ||
                        ' is: ' || v_total);
EXCEPTION
    WHEN OTHERS THEN
        DBMS_OUTPUT.PUT_LINE('Error in dynamic_query_analytics: ' ||
        ↪   SQLERRM);
END dynamic_query_analytics;
/
```

164

```
-------------------------------------------------------------------
-- Function: get_dynamic_refcursor
-- Description: Returns a SYS_REFCURSOR for a dynamically
↪  constructed query.
-- This function demonstrates the mapping of Q(P) to a result set R
↪  where the query
-- is generated at runtime based on the provided category.
-------------------------------------------------------------------
CREATE OR REPLACE FUNCTION get_dynamic_refcursor (
    p_category IN VARCHAR2
) RETURN SYS_REFCURSOR
IS
    v_cursor SYS_REFCURSOR;
    v_sql    VARCHAR2(4000);
BEGIN
    -- Dynamically construct a SQL statement to retrieve detailed
    ↪  analytics for a specified category.
    v_sql := 'SELECT ANALYTICS_ID, METRIC_NAME, METRIC_VALUE,
    ↪  REPORT_DATE ' ||
             'FROM FACT_ANALYTICS ' ||
             'WHERE CATEGORY = :category ' ||
             'ORDER BY REPORT_DATE';

    OPEN v_cursor FOR v_sql USING p_category;
    RETURN v_cursor;
EXCEPTION
    WHEN OTHERS THEN
        DBMS_OUTPUT.PUT_LINE('Error in get_dynamic_refcursor: ' ||
        ↪  SQLERRM);
        RETURN NULL;
END get_dynamic_refcursor;
/


-------------------------------------------------------------------
-- Procedure: dynamic_cursor_fetch
-- Description: Demonstrates dynamic SQL execution using the
↪  DBMS_SQL package.
-- This approach provides granular control over runtime query
↪  evaluation and row-by-row processing.
-------------------------------------------------------------------
CREATE OR REPLACE PROCEDURE dynamic_cursor_fetch (
    p_sql IN VARCHAR2
) IS
    v_cursor    INTEGER;
    v_status    INTEGER;
    v_value     VARCHAR2(4000);
    v_row_count INTEGER := 0;
BEGIN
    -- Open a dynamic cursor using DBMS_SQL.
    v_cursor := DBMS_SQL.OPEN_CURSOR;
    DBMS_SQL.PARSE(v_cursor, p_sql, DBMS_SQL.NATIVE);
```

```
    -- Define the first column assuming it returns a VARCHAR2 value.
    DBMS_SQL.DEFINE_COLUMN(v_cursor, 1, v_value, 4000);

    -- Loop through the fetched rows and display values.
    LOOP
        v_status := DBMS_SQL.FETCH_ROWS(v_cursor);
        EXIT WHEN v_status = 0;
        DBMS_SQL.COLUMN_VALUE(v_cursor, 1, v_value);
        DBMS_OUTPUT.PUT_LINE('Row ' || (v_row_count+1) || ': ' ||
        ↪  v_value);
        v_row_count := v_row_count + 1;
    END LOOP;

    DBMS_OUTPUT.PUT_LINE('Total rows fetched: ' || v_row_count);
    DBMS_SQL.CLOSE_CURSOR(v_cursor);
EXCEPTION
    WHEN OTHERS THEN
        IF DBMS_SQL.IS_OPEN(v_cursor) THEN
            DBMS_SQL.CLOSE_CURSOR(v_cursor);
        END IF;
        DBMS_OUTPUT.PUT_LINE('Error in dynamic_cursor_fetch: ' ||
        ↪  SQLERRM);
END dynamic_cursor_fetch;
/


-------------------------------------------------------------------
-- Example Execution:
-- Call dynamic_query_analytics to aggregate "Sales" metrics for the
↪  "Revenue" category.
-------------------------------------------------------------------
BEGIN
    dynamic_query_analytics(
        p_metric     => 'Sales',
        p_category   => 'Revenue',
        p_start_date => DATE '2023-10-01',
        p_end_date   => DATE '2023-10-31'
    );
END;
/


-------------------------------------------------------------------
-- Example Execution:
-- Retrieve and display analytics details using a REF CURSOR for the
↪  "Cost" category.
-------------------------------------------------------------------
DECLARE
    v_rc    SYS_REFCURSOR;
    v_id    FACT_ANALYTICS.ANALYTICS_ID%TYPE;
    v_name  FACT_ANALYTICS.METRIC_NAME%TYPE;
    v_value FACT_ANALYTICS.METRIC_VALUE%TYPE;
    v_date  FACT_ANALYTICS.REPORT_DATE%TYPE;
BEGIN
    v_rc := get_dynamic_refcursor('Cost');
```

```
LOOP
    FETCH v_rc INTO v_id, v_name, v_value, v_date;
    EXIT WHEN v_rc%NOTFOUND;
    DBMS_OUTPUT.PUT_LINE('ID: ' || v_id || ', Metric: ' ||
    ↪   v_name ||
                        ', Value: ' || v_value || ', Date: ' ||
                        ↪   TO_CHAR(v_date, 'YYYY-MM-DD'));
    END LOOP;
    CLOSE v_rc;
END;
/


----------------------------------------------------------------------
-- Example Execution:
-- Use dynamic_cursor_fetch to execute a custom dynamic SQL query
↪   that retrieves formatted dates.
----------------------------------------------------------------------
BEGIN
    dynamic_cursor_fetch('SELECT TO_CHAR(REPORT_DATE,
    ↪   ''YYYY-MM-DD'') FROM FACT_ANALYTICS WHERE METRIC_NAME =
    ↪   ''Expense'' ORDER BY REPORT_DATE');
END;
/
```

Multiple Choice Questions

1. Which of the following best describes the primary advantage
   of utilizing dynamic SQL in analytic applications?

   (a) It allows the use of precompiled and unmodifiable SQL
       queries.

   (b) It enables the construction of queries at runtime based
       on evolving parameters.

   (c) It restricts query execution to a fixed database schema.

   (d) It enforces static table names to enhance security.

2. What is the fundamental process involved in constructing a
   dynamic SQL query in PL/SQL?

   (a) Direct execution of a fully static SQL statement.

   (b) Modular assembly of query components while ensuring
       syntactic and semantic integrity.

   (c) Random selection and concatenation of SQL fragments.

   (d) Precompiling a universal query for all possible analytic
       scenarios.

3. In the formal mapping $E : Q(P) \mapsto R$ described in dynamic SQL execution semantics, what does R represent?

    (a) The set of runtime parameters.

    (b) The dynamically generated SQL query string.

    (c) The resulting data set returned by the query.

    (d) The error log output from the SQL engine.

4. How does dynamic SQL contribute to performance optimization in high-volume analytic environments?

    (a) It enforces static query plans disregarding data changes.

    (b) It generates queries that are optimized based on the current data distribution and system workload.

    (c) It minimizes the involvement of query optimization routines at runtime.

    (d) It avoids conditional logic by using a fixed query template.

5. Which attribute of dynamic SQL most effectively supports its integration with real-time analytic applications?

    (a) Its reliance on precompiled, static queries.

    (b) Its capability to adapt query construction based on live analytical requirements.

    (c) Its enforcement of a fixed query structure regardless of input.

    (d) Its limitation to a single pre-determined data source.

6. What role does conditional logic play in the assembly of dynamic SQL queries?

    (a) It simplifies the SQL syntax by removing all variable conditions.

    (b) It enables the selective inclusion or exclusion of query components based on runtime context.

    (c) It guarantees that every query is executed with an identical structure.

    (d) It automatically substitutes all parameters with fixed constants.

7. Why is modular query construction considered critical in dynamic SQL applications?

   (a) It minimizes overall code complexity by enforcing a monolithic query design.

   (b) It permits independent modification and optimization of each query segment to adapt to changing analytic demands.

   (c) It restricts flexibility by adhering to a fixed query template.

   (d) It eliminates the need for validating syntactic correctness in the final query.

Answers:

1. **B: It enables the construction of queries at runtime based on evolving parameters.**
   Dynamic SQL is defined by its ability to generate SQL queries during execution, adapting the query structure to runtime parameters and analytic requirements rather than relying on a fixed, precompiled form.

2. **B: Modular assembly of query components while ensuring syntactic and semantic integrity.**
   The construction of dynamic SQL relies on piecing together various components (e.g., SELECT, FROM, WHERE clauses) into a complete query string. This modular approach facilitates adjustments and guarantees that the final query adheres to both SQL syntax and the intended logic.

3. **C: The resulting data set returned by the query.**
   In the mapping $E : Q(P) \mapsto R$, $Q(P)$ represents the dynamically generated query based on parameters P, and R is the result set produced after the query is executed, reflecting the current state of the database.

4. **B: It generates queries that are optimized based on the current data distribution and system workload.**
   Dynamic SQL enhances performance by tailoring queries to current conditions. This adaptability allows the SQL engine's optimization routines to develop execution plans that reflect the immediate state of the data and system, thereby improving processing efficiency.

5. **B: Its capability to adapt query construction based on live analytical requirements.**
   The key to integrating dynamic SQL with real-time analytics lies in its flexibility. By synthesizing SQL commands at runtime in accordance with up-to-date input parameters, it supports the generation of customized queries that meet immediate analytic needs.

6. **B: It enables the selective inclusion or exclusion of query components based on runtime context.**
   Incorporating conditional logic during query construction allows dynamic SQL to include or omit certain clauses depending on parameters available at runtime. This results in highly tailored queries that accurately reflect the desired analytic conditions.

7. **B: It permits independent modification and optimization of each query segment to adapt to changing analytic demands.**
   A modular approach to building dynamic SQL queries allows each component to be developed, tested, and optimized separately. This independent control is crucial when queries must evolve rapidly in response to shifting analytics requirements, ensuring both flexibility and maintainability.

Chapter 18

Advanced Collections: Associative Arrays and Nested Tables

Associative Arrays: Structural Design and Dynamic Indexing

Associative arrays constitute a sophisticated data structure within PL/SQL that enables the mapping of keys to corresponding values without reliance on contiguous indexing. This data type is formally abstracted as a function $f : K \rightarrow V$, where K represents the domain of admissible keys and V denotes the set of stored values. Owing to its hash-based implementation, an associative array supports dynamic allocation and deallocation of elements, thereby permitting rapid access and modification even in the presence of sparse or highly variable indices. The internal organization of these collections favors an algorithmic perspective whereby the expected lookup operation adheres to an average time complexity of $O(1)$; however, such performance is inherently dependent on the efficiency of the underlying hash function and the management of collision resolution. The absence of a sequential ordering constraint further distinguishes associative arrays from conventional arrays, making them especially well-suited for managing datasets whose structure is not predetermined at compile time and which require adaptive indexing strategies.

Nested Tables: Hierarchical Data Structures and Set-Based Operations

Nested tables offer an alternative collection mechanism that transforms a group of scalar or composite elements into a single, compact entity. Unlike associative arrays, nested tables are designed with dense sequential storage in mind, permitting operations analogous to those supported on relational tables. The formal representation of a nested table may be characterized by the finite set $S = \{a_1, a_2, \ldots, a_n\}$, where the preservation of element ordering facilitates operations such as bulk collection manipulation and set-based transformations. The ability to seamlessly integrate nested tables into SQL queries provides a dual advantage: it bridges procedural PL/SQL constructs with declarative relational operations, and it leverages the powerful optimization strategies inherent in the underlying database engine. This data structure is particularly effective in modeling one-to-many relationships, thus supporting complex data hierarchies and enabling intricate analytic operations that require aggregation, filtering, and reordering of the dataset without forfeiting the intrinsic relational properties of the data.

Comparative Analysis and Performance Considerations

A rigorous examination of advanced collection types necessitates an in-depth comparative analysis of associative arrays and nested tables, especially from the perspectives of operational efficiency and adaptability. Associative arrays excel in scenarios demanding rapid key-based access and flexible memory allocation. Their implementation, which often mirrors that of hash tables, facilitates near constant-time access to elements under average conditions. Nevertheless, such efficiency is contingent upon the distribution of keys and the inherent capability of the hash function to minimize collisions. In contrast, nested tables capitalize on the structural benefits of dense storage, thereby enabling advanced set-based operations that are optimized within the relational paradigm. The contiguous nature of nested tables promotes efficient bulk processing and grants the database engine the leverage to apply advanced SQL optimization techniques, which are particularly advantageous when executing complex queries that involve multiset operations.

Furthermore, the trade-offs between these collection types become evident when considering the management of memory and the demands of dynamic datasets. Associative arrays, with their non-sequential indexing, may incur fragmentation and unpredictable memory utilization when faced with extensive insertions and deletions, a factor that necessitates vigilant memory management in high-throughput environments. Nested tables, by virtue of their ordered storage, often provide better predictability in memory consumption and facilitate operations that involve sorting and aggregation. The selection between these two paradigms is thus governed by the specific operational requirements of the analytic process, where associative arrays may be favored for their flexible indexing in highly dynamic contexts, while nested tables are preferable when the task demands set-oriented manipulation and direct integration with SQL-based relational processing.

Oracle 19c SQL Code Snippet

```
--------------------------------------------------------------------
-- Create a demo table to simulate analytical data points
--------------------------------------------------------------------
CREATE TABLE DATA_POINTS (
    POINT_ID    NUMBER GENERATED BY DEFAULT AS IDENTITY,
    DESCRIPTION VARCHAR2(50),
    VALUE       NUMBER,
    CREATED_AT  DATE DEFAULT SYSDATE,
    CONSTRAINT DATA_POINTS_PK PRIMARY KEY (POINT_ID)
);

-- Insert sample data into DATA_POINTS table
INSERT ALL
    INTO DATA_POINTS (DESCRIPTION, VALUE) VALUES ('Sample A', 10)
    INTO DATA_POINTS (DESCRIPTION, VALUE) VALUES ('Sample B', 20)
    INTO DATA_POINTS (DESCRIPTION, VALUE) VALUES ('Sample C', 15)
    INTO DATA_POINTS (DESCRIPTION, VALUE) VALUES ('Sample D', 25)
SELECT * FROM DUAL;
COMMIT;


--------------------------------------------------------------------
-- Demonstration of Associative Arrays (Mapping: f: K -> V)
--
-- In this block we simulate an associative array, formally
↪   abstracted as:
--       f: K -> V
-- where K represents keys (here, the DESCRIPTION field) and V the
↪   numeric VALUE.
```

```
-- The algorithm demonstrates dynamic allocation, rapid lookup
↪  (average O(1)
-- complexity under ideal conditions) and dynamic update of element
↪  values.
-------------------------------------------------------------------


DECLARE
    -- Define an associative array type: mapping VARCHAR2 keys to
    ↪  NUMBER values
    TYPE assoc_array_t IS TABLE OF NUMBER INDEX BY VARCHAR2(30);
    assoc_arr assoc_array_t;

    v_key      VARCHAR2(30);
    v_value    NUMBER;
    v_sum      NUMBER := 0;
    v_count    NUMBER := 0;
BEGIN
    -- Populate the associative array from the DATA_POINTS table
    FOR rec IN (SELECT DESCRIPTION, VALUE FROM DATA_POINTS) LOOP
        assoc_arr(rec.DESCRIPTION) := rec.VALUE;
    END LOOP;

    -- Dynamic indexing: update the value associated with key
    ↪  'Sample B'
    IF assoc_arr.EXISTS('Sample B') THEN
        assoc_arr('Sample B') := assoc_arr('Sample B') + 5;   --
        ↪  f('Sample B') is incremented by 5
    END IF;

    -- Iterate over the associative array to calculate the sum and
    ↪  compute the average
    v_key := assoc_arr.FIRST;
    WHILE v_key IS NOT NULL LOOP
        v_sum := v_sum + assoc_arr(v_key);
        v_count := v_count + 1;
        v_key := assoc_arr.NEXT(v_key);
    END LOOP;

    DBMS_OUTPUT.PUT_LINE('Associative Array Total Sum: ' || v_sum);
    DBMS_OUTPUT.PUT_LINE('Associative Array Average (f:K -> V): ' ||
    ↪  v_sum/v_count);
END;
/

-------------------------------------------------------------------
-- Demonstration of Nested Tables (Set S = {a1, a2, ..., an})
--
-- Here we use a nested table to manage a finite set S = {a1, a2,
↪  ..., an}. This block
-- performs bulk collection, set-based ordering and aggregation
↪  operations-a dual approach
-- that leverages the relational optimization inherent in Oracle's
↪  SQL engine.
```

174

```
-------------------------------------------------------------------------
DECLARE
    -- Define a nested table type for NUMBER values
    TYPE num_table_t IS TABLE OF NUMBER;
    num_table num_table_t;

    v_total NUMBER := 0;
    v_avg   NUMBER;
BEGIN
    -- Bulk collect the numeric values from DATA_POINTS into the
    ↪  nested table
    SELECT VALUE
      BULK COLLECT INTO num_table
      FROM DATA_POINTS;

    -- Iterate over the nested table to compute the aggregate sum
    FOR i IN 1..num_table.COUNT LOOP
        v_total := v_total + num_table(i);
    END LOOP;

    v_avg := v_total / num_table.COUNT;

    DBMS_OUTPUT.PUT_LINE('Nested Table Total Sum: ' || v_total);
    DBMS_OUTPUT.PUT_LINE('Nested Table Average: ' || v_avg);
END;
/


-------------------------------------------------------------------------
-- Integrative Procedure: Combining Associative Arrays and Nested
↪  Tables
--
-- This procedure encapsulates an end-to-end analytical algorithm:
-- 1. It maps data using an associative array (f: K -> V) to
↪  demonstrate dynamic indexing,
--     updates a specific element, and computes an aggregate sum and
↪  average.
-- 2. It simultaneously employs a nested table (S = {a1, a2, ...,
↪  an}) to perform bulk
--     collection and set-based operations.
--
-- The integrative analytics demonstrate key mathematical and
↪  algorithmic principles:
--   - f('key') update: f('Sample D') = f('Sample D') * 1.2
↪  [Simulating a transformation]
--   - Average computation: ( value) / n, reflecting both dynamic
↪  and static collection strategies.
-------------------------------------------------------------------------

CREATE OR REPLACE PROCEDURE analyze_data_collections IS
    -- Declaration for associative array analysis
    TYPE assoc_array_t IS TABLE OF NUMBER INDEX BY VARCHAR2(30);
    assoc_arr assoc_array_t;
```

```
      -- Declaration for nested table processing
      TYPE num_table_t IS TABLE OF NUMBER;
      num_table num_table_t;

      v_key          VARCHAR2(30);
      v_sum_assoc    NUMBER := 0;
      v_count_assoc  NUMBER := 0;

      v_sum_nested   NUMBER := 0;
      v_avg_nested   NUMBER;
BEGIN
      -- Populate the associative array from the DATA_POINTS table
      FOR rec IN (SELECT DESCRIPTION, VALUE FROM DATA_POINTS) LOOP
          assoc_arr(rec.DESCRIPTION) := rec.VALUE;
      END LOOP;

      -- Perform a dynamic update on the associative array:
      -- Increase 'Sample D' by multiplying its value by factor 1.2
      IF assoc_arr.EXISTS('Sample D') THEN
          assoc_arr('Sample D') := assoc_arr('Sample D') * 1.2;
      END IF;

      -- Compute aggregate sum and average using the associative array
      ↪   (f:K -> V fundamentals)
      v_key := assoc_arr.FIRST;
      WHILE v_key IS NOT NULL LOOP
          v_sum_assoc := v_sum_assoc + assoc_arr(v_key);
          v_count_assoc := v_count_assoc + 1;
          v_key := assoc_arr.NEXT(v_key);
      END LOOP;

      DBMS_OUTPUT.PUT_LINE('Procedure - Associative Array Sum: ' ||
      ↪   v_sum_assoc);
      DBMS_OUTPUT.PUT_LINE('Procedure - Associative Array Average: '
      ↪   || v_sum_assoc/v_count_assoc);

      -- Bulk collect data into a nested table for set-based
      ↪   operations
      SELECT VALUE BULK COLLECT INTO num_table FROM DATA_POINTS;

      -- Sum up values from the nested table using a simple iterative
      ↪   algorithm
      FOR i IN 1 .. num_table.COUNT LOOP
          v_sum_nested := v_sum_nested + num_table(i);
      END LOOP;

      v_avg_nested := v_sum_nested / num_table.COUNT;

      DBMS_OUTPUT.PUT_LINE('Procedure - Nested Table Sum: ' ||
      ↪   v_sum_nested);
      DBMS_OUTPUT.PUT_LINE('Procedure - Nested Table Average: ' ||
      ↪   v_avg_nested);
```

```
END analyze_data_collections;
/

-- Execute the integrative analytics procedure
BEGIN
    analyze_data_collections;
END;
/
```

Multiple Choice Questions

1. Which of the following best describes the primary advantage of using associative arrays in PL/SQL when handling non-sequential data?

    (a) They guarantee a sorted order of elements.

    (b) They facilitate dynamic, key-based indexing that enables near constant-time access.

    (c) They enforce dense, contiguous storage ideal for bulk operations.

    (d) They automatically integrate with SQL set-based operations.

2. In PL/SQL, the expected average time complexity for a lookup operation in an associative array is $O(1)$ primarily due to:

    (a) Sequential scanning of the entire collection.

    (b) The use of binary search on a sorted key-set.

    (c) The hash-based implementation coupled with efficient collision resolution techniques.

    (d) Direct integration with the SQL query optimizer.

3. Which statement correctly contrasts associative arrays with nested tables in PL/SQL?

    (a) Associative arrays maintain sequential ordering, whereas nested tables do not.

    (b) Associative arrays support arbitrary key types and non-sequential indexing, while nested tables are designed for dense, sequential storage.

    (c) Nested tables utilize hash-based lookups, whereas associative arrays require explicit index ordering.

(d) Nested tables are limited to scalar data, while associative arrays are intended solely for composite data types.

4. What feature of nested tables makes them especially suitable for direct integration with SQL queries?

    (a) Their inherent hash-based indexing mechanism.

    (b) Their ordered, set-like storage structure that mirrors relational table properties.

    (c) Their dynamic memory allocation that adapts to dataset changes.

    (d) Their capability to automatically resolve key collisions.

5. Regarding memory management in dynamic analytic environments, which statement is true when comparing associative arrays and nested tables?

    (a) Associative arrays provide predictable, contiguous memory usage regardless of insertions and deletions.

    (b) Nested tables typically suffer from fragmentation due to their sequential storage.

    (c) Associative arrays may experience memory fragmentation in sparse datasets, whereas nested tables generally offer predictable memory consumption due to dense storage.

    (d) Both associative arrays and nested tables manage memory identically under dynamic data manipulation.

6. When choosing between an associative array and a nested table for an analytic application in PL/SQL, which design consideration is most critical?

    (a) The trade-off between constant-time, key-based access and robust support for SQL set operations.

    (b) The decision between static versus dynamic memory allocation.

    (c) Whether the data needs to be automatically sorted.

    (d) The compatibility with external programming languages.

7. Under which condition might the performance advantage of an associative array be significantly diminished?

(a) When the dataset is strictly sequential with few insertions or deletions.

(b) When the underlying hash function produces numerous collisions due to poor key distribution.

(c) When the collection is used exclusively in set-oriented SQL queries.

(d) When the collection contains only numeric data.

Answers:

1. **B: They facilitate dynamic, key-based indexing that enables near constant-time access**
   Associative arrays map arbitrary keys to values using a hash-based mechanism, allowing for rapid lookups even when the indices are non-sequential.

2. **C: The hash-based implementation coupled with efficient collision resolution techniques**
   Associative arrays achieve an average $O(1)$ lookup time by employing a hash function to map keys to locations; efficient handling of collisions is essential for maintaining this performance.

3. **B: Associative arrays support arbitrary key types and non-sequential indexing, while nested tables are designed for dense, sequential storage**
   Unlike nested tables, which store elements in a contiguous, ordered manner conducive to SQL operations, associative arrays allow flexible and dynamic key assignment without inherent ordering.

4. **B: Their ordered, set-like storage structure that mirrors relational table properties**
   Nested tables are stored as dense collections, making them compatible with SQL operations that expect a set or table-like structure for operations such as aggregation and ordering.

5. **C: Associative arrays may experience memory fragmentation in sparse datasets, whereas nested tables generally offer predictable memory consumption due to dense storage**
   Dynamic insertion and deletion in associative arrays can lead to fragmented memory allocation, while nested tables, with

their sequential storage, provide more consistent memory usage.

6. **A: The trade-off between constant-time, key-based access and robust support for SQL set operations**
The key decision factor is whether the analytic task benefits more from the $O(1)$ access time of associative arrays or from the set-based manipulation capabilities that nested tables offer through direct SQL integration.

7. **B: When the underlying hash function produces numerous collisions due to poor key distribution**
The efficiency of associative arrays relies on a well-distributed hash function. A poor distribution causing frequent collisions can degrade performance, negating the typical $O(1)$ advantage.

Chapter 19

Crafting Table Functions for Custom Data Retrieval

Theoretical Foundations and Formal Definitions

Table functions represent an advanced construct in relational database systems whereby a function, viewed formally as $f : \mathcal{D} \rightarrow \mathcal{R}$, returns a set of rows that is amenable to full integration within SQL query formulations. In this formalism, the domain $\mathcal{D}$ encapsulates the set of permissible input parameters, while the codomain $\mathcal{R}$ is defined as a collection of rows that conform to a predetermined relational schema. This formulation allows the encapsulation of intricate procedural logic into a modular function whose output is interpreted as a relational table. Through this encapsulation, the expressiveness of procedural constructs is harnessed while preserving the declarative semantics and optimization capabilities inherent in set-based data analytics.

The abstraction effectively reduces the impedance mismatch that often exists between procedural programming constructs and relational algebra, enabling practitioners to define complex data transformations and retrieval strategies within a single coherent function. The mathematical underpinning of table functions ensures that such functions exhibit properties of determinism and composability, which are critical for reasoning about query correctness and performance within a formal database context.

Bridging Procedural Logic with Set-Based Operations

A core utility of table functions is their ability to serve as a bridge between the step-by-step procedural logic endemic to traditional algorithmic implementations and the holistic, set-oriented operations characteristic of SQL. In this context, the function encapsulates a sequential or iterative process and presents its intermediary results as a well-defined row set. This abstraction permits the invocation of table functions within FROM clauses and allows them to participate in complex joins, aggregations, and set operations without requiring external transformation of procedural results into table structures.

The operational model of a table function implicitly relies on an internal mechanism that constructs the output row set during runtime. By leveraging the execution paradigm where procedural loops and conditional branches coalesce into a single output stream, the table function acts as a conduit by which raw computational results are normalized into a relational format. This transformation is conceptually characterized by the mapping $f(x) = R_x$, where for each input $x \in \mathcal{D}$, the function f produces a subset $R_x \subset \mathcal{R}$ that is subsequently "flattened" into the composite output of the function. As a result, table functions enable the extraction of deeply nested or dynamically generated datasets and their immediate consumption in SQL-driven analytics.

Architectural and Design Considerations

The design of table functions necessitates a comprehensive evaluation of both modularity and extensibility within the broader context of database architecture. At the architectural level, table functions are conceived as encapsulated modules that abstract the intricacies of procedural data manipulation. Their design promotes separation of concerns by isolating logic that pertains to data transformation from the declarative specifications typical of SQL queries.

In designing these functions, careful attention must be paid to the schema of the row set that will be returned. A well-defined output schema is essential to ensure that the table function integrates seamlessly with subsequent relational operations. The internal implementation must efficiently handle the allocation and population of rows, which often involves dynamically managing data buffers and intermediate storage structures. Moreover, it is crucial to adhere to best practices in maintaining the logical consistency and integrity of the data transformations performed within the function.

The process of defining a table function includes specifying input parameters, internal control structures, and the expected relational output. This architectural framework facilitates the encapsulation of complex analytics routines that would otherwise be cumbersome to express solely using SQL. In this way, table functions serve as a powerful tool for implementing custom data retrieval strategies that are both robust and highly adaptable.

Performance Considerations and Efficiency Trade-offs

The performance characteristics of table functions are intimately linked to the underlying mechanisms of row set generation and the efficiency of bridging procedural execution with set-based processing. The conversion of procedural loops into a structured row set inherently involves considerations related to memory management, buffering, and runtime overhead. The computational complexity of the function is frequently characterized by the interplay between the number of iterations in the procedural logic and the efficiency of the row set assembly process.

Optimizing a table function typically requires an analysis of the time and space complexity of the operations performed during execution. Given that each invocation of the function can produce a variable number of rows, it is imperative to consider the worst-case scenario where the size of the output may approach the cardinality of the input domain. In such cases, the function may be analyzed in terms of its asymptotic behavior, often expressed as $O(n)$ with respect to the number of rows processed, where n represents the number of elements in the input dataset.

Furthermore, the integration of table functions within larger SQL queries introduces additional performance trade-offs. The execution engine must fully optimize the combination of the function's internal procedural logic with the surrounding relational operations. Thus, the design of table functions must facilitate efficient pushdown of predicates and minimize redundant computations to exploit the strengths of set-based query optimizers. The overall performance is contingent upon a balanced design that judiciously manages the inherent overhead of procedural execution while capitalizing on the parallelism and optimization inherent in relational database operations.

Oracle 19c SQL Code Snippet

```
-- Create an object type to represent a single row of results
↪    produced by the table function
CREATE OR REPLACE TYPE custom_row AS OBJECT (
    input_val    NUMBER,
    computed_val NUMBER,
    description  VARCHAR2(100)
);
/

-- Create a collection type (nested table) based on the custom_row
↪    type;
-- this will serve as the return type of the pipelined table
↪    function.
CREATE OR REPLACE TYPE custom_row_table AS TABLE OF custom_row;
/

-------------------------------------------------------------------
-- Create a pipelined table function that maps each numeric input x
↪    in a given range
-- to a computed value based on the formula: f(x) = (x * p_coef) +
↪    100.
-- This function encapsulates procedural logic (looping and
↪    conditional evaluation)
-- while returning a set of rows that can be queried within SQL.
-------------------------------------------------------------------

CREATE OR REPLACE FUNCTION generate_custom_data(
    p_start IN NUMBER,
    p_end   IN NUMBER,
    p_coef  IN NUMBER
) RETURN custom_row_table PIPELINED IS
    v_result NUMBER;
BEGIN
    FOR i IN p_start .. p_end LOOP
        -- Compute the result using the specified formula
        v_result := (i * p_coef) + 100;
```

```
            -- Use conditional logic to annotate the computed result
            IF MOD(v_result, 2) = 0 THEN
                PIPE ROW(custom_row(i, v_result, 'Even Result'));
            ELSE
                PIPE ROW(custom_row(i, v_result, 'Odd Result'));
            END IF;
        END LOOP;
        RETURN;
EXCEPTION
    WHEN OTHERS THEN
        DBMS_OUTPUT.PUT_LINE('Error in generate_custom_data: ' ||
        ↪   SQLERRM);
        RAISE;
END generate_custom_data;
/


-------------------------------------------------------------------------
-- Demonstrate the use of the table function within a SQL query.
-- The function call is embedded in the FROM clause via the TABLE
↪   operator,
-- which bridges the procedural output into a relational row set.
-------------------------------------------------------------------------


SELECT *
FROM TABLE(generate_custom_data(1, 10, 5));


-------------------------------------------------------------------------
-- Create a materialized view to precompute and store the output of
↪   the table function.
-- This approach leverages the transform of procedural logic into a
↪   persistent relational
-- structure, improving performance for repeat analytical queries.
-------------------------------------------------------------------------


CREATE MATERIALIZED VIEW MV_CUSTOM_DATA
BUILD IMMEDIATE
REFRESH ON DEMAND
AS
SELECT *
FROM TABLE(generate_custom_data(1, 20, 3));
/

-- Query the materialized view to retrieve precomputed results
SELECT * FROM MV_CUSTOM_DATA;


-------------------------------------------------------------------------
-- Performance Analysis: Examine the execution plan of a query
↪   invoking the table function.
-- This step demonstrates the integration of the table function
↪   within the SQL optimizer's
-- framework, ensuring efficient execution of complex,
↪   procedural-to-relational transformations.
```

185

```
EXPLAIN PLAN FOR
SELECT *
FROM TABLE(generate_custom_data(1, 10, 5));

-- Display the execution plan using Oracle's DBMS_XPLAN utility
SELECT PLAN_TABLE_OUTPUT
FROM TABLE(DBMS_XPLAN.DISPLAY());
```

Multiple Choice Questions

1. In the formal definition of table functions expressed as $f : \mathcal{D} \to \mathcal{R}$, what does the codomain $\mathcal{R}$ represent?

    (a) A single computed value.

    (b) A collection of rows conforming to a specified relational schema.

    (c) The set of permissible input parameters.

    (d) A pointer to a memory location used during execution.

2. What primary advantage do table functions offer when integrating procedural logic with set-based SQL operations?

    (a) They eliminate the need for procedural code by replacing it with declarative SQL.

    (b) They encapsulate iterative procedures and expose their results as relational row sets.

    (c) They automatically convert all SQL queries to procedural routines.

    (d) They enforce strict typing on procedural outputs.

3. Which architectural consideration is most critical when designing a table function for custom data retrieval?

    (a) Developing a real-time graphical user interface.

    (b) Defining a well-structured output schema for seamless SQL integration.

    (c) Optimizing network latency between distributed database nodes.

    (d) Minimizing the number of embedded SQL statements.

4. How is the transformation from procedural logic to a relational row set conceptually characterized in table functions?

   (a) $f(x) = R_x$, where each input $x \in \mathcal{D}$ yields a corresponding row set R_x.

   (b) $f(x) = 2x$, doubling the input value to generate output.

   (c) $f(x) = \text{SQL}(x)$, where each input triggers a dynamic SQL query.

   (d) $f(x) = x \mod n$, partitioning the input into n groups.

5. Which performance aspect is paramount when evaluating table functions in high-volume data processing?

   (a) The aesthetics of the output display.

   (b) The efficiency of row set assembly and memory management during iterative processing.

   (c) The version number of Oracle Database in use.

   (d) The number of input parameters defined.

6. In the context of SQL query formulation, what role do table functions primarily serve?

   (a) They restrict the output to scalar values only.

   (b) They convert procedural computations into row sets that can be joined, aggregated, and manipulated within SQL queries.

   (c) They serve exclusively as transaction control modules.

   (d) They bypass the use of optimization engines in SQL.

7. To minimize performance trade-offs when integrating table functions into broader SQL queries, which strategy is recommended?

   (a) Avoid the use of conditional logic within the function.

   (b) Implement predicate pushdown and optimize the row set generation process.

   (c) Use table functions only for small, non-critical datasets.

   (d) Increase the number of procedural loops to enhance data granularity.

Answers:

1. **B: A collection of rows conforming to a specified relational schema**

   This is correct because, in the formalism of table functions, the codomain $\mathcal{R}$ is defined specifically as the set of rows—each adhering to a predetermined schema—which the function returns for use in SQL queries.

2. **B: They encapsulate iterative procedures and expose their results as relational row sets**

   The chapter emphasizes that table functions bridge the gap between procedural logic and SQL by transforming the output of iterative, step-by-step computations into row sets directly consumable by SQL, thereby reducing the typical impedance mismatch.

3. **B: Defining a well-structured output schema for seamless SQL integration**

   A key architectural consideration is to precisely define the output row set's schema. This ensures that the table function integrates smoothly with SQL operations such as joins, aggregations, and set operations.

4. **A: $f(x) = R_x$, where each input $x \in \mathcal{D}$ yields a corresponding row set R_x**

   The conceptual model presented in the chapter describes the transformation from an input x to its corresponding output R_x via the mapping $f(x) = R_x$, which encapsulates the conversion of procedural results into relational format.

5. **B: The efficiency of row set assembly and memory management during iterative processing**

   Performance considerations focus on the overhead associated with transforming procedural loops into structured row sets. Efficient memory management and minimizing buffering overhead are critical for scaling table functions in data-intensive environments.

6. **B: They convert procedural computations into row sets that can be joined, aggregated, and manipulated within SQL queries**

   Table functions act as a bridge by packaging procedural logic into a form that fits seamlessly into the declarative, set-based paradigm of SQL, thereby enabling complex data manipulations within standard SQL queries.

7. **B: Implement predicate pushdown and optimize the row set generation process**
To minimize performance trade-offs, it is essential to design table functions that support predicate pushdown—allowing filters to be applied earlier—and to optimize the process by which procedural results are assembled into row sets, thus ensuring efficient query execution.

Chapter 20

Data Pivoting and Unpivoting Techniques

Conceptual Framework of Data Restructuring

Data pivoting refers to the systematic reorientation of a dataset wherein the distinct values of a designated attribute are transposed into separate column headers. This transformation alters the traditional row-based representation into a cross-tabulated format, thereby facilitating the aggregation of measures along specified dimensions. Conversely, unpivoting constitutes the reversal of this operation by reconstituting the columnar information back into a normalized, row-oriented structure. Such bi-directional transformations are pivotal in multi-dimensional data analysis, as they allow for both coarse-grained overviews and fine-grained inspections of underlying data trends without compromising data integrity.

In a formal setting, let D denote an original relation comprising tuples defined over a schema $S = \{C_1, C_2, \ldots, C_n\}$. A pivot operation may be conceptualized as a function $P\colon D \to D'$ such that D' embodies a restructured relation wherein one or more attributes are transposed into a series of aggregated columns. This reorientation directly supports the development of cross-tabulation matrices that enable analytical insights by exposing latent relational patterns.

Mathematical Formalization of Pivot Operations

The pivot operation can be rigorously defined as an operator $P \colon \mathbb{D} \to \mathbb{D}'$, where $\mathbb{D}$ is the set of all permissible tuples over a given schema and $\mathbb{D}'$ represents the set of transformed tuples. Consider a pivot attribute C_p with a distinct set of values $V = \{v_1, v_2, \ldots, v_m\}$. The transformation effectively remaps the original relation such that for each unique $v_i \in V$, a corresponding column in the transformed relation is generated. If M denotes an attribute designated for aggregation, then an aggregate function $F \colon \mathbb{R}^{|T|} \to \mathbb{R}$ may be applied over groups of tuples sharing a common key. The output relation, therefore, is characterized by a function P that aggregates and reorients data in a manner that adheres to the mapping

$$P(t) = \{(k, F(M_{v_1}), F(M_{v_2}), \ldots, F(M_{v_m})) \mid t \in D\},$$

where k denotes the grouping key derived from non-pivot attributes. This formalization ensures that data integrity is maintained while providing a transformation that is both expressive and amenable to subsequent analytic operations.

Mathematical Formalization of Unpivot Operations

Given a pivoted relation D' in which the values originally contained in a single attribute have been distributed across multiple columns, the unpivot operation serves to restore the data to its canonical, normalized form. Formally, the unpivot transformation is defined as a function $U \colon \mathbb{D}' \to \mathbb{D}$, which satisfies the property

$$U(P(t)) = t, \quad \forall t \in D,$$

under conditions where the transformation is lossless. In this context, suppose D' contains attributes $\{A_1, A_2, \ldots, A_r, v_1, v_2, \ldots, v_m\}$, where v_i $(1 \leq i \leq m)$ represent the pivot-generated columns. The operation U systematically converts these multiple columns back to a single attribute C_p, reintroducing a new column that captures the previously distributed values along with an associated measure for aggregation. The design of U must address any potential ambiguities arising from non-unique mappings and ensure that a well-defined inverse relationship is preserved under the mapping, often by incorporating additional grouping or identification mechanisms to maintain relational consistency.

Operational Considerations in Data Restructuring

The execution of pivot and unpivot operations within relational databases necessitates a careful consideration of both computational and storage implications. Given a relation comprising n tuples and a pivot attribute exhibiting m distinct values, the pivot operation inherently possesses a time complexity that is generally bounded by $O(n \cdot m)$, particularly when each tuple contributes to one or more of the m output columns. In addition, the memory requirements for such transformations can be significant, especially in scenarios where intermediate representations of the data are constructed prior to aggregation. The implementation must therefore optimize buffering strategies and leverage set-based processing techniques that are intrinsic to modern relational query optimizers.

Furthermore, the architectural design of these transformations must take into account the scalability of the operation. This involves ensuring that the underlying operations are compatible with parallel processing paradigms and that indexing strategies are suitably adapted to handle the dynamic restructuring of the data. These considerations are critical in environments where high-volume data processing is required, as the efficiency of the pivot/unpivot cycle directly impacts the feasibility of cross-tabulated data analysis in large-scale data management systems.

Analytical Implications and Cross-Tabulation Structures

The restructuring of data via pivot operations yields a cross-tabulated matrix that encapsulates the interplay between categorical variables and aggregated measures. Such a matrix, denoted as $M \in \mathbb{R}^{r \times c}$ where r represents the number of groups and c corresponds to the number of aggregated columns, offers a simplified yet expressive overview of data trends. The conversion to a matrix form streamlines the application of both descriptive and inferential statistical methods, enabling the identification and analysis of patterns that may be obscured within a normalized dataset.

Cross-tabulation inherently enhances the interpretability of complex datasets by aligning the data with a format that is both visually and analytically tractable. By recasting relational data into a form amenable to linear algebraic manipulations, pivot operations facilitate the extraction of key insights regarding the distribution and correlation of variables. The subsequent unpivoting operation ensures that detailed, row-level information can be recovered when granular analysis is required. This dual capacity renders the pivot/unpivot paradigm an indispensable tool in the arsenal of techniques employed for advanced data analysis, particularly in settings where both aggregate and detailed views of the data are paramount.

Oracle 19c SQL Code Snippet

```
-- Create the ANALYTICS_DATA table to simulate a dataset with pivot
↪   attributes
CREATE TABLE ANALYTICS_DATA (
    ID          NUMBER GENERATED BY DEFAULT AS IDENTITY,
    GROUP_KEY   VARCHAR2(50),
    ASPECT      VARCHAR2(50),
    MEASURE     NUMBER,
    ENTRY_DATE  DATE,
    CONSTRAINT ANALYTICS_DATA_PK PRIMARY KEY (ID)
);
COMMIT;

-- Insert sample data into ANALYTICS_DATA to represent measures for
↪   different aspects
INSERT ALL
    INTO ANALYTICS_DATA (GROUP_KEY, ASPECT, MEASURE, ENTRY_DATE)
        VALUES ('Group1', 'Sales', 1000, DATE '2023-10-01')
    INTO ANALYTICS_DATA (GROUP_KEY, ASPECT, MEASURE, ENTRY_DATE)
        VALUES ('Group1', 'Profit', 300, DATE '2023-10-01')
    INTO ANALYTICS_DATA (GROUP_KEY, ASPECT, MEASURE, ENTRY_DATE)
        VALUES ('Group1', 'Cost', 700, DATE '2023-10-01')
    INTO ANALYTICS_DATA (GROUP_KEY, ASPECT, MEASURE, ENTRY_DATE)
        VALUES ('Group2', 'Sales', 1500, DATE '2023-10-02')
    INTO ANALYTICS_DATA (GROUP_KEY, ASPECT, MEASURE, ENTRY_DATE)
        VALUES ('Group2', 'Profit', 450, DATE '2023-10-02')
    INTO ANALYTICS_DATA (GROUP_KEY, ASPECT, MEASURE, ENTRY_DATE)
        VALUES ('Group2', 'Cost', 1050, DATE '2023-10-02')
SELECT * FROM DUAL;
COMMIT;
```

```
-- Display the inserted data for verification
SELECT * FROM ANALYTICS_DATA;


------------------------------------------------------------------------
-- Pivot Query: Transform row data into a cross-tabulated format.
-- This query implements the pivot operator P defined as:
--    P(t) = { (k, F(M_{v_1}), F(M_{v_2}), ..., F(M_{v_m})) }
-- where k is the grouping key, F denotes an aggregate function (SUM
↪   here),
-- and v_i represents distinct values of the pivot attribute
↪   (ASPECT).
------------------------------------------------------------------------
SELECT *
FROM (
    SELECT GROUP_KEY, ASPECT, MEASURE
    FROM ANALYTICS_DATA
)
PIVOT (
    SUM(MEASURE) AS TOTAL
    FOR ASPECT IN ('Sales' AS SALES, 'Profit' AS PROFIT, 'Cost' AS
    ↪   COST)
)
ORDER BY GROUP_KEY;


------------------------------------------------------------------------
-- Unpivot Query: Convert the cross-tabulated data back to the
↪   normalized row format.
-- This operation demonstrates the unpivot operator U that
↪   satisfies:
--    U(P(t)) = t,  for all t in the original dataset D.
------------------------------------------------------------------------
SELECT GROUP_KEY, ASPECT, TOTAL_MEASURE
FROM (
    SELECT GROUP_KEY,
           SALES_TOTAL, PROFIT_TOTAL, COST_TOTAL
    FROM (
        SELECT GROUP_KEY, ASPECT, MEASURE
        FROM ANALYTICS_DATA
    )
    PIVOT (
        SUM(MEASURE) AS TOTAL
        FOR ASPECT IN ('Sales' AS SALES, 'Profit' AS PROFIT, 'Cost'
        ↪   AS COST)
    )
)
UNPIVOT (
    TOTAL_MEASURE FOR ASPECT IN (
        SALES_TOTAL AS 'Sales',
        PROFIT_TOTAL AS 'Profit',
        COST_TOTAL AS 'Cost'
    )
)
ORDER BY GROUP_KEY, ASPECT;
```

```
----------------------------------------------------------------
-- Dynamic Pivot: Use PL/SQL to dynamically construct and execute a
↪  pivot query.
-- This is particularly useful when the set of pivot values (ASPECT)
↪  is not known beforehand.
----------------------------------------------------------------
DECLARE
    v_sql       VARCHAR2(4000);
    v_columns   VARCHAR2(1000);
BEGIN
    -- Generate a dynamic list of distinct ASPECT values formatted
    ↪  for the pivot IN clause
    SELECT LISTAGG('''' || ASPECT || ''' AS "' || ASPECT || '"', ',
    ↪  ')
            WITHIN GROUP (ORDER BY ASPECT)
      INTO v_columns
      FROM (SELECT DISTINCT ASPECT FROM ANALYTICS_DATA);

    -- Build the dynamic pivot query using the generated column
    ↪  list.
    v_sql := 'SELECT * FROM ( ' ||
             ' SELECT GROUP_KEY, ASPECT, MEASURE FROM
                ↪  ANALYTICS_DATA ' ||
             ') PIVOT ( ' ||
             ' SUM(MEASURE) AS TOTAL ' ||
             ' FOR ASPECT IN (' || v_columns || ') ' ||
             ') ORDER BY GROUP_KEY';

    DBMS_OUTPUT.PUT_LINE('Dynamic Pivot SQL:');
    DBMS_OUTPUT.PUT_LINE(v_sql);

    -- Execute the dynamic SQL. In production, you might open a ref
    ↪  cursor to fetch results.
    EXECUTE IMMEDIATE v_sql;
EXCEPTION
    WHEN OTHERS THEN
        DBMS_OUTPUT.PUT_LINE('Error executing dynamic pivot: ' ||
        ↪  SQLERRM);
END;
/


----------------------------------------------------------------
-- Window Function Demonstration: Calculate a running total for
↪  Sales.
-- This query utilizes analytic window functions to compute a
↪  running aggregate,
-- enhancing the capability for rolling analytics.
----------------------------------------------------------------
SELECT GROUP_KEY,
       SALES_TOTAL,
       SUM(SALES_TOTAL) OVER (PARTITION BY GROUP_KEY
                              ORDER BY GROUP_KEY
```

```
                          ROWS BETWEEN UNBOUNDED PRECEDING AND
                          ↪   CURRENT ROW) AS
                          ↪   RUNNING_SALES_TOTAL
FROM (
    SELECT GROUP_KEY, SALES_TOTAL
    FROM (
        SELECT GROUP_KEY, ASPECT, MEASURE
        FROM ANALYTICS_DATA
    )
    PIVOT (
        SUM(MEASURE) AS TOTAL
        FOR ASPECT IN ('Sales' AS SALES)
    )
)
ORDER BY GROUP_KEY;
```

Multiple Choice Questions

1. Which of the following best describes the primary goal of a data pivot operation as discussed in this chapter?

    (a) To eliminate duplicate records from a dataset.

    (b) To transpose unique attribute values into individual column headers, forming a cross-tabulated structure.

    (c) To convert numerical data into categorical bins.

    (d) To join unrelated datasets into a single table.

2. In the formal mathematical representation of the pivot operation described in the chapter, the function $P: D \to D'$ is primarily responsible for:

    (a) Encrypting sensitive data before analysis.

    (b) Aggregating data and creating new columns corresponding to distinct values of a pivot attribute.

    (c) Sorting the dataset in ascending order.

    (d) Normalizing the data to remove redundancy.

3. Given an aggregation function F used during pivot operations, what is its central role?

    (a) To partition the data into smaller clusters.

    (b) To combine multiple values from tuples sharing the same grouping key into a single summarized value.

196

(c) To filter out incomplete records.

(d) To rearrange data based on lexicographical order.

4. Which of the following statements accurately captures the essence of the unpivot operation as defined in the chapter?

   (a) It splits a single aggregated column into several discrete variables.

   (b) It aggregates row-level data into a higher-level summary.

   (c) It reverses the pivot operation by converting multiple aggregated columns back into a normalized, row-based format.

   (d) It duplicates column values into multiple rows for redundancy.

5. Considering computational complexity, if a dataset contains n tuples and the pivot attribute has m distinct values, what is the typical time complexity of the pivot operation?

   (a) $O(n)$

   (b) $O(m)$

   (c) $O(n \cdot m)$

   (d) $O(1)$

6. Which operational consideration is most critical when implementing pivot and unpivot operations on large-scale datasets?

   (a) Ensuring compliance with encryption protocols.

   (b) Optimizing buffering strategies and utilizing set-based processing techniques to efficiently manage memory and compute resources.

   (c) Converting all numerical values to string format.

   (d) Minimizing the number of columns created during pivoting.

7. How does the cross-tabulated matrix produced by a pivot operation enhance advanced analytical methods, as discussed in the chapter?

   (a) It removes the need for aggregation functions in subsequent analyses.

(b) It simplifies the application of both descriptive statistics and linear-algebraic methods by aligning data in an easily interpretable matrix format.

(c) It increases data redundancy, which is beneficial for backup operations.

(d) It transforms categorical variables into continuous scales for easier plotting.

Answers:

1. **B: To transpose unique attribute values into individual column headers, forming a cross-tabulated structure.** Explanation: The chapter explains that pivoting reorients data by transposing distinct attribute values into separate columns, which supports cross-tabulation and facilitates aggregated analysis.

2. **B: Aggregating data and creating new columns corresponding to distinct values of a pivot attribute.** Explanation: The formal definition provided uses the function P to describe how data is aggregated and restructured, with each distinct value of the pivot attribute becoming its dedicated column in the transformed relation.

3. **B: To combine multiple values from tuples sharing the same grouping key into a single summarized value.** Explanation: The aggregation function F is used to consolidate data within each group determined by a key, thereby summarizing multiple records into one aggregated output per pivot attribute value.

4. **C: It reverses the pivot operation by converting multiple aggregated columns back into a normalized, row-based format.** Explanation: Unpivoting is defined as the inverse of pivoting; it restores the original normalized form by taking the multiple aggregated columns and reorganizing them into a single column representing the pivot attribute.

5. **C:** $O(n \cdot m)$ Explanation: The chapter details that the pivot operation's complexity is generally proportional to the product of the number of tuples n and the number of distinct pivot values m, reflecting the need to process each tuple for each pivot-generated column.

6. **B: Optimizing buffering strategies and utilizing set-based processing techniques to efficiently manage memory and compute resources.** Explanation: Operational considerations emphasize the importance of performance optimization, particularly through effective buffering and set-based operations, to handle the often significant computational and storage demands of pivot/unpivot operations.

7. **B: It simplifies the application of both descriptive statistics and linear-algebraic methods by aligning data in an easily interpretable matrix format.** Explanation: The cross-tabulated structure generated by pivoting makes it easier to apply various analytical techniques, including statistical analysis and matrix operations, thus enhancing the interpretability and usability of the data.

Chapter 21

Hierarchical Data Processing and Recursive Queries

Hierarchical Data Structures in Relational Databases

Hierarchical data structures in relational databases are typically represented by self-referential relations, wherein each record may include a reference to its parent node. Such data models can be mathematically formulated as a directed graph $G = (V, E)$, where V denotes the set of records and $E \subseteq V \times V$ represents the parent-child associations. Within this framework, a record containing a reference to another record establishes an intrinsic hierarchy, enabling the modeling of complex relationships such as organizational charts, file systems, or nested categories. The inherent self-referentiality of these data models necessitates specialized query mechanisms capable of traversing variable-depth hierarchies while preserving the logical connections between nodes.

Recursive Query Constructs in PL/SQL

Recursive queries in PL/SQL are designed to address the challenge of navigating hierarchical data by allowing a query to reference its own result set iteratively. The recursive query paradigm is typically structured into two principal components: an anchor member and a recursive member. The anchor member defines the base case by selecting the root nodes of the hierarchy, whereas the recursive member operates on the result of the previous iteration to locate immediate descendants. This dual-part construction can be conceptually denoted as

$$Q = A \cup R(A),$$

where A represents the anchor query and $R(A)$ encapsulates the recursive expansion. The recursive member is repeatedly executed until the union of the results reaches a fixed point, thereby ensuring that the entire hierarchy is thoroughly processed. This approach is instrumental in exploring self-referential datasets where the level of nesting is not predetermined.

Mathematical Foundations of Recursion in Data Queries

The mathematical underpinning of recursive queries is closely aligned with fixed-point theory. Consider a function $F : \mathcal{P}(V) \to \mathcal{P}(V)$, where $\mathcal{P}(V)$ is the power set of the set of nodes V. The function F maps a subset of nodes to their corresponding immediate descendants. The objective of a recursive query is to compute the transitive closure

$$T = \bigcup_{i=0}^{\infty} F^i(S),$$

in which S denotes the set of anchor nodes and F^i represents the composition of F with itself i times. Termination is achieved upon the existence of a nonnegative integer k such that

$$F^k(S) = F^{k+1}(S).$$

This fixed-point condition guarantees that no new nodes are added upon further recursive iterations, thereby indicating that the entire hierarchical structure has been explored.

PL/SQL Techniques for Analyzing Self-Referential Data

PL/SQL provides a robust environment for the analysis of self-referential data through the integration of recursive constructs and procedural logic. Techniques for hierarchical data processing in PL/SQL include the employment of recursive subprograms and controlled iterative loops that simulate recursion. The language's ability to combine set-based operations with procedural constructs allows for the systematic traversal of hierarchies and the aggregation of information across multiple levels. In the context of self-referential data analysis, it is crucial to implement mechanisms that enforce termination conditions and to structure queries in a manner that prevents redundant processing of nodes. These techniques ensure that hierarchical relationships are accurately maintained while facilitating the extraction of multilevel insights from complex datasets.

Advanced Optimization and Algorithmic Strategies

The execution efficiency of recursive queries is paramount when dealing with large-scale hierarchical datasets. Optimization strategies for recursive queries involve careful analysis of execution paths and the application of algorithmic principles aimed at minimizing unnecessary computations. Techniques such as early termination, result memoization, and the utilization of effective indexing on self-referential keys contribute significantly to reducing computational overhead. In formal terms, the worst-case time complexity of processing a hierarchy can be modeled as proportional to the product of the number of records and the maximum depth of the hierarchy, that is, $O(|V| \cdot d)$, where $|V|$ is the cardinality of the set of nodes and d denotes the deepest level within the hierarchy. These strategies serve not only to expedite recursive operations but also to ensure that query execution remains scalable in the presence of highly nested or extensive hierarchical structures.

Oracle 19c SQL Code Snippet

```sql
-- Create HIERARCHY_NODES table to store self-referential
   hierarchical data

CREATE TABLE HIERARCHY_NODES (
    NODE_ID         NUMBER GENERATED BY DEFAULT AS IDENTITY,
    PARENT_NODE_ID  NUMBER,
    NODE_NAME       VARCHAR2(100),
    CONSTRAINT HIERARCHY_NODES_PK PRIMARY KEY (NODE_ID)
);

-- Establish self-reference constraint on PARENT_NODE_ID
ALTER TABLE HIERARCHY_NODES
ADD CONSTRAINT FK_PARENT
FOREIGN KEY (PARENT_NODE_ID)
REFERENCES HIERARCHY_NODES(NODE_ID);


-- Insert sample data representing an organizational hierarchy
--
-- The data model represents a directed graph G = (V, E) where each
   record is a
-- node and the PARENT_NODE_ID defines an edge from a node to its
   parent.

INSERT ALL
    INTO HIERARCHY_NODES (PARENT_NODE_ID, NODE_NAME) VALUES (NULL,
       'CEO')            -- Root node (anchor)
    INTO HIERARCHY_NODES (PARENT_NODE_ID, NODE_NAME) VALUES (1, 'VP
       Sales')
    INTO HIERARCHY_NODES (PARENT_NODE_ID, NODE_NAME) VALUES (1, 'VP
       Marketing')
    INTO HIERARCHY_NODES (PARENT_NODE_ID, NODE_NAME) VALUES (2,
       'Sales Manager')
    INTO HIERARCHY_NODES (PARENT_NODE_ID, NODE_NAME) VALUES (2,
       'Account Manager')
    INTO HIERARCHY_NODES (PARENT_NODE_ID, NODE_NAME) VALUES (3,
       'Marketing Manager')
SELECT * FROM DUAL;
COMMIT;


-- Recursive Query using Common Table Expression (CTE)
--
-- This query demonstrates the recursive expansion of
   self-referential data.
-- It embodies the fixed-point iteration: T = A  R(A) where the
   recursion stops
-- once F^(k)(S) = F^(k+1)(S). The PATH column visually tracks the
   derivation sequence.
```

```
WITH Hierarchy_CTE (NODE_ID, PARENT_NODE_ID, NODE_NAME, LEVEL, PATH)
↪   AS (
    -- Anchor member: select root nodes where PARENT_NODE_ID is NULL
    SELECT
        NODE_ID,
        PARENT_NODE_ID,
        NODE_NAME,
        1 AS LEVEL,
        TO_CHAR(NODE_ID) AS PATH
    FROM HIERARCHY_NODES
    WHERE PARENT_NODE_ID IS NULL

    UNION ALL

    -- Recursive member: join the table with the CTE to fetch child
    ↪   nodes
    SELECT
        h.NODE_ID,
        h.PARENT_NODE_ID,
        h.NODE_NAME,
        hc.LEVEL + 1,
        hc.PATH || '->' || TO_CHAR(h.NODE_ID) AS PATH
    FROM HIERARCHY_NODES h
    INNER JOIN Hierarchy_CTE hc ON h.PARENT_NODE_ID = hc.NODE_ID
)
-- Retrieve entire hierarchical data, ordered by the derived path
SELECT NODE_ID, PARENT_NODE_ID, NODE_NAME, LEVEL, PATH
FROM Hierarchy_CTE
ORDER BY PATH;


-- PL/SQL Function to Count Total Descendants (Transitive Closure)
--
-- This function illustrates the algorithmic principle of
↪   fixed-point recursion.
-- It computes the number of nodes in the transitive closure T =
↪   _{i=0}^ F^i(S)
-- for a given anchor node (p_node_id). The recursive subquery
↪   (Descendants_CTE)
-- iteratively gathers all descendant nodes.

CREATE OR REPLACE FUNCTION count_descendants(p_node_id IN NUMBER)
↪   RETURN NUMBER IS
    v_count NUMBER := 0;
BEGIN
    FOR rec IN (
        WITH Descendants_CTE (NODE_ID) AS (
            -- Anchor: immediate children of the specified node
            SELECT NODE_ID
            FROM HIERARCHY_NODES
            WHERE PARENT_NODE_ID = p_node_id
```

```
    UNION ALL

    -- Recursive member: fetch further descendants
    ↳  iteratively
    SELECT h.NODE_ID
    FROM HIERARCHY_NODES h
    INNER JOIN Descendants_CTE d ON h.PARENT_NODE_ID =
    ↳  d.NODE_ID
)
    SELECT NODE_ID FROM Descendants_CTE
) LOOP
    v_count := v_count + 1;
END LOOP;
RETURN v_count;
EXCEPTION
    WHEN OTHERS THEN
        ROLLBACK;
        RAISE;
END;
/

-- Test the function for the root node 'CEO' (assuming NODE_ID = 1)
DECLARE
    total_descendants NUMBER;
BEGIN
    total_descendants := count_descendants(1);
    DBMS_OUTPUT.PUT_LINE('Total descendants for node 1 (CEO): ' ||
    ↳  total_descendants);
END;
/

-------------------------------------------------------------------------
-- Index Creation for Optimization
--
-- Create an index on PARENT_NODE_ID to expedite hierarchical
↳  traversals,
-- especially useful when processing large and deeply nested
↳  datasets.
-------------------------------------------------------------------------
CREATE INDEX IDX_PARENT_NODE ON HIERARCHY_NODES (PARENT_NODE_ID);
```

Multiple Choice Questions

1. Hierarchical data structures in relational databases are mathematically modeled as which of the following?

    (a) An undirected graph

    (b) A directed graph

    (c) A weighted graph

(d) A cyclic graph

2. Recursive queries in PL/SQL are typically structured with which two principal components?

    (a) Base case and termination clause

    (b) Anchor member and recursive member

    (c) Primary query and secondary query

    (d) Initialization phase and iterative phase

3. The termination of a recursive query is achieved when a fixed point is reached. This occurs when:

    (a) The anchor member returns no rows.

    (b) The recursive member returns an empty set.

    (c) The result of one recursive iteration is identical to that of the previous iteration.

    (d) The total number of iterations exceeds the number of nodes.

4. Given a function F: (V) → (V) (with (V) indicating the power set of nodes V) that maps a set of nodes to their immediate descendants, the transitive closure T computed by a recursive query is defined as:

    (a) $T = \bigcap_{i=0}^{\infty} F^i(S)$

    (b) $T = \prod_{i=0}^{\infty} F^i(S)$

    (c) $T = \bigcup_{i=0}^{\infty} F^i(S)$

    (d) $T = F(S)$

5. Which of the following PL/SQL techniques is recommended for analyzing self-referential data structures?

    (a) Exclusively using set-based SQL queries without procedural extensions

    (b) Utilizing recursive subprograms and controlled iterative loops

    (c) Relying solely on dynamic SQL execution

    (d) Applying only non-recursive analytical functions

6. In the context of processing hierarchical data, the worst-case time complexity of recursive queries is modeled as:

(a) $O(|V| + d)$

(b) $O(|V| \cdot d)$

(c) $O(|V|^2)$

(d) $O(|V| / d)$

7. Which advanced optimization strategy can effectively reduce the computational overhead of recursive queries in PL/SQL?

   (a) Ignoring indexing on self-referential keys to speed up insertions

   (b) Early termination, result memoization, and effective indexing on self-referential keys

   (c) Increasing the number of recursive iterations regardless of redundancy

   (d) Converting recursive queries into simple linear scans

Answers:

1. **B: A directed graph**
   Hierarchical data is modeled as a directed graph $G = (V, E)$ where each record (node) can reference its parent (directed edge), capturing the parent-child relationships inherent in the structure.

2. **B: Anchor member and recursive member**
   Recursive queries in PL/SQL consist of an anchor member, which identifies the base or root nodes of the hierarchy, and a recursive member, which iteratively finds the subsequent descendants until the entire hierarchy is traversed.

3. **C: The result of one recursive iteration is identical to that of the previous iteration**
   The recursive process terminates when a fixed point is reached, meaning that executing the recursive member yields no new nodes compared to the prior iteration, fulfilling the fixed-point condition.

4. **C:** $T = \bigcup_{i=0}^{\infty} F^i(S)$
   The transitive closure is defined as the union over all iterations ($F^i(S)$, starting with $i = 0$) of the immediate descendants function, ensuring that all reachable nodes are included.

5. **B: Utilizing recursive subprograms and controlled iterative loops**
   To handle self-referential (hierarchical) data in PL/SQL, combining recursive subprograms with iterative loops offers both the flexibility of procedural logic and the power to traverse variable-depth hierarchies effectively.

6. **B: $O(|V| \cdot d)$**
   The worst-case time complexity is modeled as $O(|V| \cdot d)$, where $|V|$ represents the total number of nodes and d the maximum depth of the hierarchy, reflecting the potential multiplication of nodes processed at each level.

7. **B: Early termination, result memoization, and effective indexing on self-referential keys**
   Optimization strategies such as early termination (stopping once no new nodes are found), result memoization (caching previously computed results), and proper indexing on the keys involved in self-referential relationships greatly minimize redundant computations and enhance performance.

Chapter 22

Implementing Window Functions for Rolling Analytics

Mathematical Foundations and Formal Definitions

Window functions are defined over a set of rows extracted from a relation, where the selection of rows is determined by an explicit window specification. Formally, given a relation R and an expression f that performs an aggregate or analytic computation, a window function computes a value for each row based on a defined subset of rows. Consider a partition of R by a predicate P, and an ordering of rows according to a criterion O. The window frame for a given row r_i is a subset $W(r_i) \subset R$ such that each row $r_j \in W(r_i)$ satisfies the conditions determined by P and O. In mathematical notation, if f denotes an aggregate operator, a rolling aggregate for row r_i can be expressed as

$$A(r_i) = f\left(\{x_j : r_j \in W(r_i)\}\right).$$

This formalism encapsulates operations ranging from simple running totals to more nuanced moving averages.

Partitioning, Ordering, and Frame Specification

The effectiveness of window functions hinges on the precise configuration of partitioning and ordering, which collectively define the frame for each computation. Partitioning divides the relation into subsets such that only rows within the same partition are considered for the analytic operation. When a relation is partitioned by a key attribute p, the evaluation space is restricted to rows for which the value of p is identical. The ordering clause then imposes a total order on the rows within each partition, commonly based on a time-stamp or sequential identifier. Let $r_1, r_2, \ldots, r_n$ denote the ordered rows within a partition. The window frame for each row is defined relative to its position in this ordering, with boundaries that can be specified absolute or relative to the current row. In essence, the window frame $F(r_i)$ may be described as

$$F(r_i) = \{r_j \in R : \text{lower}(r_i) \leq j \leq \text{upper}(r_i)\},$$

where the functions $\text{lower}(r_i)$ and $\text{upper}(r_i)$ determine the extent of the preceding and following rows that are included.

1 Computing Running Totals

Running totals represent a cumulative calculation where each row reflects the aggregate of all qualifying preceding values according to the defined order. Let x_i denote the numeric value associated with row r_i. The running total y_i for the row positioned at index i is computed as

$$y_i = \sum_{j=1}^{i} x_j.$$

This computation takes advantage of the fact that successive window frames have significant overlap, making it amenable to optimizations through incremental aggregation. The rolling total, when computed over a partition ordered by time, reveals the cumulative evolution of the measure of interest and is central to many time-series analyses.

2 Evaluating Moving Averages

Moving averages provide a smoothing mechanism that reduces the influence of short-term fluctuations and highlights overall trends.

For a fixed window of size k, the moving average m_i at position i is defined as

$$m_i = \frac{1}{k} \sum_{j=i-k+1}^{i} x_j,$$

provided that the window contains k elements. Alternative formulations may involve weighted averages where individual elements within the frame are assigned different coefficients to adjust the sensitivity to recent values. This approach facilitates the extraction of trend components from noisy data, particularly in contexts where periodicity and seasonal variations are present. The determination of the frame limits, whether it is a fixed number of rows or a dynamic range based on temporal intervals, is critical for obtaining meaningful and statistically robust averages in rolling analytics.

Temporal Considerations in Rolling Analytics

Time-series data inherently possess a sequential structure defined by timestamps or similar monotonically increasing attributes. In the context of rolling analytics, window functions exploit this temporal ordering to compute aggregates that evolve temporally. When the ordering column is derived from time, the window frame for each row corresponds to a specific temporal interval. This allows for the generation of metrics, such as cumulative sums and moving averages, that are aligned with the natural progression of time. The mathematical structure of these computations ensures that, for each temporal slice, the aggregate value succinctly encapsulates the historical behavior up to and including that time point. In scenarios where intervals vary in size or density, defining dynamic window frames becomes essential to accommodate irregular time-series data, thereby preserving the integrity of the analytic observation.

Algorithmic Efficiency in Window Function Evaluations

The computation of window functions over large datasets requires careful consideration of algorithmic efficiency. Although each window function operation is applied to a moving frame that exhibits significant overlap with adjacent frames, inefficient evaluation strategies can lead to redundant calculations. By leveraging the overlapping nature of the window frames, rolling aggregates such as running totals and moving averages can be updated incrementally. For instance, the computation of a running total y_i can be optimized by reusing the result from row $i-1$, adjusting it by adding the contribution of the current row. In formal terms, if y_{i-1} equals $\sum_{j=1}^{i-1} x_j$, then

$$y_i = y_{i-1} + x_i.$$

Similar incremental strategies may be employed for moving averages by maintaining a sliding buffer of values. The use of such techniques reduces the per-row computational cost from a linear aggregation over the window size to an amortized constant-time update in many practical implementations. The overall time complexity for the evaluation of window functions across n rows, although theoretically bounded by $O(n)$ per row in a naive approach, is effectively improved by these optimizations. Memory management and efficient data access patterns are additional factors that influence performance, particularly when working with extensive time-series datasets where both computational efficiency and scalability are paramount.

Oracle 19c SQL Code Snippet

```
-- Create a table to simulate time-series data for rolling analytics
↪   demonstration
CREATE TABLE ROLLING_ANALYTICS (
    ENTRY_ID     NUMBER GENERATED BY DEFAULT AS IDENTITY,
    TRANS_DATE   DATE,
    CATEGORY     VARCHAR2(20),
    X_VALUE      NUMBER,
    CONSTRAINT ROLLING_ANALYTICS_PK PRIMARY KEY (ENTRY_ID)
);

-- Insert sample data into ROLLING_ANALYTICS with two categories
↪   (for partitioning demonstration)
INSERT ALL
    INTO ROLLING_ANALYTICS (TRANS_DATE, CATEGORY, X_VALUE)
        VALUES (DATE '2023-09-01', 'A', 100)
    INTO ROLLING_ANALYTICS (TRANS_DATE, CATEGORY, X_VALUE)
        VALUES (DATE '2023-09-02', 'A', 150)
    INTO ROLLING_ANALYTICS (TRANS_DATE, CATEGORY, X_VALUE)
        VALUES (DATE '2023-09-03', 'A', 200)
    INTO ROLLING_ANALYTICS (TRANS_DATE, CATEGORY, X_VALUE)
        VALUES (DATE '2023-09-04', 'A', 250)
```

```
        INTO ROLLING_ANALYTICS (TRANS_DATE, CATEGORY, X_VALUE)
            VALUES (DATE '2023-09-05', 'A', 300)
        INTO ROLLING_ANALYTICS (TRANS_DATE, CATEGORY, X_VALUE)
            VALUES (DATE '2023-09-01', 'B', 120)
        INTO ROLLING_ANALYTICS (TRANS_DATE, CATEGORY, X_VALUE)
            VALUES (DATE '2023-09-02', 'B', 130)
        INTO ROLLING_ANALYTICS (TRANS_DATE, CATEGORY, X_VALUE)
            VALUES (DATE '2023-09-03', 'B', 140)
        INTO ROLLING_ANALYTICS (TRANS_DATE, CATEGORY, X_VALUE)
            VALUES (DATE '2023-09-04', 'B', 150)
        INTO ROLLING_ANALYTICS (TRANS_DATE, CATEGORY, X_VALUE)
            VALUES (DATE '2023-09-05', 'B', 160)
SELECT * FROM DUAL;
COMMIT;


------------------------------------------------------------------------
-- Compute Running Totals
-- The rolling total for each row is computed using a window
↪  function that sums
-- the X_VALUE over all rows preceding and including the current
↪  row.
-- This implements the equation:
--    y_i = SUM(x_j) for all j such that 1 <= j <= i
------------------------------------------------------------------------


SELECT
    ENTRY_ID,
    TRANS_DATE,
    CATEGORY,
    X_VALUE,
    SUM(X_VALUE) OVER (
        PARTITION BY CATEGORY
        ORDER BY TRANS_DATE
        ROWS BETWEEN UNBOUNDED PRECEDING AND CURRENT ROW
    ) AS RUNNING_TOTAL
FROM ROLLING_ANALYTICS
ORDER BY CATEGORY, TRANS_DATE;


------------------------------------------------------------------------
-- Compute Moving Averages
-- The moving average is calculated over a fixed window of 3 rows,
↪  i.e.,
--    m_i = (1/3) * (x_{i-2} + x_{i-1} + x_i)
-- when at least three rows are present in the defined window.
------------------------------------------------------------------------


SELECT
    ENTRY_ID,
    TRANS_DATE,
    CATEGORY,
    X_VALUE,
    AVG(X_VALUE) OVER (
        PARTITION BY CATEGORY
```

```
        ORDER BY TRANS_DATE
        ROWS BETWEEN 2 PRECEDING AND CURRENT ROW
    ) AS MOVING_AVERAGE
FROM ROLLING_ANALYTICS
ORDER BY CATEGORY, TRANS_DATE;


-- Demonstrate Incremental Aggregation for Efficiency
-- The aggregate operation used for running totals leverages an
↪   incremental update:
--     y_i = y_{i-1} + x_i
-- Although Oracle's analytic functions perform the aggregation
↪   internally,
-- the following query simulates this concept by showing the
↪   cumulative sum.


SELECT
    ENTRY_ID,
    TRANS_DATE,
    CATEGORY,
    X_VALUE,
    SUM(X_VALUE) OVER (
        PARTITION BY CATEGORY
        ORDER BY TRANS_DATE
        ROWS BETWEEN UNBOUNDED PRECEDING AND CURRENT ROW
    ) AS INCREMENTAL_RUNNING_TOTAL
FROM ROLLING_ANALYTICS
ORDER BY CATEGORY, TRANS_DATE;
```

Multiple Choice Questions

1. Which of the following best represents the formal expression for computing a rolling aggregate $A(r\_i)$ using a window function?

   (a) $A(r\_i) = f\Big(\{x\_j : r\_j \in R\}\Big) A(r\_i) = f\Big(\{x\_j : r\_j \notin W(r\_i)\}\Big)$

   (b) $A(r\_i) = f\Big(\{x\_j : r\_j \in W(r\_i)\}\Big) A(r\_i) = f\Big(\{x\_j : x\_j \text{ is independent of } r\_i\}\Big)$

2. In the context of window functions, what is the primary purpose of the partitioning clause?

   (a) To enforce a global ordering on the entire relation

(b) To divide the relation into subsets so that the computation is restricted to rows with identical partition key values

(c) To filter out rows that are irrelevant to the computation

(d) To define the boundaries of the sliding window based solely on time intervals

3. What role does the ordering clause play when defining a window frame within a partition?

(a) It determines the group of rows to be discarded before aggregation.

(b) It imposes a total order on rows within each partition, thereby defining the relative position of each row for frame specification.

(c) It segregates rows into non-overlapping batches.

(d) It creates duplicate rows for enhanced redundancy in calculations.

4. Which incremental update formula correctly computes a running total y_i over a dataset ordered in a window function?

(a) $y\_i = y\_{i\text{-}1} \times x\_i$

(b) $y\_i = y\_{i\text{-}1} + x\_i$

(c) $y\_i = y\_{i\text{-}1} - x\_i$

(d) $y\_i = y\_{i\text{-}1} + x\_i_{\overline{2}}$

5. For computing a fixed-size moving average m_i over a window of size k, which of the following expressions is correct?

(a) $m\_i = \max\{x\_i - k + 1, \ldots, x\_i\} \quad m\_i = \frac{1}{k} \sum_{j=i}^{i+k-1} x\_j$

(b) $m\_i = 1 \frac{1}{k \sum_{j=i-k+1}^{i} x\_j} \quad m\_i = \frac{1}{k} \prod_{j=i-k+1}^{i} x\_j$

(6) When applying window functions to time-series data, why is it important to use a time-based ordering column?

(a) It guarantees that no rows are omitted from the analysis.

(b) It aligns the window frames with the chronological sequence of events, ensuring that each aggregate reflects the temporal evolution of the data.

(c) It minimizes the number of partitions created.

(d) It removes the need for incremental aggregation.

7. Which of the following techniques most effectively reduces redundant computations when evaluating overlapping window frames on large datasets?

(a) Recomputing the full aggregate function for each window independently.

(b) Utilizing incremental aggregation with sliding buffers to update the aggregate based on previous computations.

(c) Disabling frame overlaps to force recalculation each time.

(d) Reordering the dataset randomly to break dependence between windows.

Answers:

1. **C:** $A(r_i) = f\Big(\{x_j : r_j \in W(r_i)\}\Big)$

   This expression correctly encapsulates the concept that the aggregate function f is applied over the set of values x_j corresponding to the rows r_j within the window frame $W(r_i)$ for a given row r_i.

2. **B:** To divide the relation into subsets so that the computation is restricted to rows with identical partition key values.

   Partitioning is used to segment the dataset so that the window function operates only within rows sharing the same partition attributes, ensuring that aggregates are computed over relevant subsets.

3. **B:** It imposes a total order on rows within each partition, thereby defining the relative position of each row for frame specification.

   The ordering clause specifies a sequence within the partition, which is essential for determining the boundaries (lower and upper limits) of the window frame for each row.

4. **B:** $y_i = y_{i-1} + x_i$

   This incremental update formula efficiently computes the running total by adding the current row's value x_i to the previously computed total y_{i-1}, taking advantage of the overlapping window frames.

5. **C:** $m_i = \frac{1}{k} \sum_{j=i-k+1}^{i} x_j$

   This formula correctly computes the moving average over a fixed window of size k by summing the k most recent values and dividing by k.

6. **B:** It aligns the window frames with the chronological sequence of events, ensuring that each aggregate reflects the temporal evolution of the data.

   Using a time-based ordering column is crucial in time-series analysis since it preserves the natural progression of events, thereby making the rolling aggregates (e.g., moving averages, running totals) meaningful and temporally accurate.

7. **B:** Utilizing incremental aggregation with sliding buffers to update the aggregate based on previous computations.

   This technique minimizes redundant calculations by taking advantage of the overlap between successive window frames, enabling efficient updates rather than recomputing aggregates from scratch for each new row.

Chapter 23

Automating Data Updates with Database Triggers

Theoretical Foundations and Formal Modeling

A database trigger is conceptualized as a declarative mechanism that is automatically invoked in response to data modification events. Formally, a trigger T is defined by the tuple

$$T = (E, \Theta, A),$$

where E represents a data manipulation event such as $INSERT$, $UPDATE$, or $DELETE$, Θ denotes a predicate condition under which the trigger is activated, and A specifies the sequence of actions executed as a consequence of the event. In a relational database system, consider a database state S and an update operation δ. When δ is applied to S, generating an intermediate state S', the trigger mechanism evaluates the condition $\Theta(S, \delta)$. If the condition holds, the subsequent execution of action A is initiated, transitioning the state from S' to a final state S''. This formalism ensures that the invariant properties defined on the analytical dataset are systematically enforced, thereby maintaining data consistency.

1 Formal Definition and Invariant Preservation

Within the formal framework, triggers serve as invariant-preserving functions. Let $A(S)$ denote an analytic aggregate derived from the current state S. The application of an update δ that modifies a subset of S, coupled with the execution of a trigger T, enforces the requirement that

$$A(S'') = A(S') + \Delta A,$$

where ΔA encapsulates the incremental change due to δ and the corresponding trigger action A. Such a formulation is crucial in scenarios where real-time analytical datasets require immediate synchronization with underlying operational data. The correctness of the trigger mechanism, therefore, hinges on its ability to consistently uphold the defined invariants throughout each transactional boundary.

Trigger Activation Dynamics and Execution Semantics

The activation of database triggers is governed by precise execution semantics that differentiate between timing attributes and operational contexts. Triggers can be classified into two primary categories based on their temporal invocation relative to the data modification event: $BEFORE$ triggers and $AFTER$ triggers. In the case of $BEFORE$ triggers, the trigger's action is performed prior to the finalization of the event, allowing for preemptive validation or modification of the incoming data. Conversely, $AFTER$ triggers execute subsequent to the committed change, thereby ensuring that the post-update state is fully available for auxiliary processing.

Given an ordered sequence of data modification events $\{\delta_1, \delta_2, \ldots, \delta_n\}$, the trigger mechanism can be modeled as a composite function

$$T_i : S \times \delta_i \rightarrow S_i,$$

with each T_i preserving atomicity and isolation within the corresponding transaction block. The precise application of these functions guarantees that overlapping events affecting a common dataset are handled in a manner that forestalls inconsistencies and race conditions.

1 Pre- and Post-Action Trigger Semantics

Within the domain of automated data updates, the distinction between pre-action and post-action triggers is pivotal. In the pre-action scenario, modifications to the incoming data can be enacted or rejected based upon the evaluation of $\Theta(S, \delta)$, thereby precluding the propagation of erroneous data into the analytical framework. In the post-action setting, the trigger operates on the fully materialized data, facilitating the update of derived values or aggregated statistics. This bifurcation in timing semantics ensures that the automatic synchronizations executed by triggers are both context-sensitive and adaptable to the dynamic conditions of the dataset.

Ensuring Analytical Dataset Consistency Through Automated Responses

The primary objective of implementing database triggers within an analytical environment is to guarantee that data used in aggregate computations and statistical analyses remains current and consistent in the face of continual data modifications. Automated trigger actions operate as an intermediate layer that bridges the gap between operational data changes and the maintenance of analytical views. In formal terms, if D represents an analytical dataset derived from one or more operational tables, then for every update δ to the underlying data, there exists a trigger T such that

$$D' = D + f(\delta),$$

where D' is the updated analytical dataset and $f(\delta)$ represents the transformation function effected by T. This synchronization mechanism is particularly valuable in environments characterized by high transaction volumes, where manual intervention to update aggregated metrics is impractical and error-prone.

Design Considerations and Performance Analysis

The deployment of database triggers in a high-performance analytical system necessitates careful deliberation regarding design trade-offs and the inherent complexity of automated updates. A primary consideration is the avoidance of recursive trigger invocations, which can lead to unintended cascades of updates and potential deadlock scenarios. Mechanisms to detect and prevent such recursive activity are indispensable.

Furthermore, the computational cost associated with a trigger's action must be evaluated in the context of overall system performance. If n rows are impacted by a data modification event, the incremental cost function $C(n)$, defined in terms of the trigger's operational steps, should ideally exhibit sublinear growth relative to n. This optimization is achievable through the utilization of incremental aggregation techniques that update analytical measures in constant or logarithmic time per affected row. Concomitantly, the integration of triggers within transactional boundaries has a direct impact on system throughput. The commitment of a transaction is deferred until all associated trigger actions are executed, thereby necessitating the design of lightweight procedures that minimize contention and lock durations.

In summary, the robust design of database triggers for automated data updates pivots upon a nuanced balance between the enforcement of invariant properties, the precise control of trigger execution timing, and the minimization of performance overhead under high transactional loads.

Oracle 19c SQL Code Snippet

```
-- Create OPERATIONAL_DATA table to simulate input data for
↪   automated analytical updates
CREATE TABLE OPERATIONAL_DATA (
    ID          NUMBER GENERATED BY DEFAULT AS IDENTITY,
    OP_VALUE    NUMBER,
    OP_DATE     DATE DEFAULT SYSDATE,
    CONSTRAINT OPERATIONAL_DATA_PK PRIMARY KEY (ID)
);

-- Create AGG_ANALYTICS table to store aggregated analytics,
-- ensuring the invariant: A(S'') = A(S') + A is maintained.
CREATE TABLE AGG_ANALYTICS (
    AGG_ID        NUMBER GENERATED BY DEFAULT AS IDENTITY,
    TOTAL_SUM     NUMBER,
    CREATED_DATE DATE DEFAULT SYSDATE,
    CONSTRAINT AGG_ANALYTICS_PK PRIMARY KEY (AGG_ID)
);

-- Initialize the AGG_ANALYTICS table with an initial row as the
↪   aggregation baseline.
```

```
INSERT INTO AGG_ANALYTICS (TOTAL_SUM)
VALUES (0);
COMMIT;


------------------------------------------------------------------------
-- BEFORE trigger for pre-action validation to enforce data quality
------------------------------------------------------------------------
CREATE OR REPLACE TRIGGER BI_VALIDATE_OP_VALUE
BEFORE INSERT OR UPDATE ON OPERATIONAL_DATA
FOR EACH ROW
BEGIN
    -- Validate that the incoming analytic value is non-negative.
    IF :NEW.OP_VALUE < 0 THEN
        RAISE_APPLICATION_ERROR(-20001, 'OP_VALUE must be
        ↪ non-negative.');
    END IF;
END;
/


------------------------------------------------------------------------
-- AFTER trigger for automated aggregate updates (post-action
↪ trigger semantics)
-- This trigger implements the invariant update:
-- A(S'') = A(S') + A, where A is the change induced by the DML
↪ operation.
------------------------------------------------------------------------
CREATE OR REPLACE TRIGGER TRG_UPDATE_AGGREGATE
AFTER INSERT OR UPDATE OR DELETE ON OPERATIONAL_DATA
FOR EACH ROW
DECLARE
    v_delta NUMBER := 0;
BEGIN
    -- Determine the incremental change (A) based on the type of DML
    ↪ operation
    IF INSERTING THEN
        v_delta := :NEW.OP_VALUE;              -- New insert
        ↪ contributes its value
    ELSIF UPDATING THEN
        v_delta := :NEW.OP_VALUE - :OLD.OP_VALUE; -- Update
        ↪ contributes the differential change
    ELSIF DELETING THEN
        v_delta := - :OLD.OP_VALUE;            -- Deletion
        ↪ subtracts the removed value
    END IF;

    -- Update the aggregated analytics record to reflect the change:
    -- Ensuring the invariant: A(S'') = A(S') + A
    UPDATE AGG_ANALYTICS
    SET TOTAL_SUM = TOTAL_SUM + v_delta
    WHERE AGG_ID = 1; -- Assuming a single aggregate record
    ↪ representing the analytical dataset

EXCEPTION
```

```
WHEN OTHERS THEN
        -- In production triggers, avoid explicit rollbacks.
        RAISE;
END;
/


---------------------------------------------------------------------
-- Demonstration of DML operations triggering automatic data updates
---------------------------------------------------------------------


-- Insert a new record into OPERATIONAL_DATA (A = 100)
INSERT INTO OPERATIONAL_DATA (OP_VALUE) VALUES (100);
COMMIT;

-- Update the existing record (e.g., change from 100 to 150; A = 50)
UPDATE OPERATIONAL_DATA
   SET OP_VALUE = 150
 WHERE ID = 1;
COMMIT;

-- Delete the record (A = -150)
DELETE FROM OPERATIONAL_DATA
 WHERE ID = 1;
COMMIT;

-- Query the aggregated result to verify that the invariant
↪   TOTAL_SUM is maintained
SELECT TOTAL_SUM FROM AGG_ANALYTICS WHERE AGG_ID = 1;
```

Multiple Choice Questions

1. In the formal trigger definition

$$T = (E, \Theta, A),$$

what does the component E represent?

(a) The sequence of actions performed after an event.

(b) The predicate condition that governs trigger activation.

(c) The data manipulation event (e.g., INSERT, UPDATE, DELETE).

(d) The transactional boundary limiting trigger execution.

2. Consider the formal invariant preservation equation:

$$A(S'') = A(S') + \Delta A.$$

What does ΔA primarily denote?

(a) The total error accumulated during the update.

(b) The incremental change in the analytical aggregate due to the update and trigger actions.

(c) The overall difference between the initial and the final database states.

(d) A constant offset maintained across transactions.

3. Which statement best distinguishes the roles of BEFORE and AFTER triggers in the execution semantics of automated data updates?

(a) BEFORE triggers execute post-commit, while AFTER triggers preemptively validate incoming data.

(b) BEFORE triggers are invoked prior to the finalization of the data modification event, enabling preemptive validation or modification; AFTER triggers execute once the data modification is fully materialized.

(c) Both BEFORE and AFTER triggers execute simultaneously at the same transactional moment.

(d) BEFORE triggers log data changes whereas AFTER triggers perform corrective actions.

4. The chapter models the trigger mechanism for a sequence of data modification events using a composite function:

$$T_i : S \times \delta_i \to S_i.$$

Which key property does this functional model ensure in a transactional setting?

(a) The immutability of the database schema.

(b) The preservation of atomicity and isolation for each individual event.

(c) The decoupling of trigger actions from underlying data operations.

(d) The deterministic ordering of all concurrent transactions.

5. In designing triggers for high transactional loads, why is it critical to implement lightweight procedures?

(a) To minimize overall memory usage of the database server.

(b) To reduce lock durations and contention, thereby enhancing overall transaction throughput.

(c) To simplify trigger code for educational purposes.

(d) To permit bypassing of trigger logic during batch processing.

6. Recursive trigger invocations can lead to which of the following issues in an analytical environment?

(a) Inadequate validation of incoming data.

(b) Unintended cascades of updates that may result in deadlocks.

(c) Violation of referential integrity constraints.

(d) Overuse of dynamic SQL which complicates maintenance.

7. How do incremental aggregation techniques contribute to the performance of trigger-based updates when n rows are affected by a data modification event?

(a) They enable the aggregation function to be updated in constant or logarithmic time per row, leading to sublinear growth of the cost function.

(b) They force a linear reevaluation of all aggregates regardless of the number of rows.

(c) They defer the aggregation until after all trigger actions are completed.

(d) They eliminate the need for triggers by pre-computing aggregates.

Answers:

1. **C: The data manipulation event (e.g., INSERT, UPDATE, DELETE)**
Explanation: In the formal model $T = (E, \Theta, A)$, E specifically represents the event that triggers the execution of actions, such as an INSERT, UPDATE, or DELETE operation.

2. **B: The incremental change in the analytical aggregate due to the update and trigger actions**
Explanation: The term ΔA encapsulates the net effect of both the direct update δ and the subsequent trigger action A, ensuring that the analytic aggregate correctly reflects the change.

3. **B: BEFORE triggers are invoked prior to the finalization of the data modification event, enabling preemptive validation or modification; AFTER triggers execute once the data modification is fully materialized**
Explanation: This captures the essential distinction: BEFORE triggers allow for validation or changes before the event is committed, whereas AFTER triggers operate on the finalized state for auxiliary processing or updates.

4. **B: The preservation of atomicity and isolation for each individual event**
Explanation: Modeling each trigger activation as $T_i : S \times \delta_i \to S_i$ ensures that each data modification event is handled within its own atomic transaction, preserving isolation and preventing interference from concurrent updates.

5. **B: To reduce lock durations and contention, thereby enhancing overall transaction throughput**
Explanation: Lightweight procedures are critical in high transactional environments because complex or slow triggers can hold locks longer, impeding performance and reducing overall throughput.

6. **B: Unintended cascades of updates that may result in deadlocks**
Explanation: Recursive trigger invocations can create a cascade effect where one trigger activates another repeatedly, potentially leading to deadlocks or excessive processing, jeopardizing system stability.

7. **A: They enable the aggregation function to be updated in constant or logarithmic time per row, leading to sublinear growth of the cost function**
Explanation: Incremental aggregation techniques allow the system to update analytical metrics efficiently. By ensuring that the per-row cost remains constant or logarithmic, the overall cost function $C(n)$ grows sublinearly, which is vital for scalability under high data volumes.

Chapter 24

Query Performance Optimization in PL/SQL

Theoretical Framework for Query Cost Modeling

Query performance optimization in PL/SQL is grounded in a rigorous theoretical framework that quantifies the resource expenditures associated with different execution plans. Within this framework, each candidate plan, denoted by π, is evaluated via a cost function $C(\pi)$ that aggregates multiple factors such as CPU time, memory usage, and disk I/O operations. A typical formulation is expressed as

$$C(\pi) = \sum_{i=1}^{k} \alpha_i \cdot f_i(\pi),$$

where α_i represents the weighting associated with the ith resource metric, and $f_i(\pi)$ is the estimated resource cost incurred by plan π. This mathematical modeling allows for the identification of plans that minimize the cumulative cost, thereby promising enhanced execution speed and lower overall system load. Statistical metadata and cardinality estimations further refine these estimates, enabling the optimizer to assess trade-offs between alternative query execution strategies in actual PL/SQL environments.

Static Query Analysis and Logical Rewriting

The process of static query analysis involves the examination and transformation of SQL statements prior to execution. Logical rewriting techniques take an original query Q and produce an alternative formulation $\mathcal{R}(Q)$, such that the semantic equivalence $Q \equiv \mathcal{R}(Q)$ is preserved while ensuring that

$$C(\mathcal{R}(Q)) < C(Q).$$

This transformation may include reordering of join operations, predicate pushdown, and the elimination of unnecessary projections. By restructuring the logical plan, the number of intermediate results and the associated computational overhead are reduced. The success of these methods is predicated on the robust application of relational algebra properties and on the prudent exploitation of query monotonicity. In the PL/SQL context, where SQL statements are frequently embedded within procedural code, such rewritings contribute vitally toward the acceleration of data analytics processing.

PL/SQL Procedural Optimization Techniques

Optimizing the performance of PL/SQL extends beyond static SQL query tuning and encompasses techniques aimed at refining the procedural code itself. A significant aspect of this is the reduction of context switching between the PL/SQL engine and the SQL engine. Minimizing these transitions contributes to a decrease in processing overhead, which otherwise may result from repeated interactions between different execution environments. The consolidation of iterative data operations into bulk processing constructs allows for the efficient management of large data volumes, thus curtailing the cumulative execution time. This efficiency gain can be quantified by the metric

$$\Delta T = T_{\text{pre-optimization}} - T_{\text{post-optimization}},$$

where ΔT represents the time savings achieved through procedural refinement. These optimization strategies demand careful consideration of both algorithmic design and resource allocation, ensuring that procedural logic is optimized to support high-velocity analytic operations without incurring unnecessary system latency.

Resource-Aware Optimization and Concurrency Considerations

In high-throughput environments, query performance optimization must concurrently address issues related to resource contention and concurrency control. Execution plans that perform optimally in isolation may encounter performance degradation when subjected to concurrent workloads. To mitigate this, resource-aware strategies are applied, incorporating parallel processing capabilities and refined lock management mechanisms. Concurrency control, often managed via protocols such as multiversion concurrency control (MVCC), ensures that optimized queries maintain their performance characteristics under simultaneous access. The effectiveness of these strategies can be captured by the performance improvement ratio

$$\Delta P = \frac{P_{\text{optimized}}}{P_{\text{baseline}}},$$

where $\Delta P > 1$ indicates a measurable gain in throughput and responsiveness. This holistic approach to resource management—integration of empirical system profiling with theoretical cost models—ensures that both the logical plan and the procedural execution in PL/SQL are finely tuned to deliver superior query performance and efficient data analytics processing.

Oracle 19c SQL Code Snippet

```
-- *************************************************************
-- Section 1: Query Cost Modeling Using a Cost Function
-- The cost of each query plan  is modeled as:
--   C() =  (_i * f_i())
-- For demonstration purposes, we use three resource metrics: CPU,
↪  Memory, and Disk I/O.
-- The weight factors are set as: _CPU = 1.5, _MEM = 1.0, _IO = 2.0.
-- *************************************************************

-- Create table to store simulated query plans and resource cost
↪  metrics.
CREATE TABLE QUERY_PLANS (
    PLAN_ID     NUMBER GENERATED BY DEFAULT AS IDENTITY,
```

```
    CPU_COST    NUMBER,    -- Represents f_1()
    MEM_COST    NUMBER,    -- Represents f_2()
    IO_COST     NUMBER,    -- Represents f_3()
    -- Virtual column that computes overall cost C() = 1.5*CPU_COST
    ↪    + 1.0*MEM_COST + 2.0*IO_COST
    OVERALL_COST NUMBER GENERATED ALWAYS AS (1.5 * CPU_COST + 1.0 *
    ↪    MEM_COST + 2.0 * IO_COST) VIRTUAL,
    CONSTRAINT QUERY_PLANS_PK PRIMARY KEY (PLAN_ID)
);

-- Insert sample query plans with estimated resource costs.
INSERT INTO QUERY_PLANS (CPU_COST, MEM_COST, IO_COST) VALUES (100,
↪    50, 20);
INSERT INTO QUERY_PLANS (CPU_COST, MEM_COST, IO_COST) VALUES (90,
↪    60, 30);
INSERT INTO QUERY_PLANS (CPU_COST, MEM_COST, IO_COST) VALUES (110,
↪    40, 25);
COMMIT;

-- Create a PL/SQL function to calculate the overall cost based on
↪    input parameters.
CREATE OR REPLACE FUNCTION calculate_plan_cost(
    p_cpu IN NUMBER,
    p_mem IN NUMBER,
    p_io  IN NUMBER
) RETURN NUMBER IS
    v_cost NUMBER;
BEGIN
    -- Implements the cost equation: C() = 1.5*p_cpu + 1.0*p_mem +
    ↪    2.0*p_io
    v_cost := 1.5 * p_cpu + 1.0 * p_mem + 2.0 * p_io;
    RETURN v_cost;
END calculate_plan_cost;
/

-- Display all query plans with calculated overall costs via the
↪    function.
SELECT PLAN_ID, CPU_COST, MEM_COST, IO_COST,
       calculate_plan_cost(CPU_COST, MEM_COST, IO_COST) AS
       ↪    CALCULATED_COST
FROM QUERY_PLANS;

-----------------------------------------------------------------------
-- Section 2: Static Query Analysis and Logical Rewriting Simulation
-- Original query Q and its rewritten alternative R(Q) are
↪    demonstrated.
-- The rewritten query is expected to have a lower cost, i.e.,
↪    C(R(Q)) < C(Q).
-----------------------------------------------------------------------

-- Assume we have a table SAMPLE_DATA that holds raw analytical
↪    data.
CREATE TABLE SAMPLE_DATA (
```

```
    ID              NUMBER PRIMARY KEY,
    REGION          VARCHAR2(50),
    STATUS          VARCHAR2(20),
    CREATED_DATE    DATE
);

-- Insert sample data into SAMPLE_DATA.
INSERT ALL
    INTO SAMPLE_DATA (ID, REGION, STATUS, CREATED_DATE) VALUES (1,
    ↪  'North', 'ACTIVE', SYSDATE)
    INTO SAMPLE_DATA (ID, REGION, STATUS, CREATED_DATE) VALUES (2,
    ↪  'South', 'INACTIVE', SYSDATE)
    INTO SAMPLE_DATA (ID, REGION, STATUS, CREATED_DATE) VALUES (3,
    ↪  'East', 'ACTIVE', SYSDATE)
SELECT * FROM DUAL;
COMMIT;

-- Original query Q without optimization (hint disabled).
SELECT /*+ NO_REWRITE */
       REGION,
       COUNT(*) AS TOTAL_ROWS
FROM   SAMPLE_DATA
GROUP BY REGION;

-- Rewritten query R(Q) with predicate pushdown and join reordering
↪  hint to reduce cost.
SELECT /*+ PUSH_PRED */
       REGION,
       COUNT(*) AS TOTAL_ROWS
FROM   SAMPLE_DATA
WHERE  STATUS = 'ACTIVE'
GROUP BY REGION;

---------------------------------------------------------------------
-- Section 3: PL/SQL Procedural Optimization with Bulk Processing
-- Demonstrates reduction in context switching via BULK COLLECT and
↪  iterative processing.
---------------------------------------------------------------------

DECLARE
    -- Define a collection type corresponding to rows of
    ↪  SAMPLE_DATA.
    TYPE data_tbl_type IS TABLE OF SAMPLE_DATA%ROWTYPE;
    v_data data_tbl_type;
BEGIN
    -- Bulk collect rows matching the 'ACTIVE' status to minimize
    ↪  row-by-row context switches.
    SELECT * BULK COLLECT INTO v_data
    FROM SAMPLE_DATA
    WHERE STATUS = 'ACTIVE';

    -- Process each row in the collection (simulate iterative
    ↪  computations or logging).
```

```
    FOR i IN v_data.FIRST .. v_data.LAST LOOP
        DBMS_OUTPUT.PUT_LINE('Processing Record - ID: ' ||
        ↪  v_data(i).ID || ', REGION: ' || v_data(i).REGION);
    END LOOP;
END;
/


-------------------------------------------------------------------
-- Section 4: Performance Measurement and Procedural Optimization
↪    Metrics
-- Calculates time savings (T) before and after optimization.
-------------------------------------------------------------------


DECLARE
    v_start NUMBER;
    v_end   NUMBER;
    v_delta NUMBER;
BEGIN
    -- Capture start time (in 100th of seconds).
    v_start := DBMS_UTILITY.GET_TIME;

    -- Simulated optimized processing block.
    NULL;  -- (Replace with actual PL/SQL processing logic)

    -- Capture end time.
    v_end := DBMS_UTILITY.GET_TIME;

    -- Time saving: T = T_pre-optimization - T_post-optimization.
    v_delta := v_end - v_start;
    DBMS_OUTPUT.PUT_LINE('Time Savings (Delta T): ' || v_delta || '
    ↪  (in 100th sec units)');
END;
/


-------------------------------------------------------------------
-- Section 5: Resource-Aware Optimization and Concurrency
↪    Considerations
-- Calculate performance improvement ratio (P) and demonstrate
↪    parallel query execution.
-------------------------------------------------------------------


-- Calculate the performance improvement ratio P = P_optimized /
↪  P_baseline.
DECLARE
    P_baseline NUMBER := 100;  -- baseline throughput metric (e.g.,
    ↪  rows/sec)
    P_optimized NUMBER := 150; -- optimized throughput metric
    Delta_P NUMBER;
BEGIN
    Delta_P := P_optimized / P_baseline;
    IF Delta_P > 1 THEN
        DBMS_OUTPUT.PUT_LINE('Improved Throughput, Delta P: ' ||
        ↪  Delta_P);
```

```
    ELSE
        DBMS_OUTPUT.PUT_LINE('No measurable improvement in
        ↪    throughput, Delta P: ' || Delta_P);
    END IF;
END;
/

-- Execute an analytical query using a parallel hint to simulate
↪  resource-aware optimization.
SELECT /*+ PARALLEL(SAMPLE_DATA, 4) */
        REGION,
        COUNT(*) AS ROW_COUNT
FROM    SAMPLE_DATA
GROUP BY REGION;
```

Multiple Choice Questions

1. Which element in the cost function

$$C(\pi) = \sum_{i=1}^{k} \alpha_i \cdot f_i(\pi)$$

best represents the relative importance of each resource metric?

   (a) The candidate plan π
   (b) The weighting factor α_i
   (c) The cost estimation function $f_i(\pi)$
   (d) The total number of resource metrics k

2. In static query analysis and logical rewriting, what is the primary objective when transforming an original query Q into an alternative formulation $\mathcal{R}(Q)$?

   (a) To alter the semantic meaning of the query in order to explore new data relationships
   (b) To increase the number of join operations for comprehensive data aggregation
   (c) To preserve semantic equivalence while reducing the estimated cost, such that

$$C(\mathcal{R}(Q)) < C(Q)$$

   (d) To obfuscate the query logic to enhance security

3. In the context of PL/SQL procedural optimization, reducing context switching between the PL/SQL engine and the SQL engine primarily leads to:

    (a) Increased memory allocation for intermediate results

    (b) A reduction in processing overhead and improved runtime performance

    (c) More detailed logging of individual SQL operations

    (d) Enhanced readability of the PL/SQL code without affecting performance

4. What is the principal benefit of consolidating iterative data operations into bulk processing constructs in PL/SQL?

    (a) It facilitates debugging by processing rows individually.

    (b) It significantly decreases cumulative execution time by reducing the number of individual operations.

    (c) It increases the complexity and variety of error-handling routines.

    (d) It ensures that queries are executed in a strictly linear, row-by-row manner.

5. Within resource-aware optimization strategies, a performance improvement ratio defined by

$$\Delta P = \frac{P_{\text{optimized}}}{P_{\text{baseline}}}$$

greater than 1 indicates:

    (a) A measurable gain in throughput and responsiveness compared to the baseline.

    (b) An increase in the resource cost despite optimization attempts.

    (c) No significant change in performance between the optimized and baseline implementations.

    (d) That the baseline system performance is superior to the optimized system.

6. Which of the following techniques is typically NOT a part of static query analysis and logical rewriting in PL/SQL?

(a) Reordering join operations to reduce intermediate results.

(b) Applying predicate pushdown to filter data early.

(c) Eliminating unnecessary projections to streamline query processing.

(d) Increasing context switches between the PL/SQL and SQL engines.

7. The metric

$$\Delta T = T_{\text{pre-optimization}} - T_{\text{post-optimization}}$$

in PL/SQL procedural optimization is used to quantify:

(a) The cumulative discrepancy between the estimated and actual cost functions.

(b) The time savings achieved through procedural refinement.

(c) The ratio of successful query executions to errors encountered.

(d) The difference in resource usage between optimized and unoptimized queries.

Answers:

1. **B: The weighting factor α_i**
   Explanation: In the cost function, α_i represents the weight assigned to the ith resource metric. It scales the estimated cost $f_i(\pi)$ for that metric, thereby quantifying its relative importance in determining the overall cost $C(\pi)$.

2. **C: To preserve semantic equivalence while reducing the estimated cost, such that**

$$C(\mathcal{R}(Q)) < C(Q)$$

   Explanation: Logical rewriting transforms the original query Q into an alternative formulation $\mathcal{R}(Q)$ without altering its meaning (semantic equivalence) but aims to lower the overall cost to achieve better performance.

3. **B: A reduction in processing overhead and improved runtime performance**
   Explanation: Minimizing context switching between the PL/SQL engine and the SQL engine significantly reduces the overhead associated with these transitions, leading to more efficient execution and improved overall performance.

4. **B: It significantly decreases cumulative execution time by reducing the number of individual operations**
   Explanation: Consolidating iterative operations into bulk processing constructs reduces the number of discrete steps required to process large data volumes, thereby curtailing execution time and enhancing performance.

5. **A: A measurable gain in throughput and responsiveness compared to the baseline**
   Explanation: The performance improvement ratio ΔP compares the throughput of the optimized implementation to that of the baseline. A ΔP greater than 1 indicates that the optimized system delivers improved performance in terms of throughput and responsiveness.

6. **D: Increasing context switches between the PL/SQL and SQL engines**
   Explanation: Static query analysis and logical rewriting focus on transforming the query for efficiency—techniques like join reordering, predicate pushdown, and projection elimination are employed. Increasing context switches would, in contrast, add overhead and is not a technique aimed at enhancing query performance.

7. **B: The time savings achieved through procedural refinement**
   Explanation: The metric ΔT is defined as the difference between the execution time before optimization and after optimization. It directly quantifies the reduction in execution time, reflecting the effectiveness of the procedural optimization techniques applied.

Chapter 25

Utilizing Optimizer Hints in PL/SQL Queries

Theoretical Foundations of Optimizer Hints

Optimizer hints are specialized annotations that influence the behavior of the query optimizer by modifying the cost model that governs the selection of execution plans. In a cost-based optimization framework, each candidate plan is associated with an estimated cost, $C(\pi)$, derived from various resource metrics. The injection of optimizer hints alters the traditional optimization pathway by biasing the evaluation of these cost metrics. By modifying parameters within the cost function, hints serve to prioritize certain access paths or join methods over those determined solely via automated analysis. This mechanism can be conceptualized as a perturbation of the base cost function, such that the modified cost, $C'(\pi)$, satisfies

$$C'(\pi) = C(\pi) + \Delta C(h),$$

where $\Delta C(h)$ reflects the adjustment instigated by the hint h. This theoretical model encapsulates the fundamental role of optimizer hints in shaping the query planning process in a statistically guided and analytically justifiable manner.

Mechanisms and Implementation within PL/SQL

In the domain of PL/SQL, optimizer hints are integrated directly into SQL statements embedded within procedural code. The embedding mechanism operates by tagging the SQL statement with a specially formatted comment directive that is interpreted by the query optimizer. These hints determine not only the join order or the access method for tables but also dictate the parallel execution parameters and other optimizer-specific options. The syntax of these hints adheres to strict formatting rules, ensuring they are recognized as non-executable annotations. Their implementation leverages the internal representation of the query plan, effectively translating syntactic hints into modifications of execution parameters. Such modifications may include adjustments to the join algorithms, use of index scans over full table scans, or the enforcement of a specific join method. The resulting plan, denoted as π_h, is thereby a function of both the intrinsic query structure and the externally imposed hints.

Analytic Impact on Complex Query Performance

When applied to complex analytic queries, optimizer hints have the potential to enhance performance by addressing intrinsic computational bottlenecks. Complex queries, involving multi-dimensional joins and aggregations over large data sets, often suffer from suboptimal plan choices due to cardinality misestimations. By explicitly directing the optimizer towards more favorable execution paths, hints can substantially reduce the overhead associated with disk I/O, CPU utilization, and memory consumption. This targeted guidance is critical when handling queries exhibiting non-trivial correlation properties among tables or when the structure of the query leads to an exponential increase in the number of intermediate relations. Statistically, if the baseline performance is represented by a throughput $P_{baseline}$ and the optimized performance by $P_{optimized}$, the effect of utilizing optimizer hints is often quantified in terms of the performance improvement ratio,

$$\Delta P = \frac{P_{optimized}}{P_{baseline}},$$

238

with values of ΔP significantly greater than 1 indicating a successful application of the hints in enhancing query execution.

Challenges and Nuances in Hint Utilization

The application of optimizer hints entails a detailed understanding of both the underlying data distribution and the query execution environment. Since the query optimizer relies on cardinality estimations and statistical metadata to generate its cost model, any hint that conflicts with these parameters may inadvertently lead to plans that are inferior to the optimizer's natural selection. Furthermore, hints must be crafted with precision, as their effect is highly context-sensitive; a hint that yields performance benefits in one scenario may induce inefficiency in another due to factors such as changing data distributions or schema modifications. The challenge lies in balancing the aggressive guidance provided by a hint with the dynamic nature of the underlying data. Analytical frameworks that model the sensitivity of the cost function to such hints, represented by the derivative $\frac{\partial C}{\partial h}$, are invaluable in understanding the marginal impact of a given optimizer hint. Such analyses enable the calibration of hints to achieve the desired cost reduction without compromising the overall stability and adaptability of the PL/SQL execution environment.

Oracle 19c SQL Code Snippet

```
----------------------------------------------------------------
-- Create a table to store query cost and performance evaluation
↪   metrics.
-- This simulates the theoretical model:
--   Base cost: C()
--   Cost adjustment by hint: C(h)
--   Adjusted cost: C'() = C() + C(h)
--   Performance improvement: P = P_optimized / P_baseline
----------------------------------------------------------------
CREATE TABLE QUERY_COST_EVALUATION (
    QUERY_ID            NUMBER PRIMARY KEY,
    DESCRIPTION         VARCHAR2(100),
    BASE_COST           NUMBER,        -- C()
    COST_DELTA          NUMBER,        -- C(h)
    ADJUSTED_COST       NUMBER,        -- C'() = C() + C(h)
    BASE_PERFORMANCE    NUMBER,        -- P_baseline
```

```
    OPTIMIZED_PERFORMANCE NUMBER,        -- P_optimized
    IMPROVEMENT_RATIO      NUMBER        -- P = P_optimized /
    ↪  P_baseline
);
/


--------------------------------------------------------------------------
-- Insert sample data simulating an analytic query affected by an
↪  optimizer hint.
INSERT INTO QUERY_COST_EVALUATION (
    QUERY_ID, DESCRIPTION, BASE_COST, COST_DELTA, ADJUSTED_COST,
    BASE_PERFORMANCE, OPTIMIZED_PERFORMANCE, IMPROVEMENT_RATIO
) VALUES (
    1, 'Complex analytic query with optimizer hint', 100, 20, 0,
    ↪  150, 300, 0
);
COMMIT;


--------------------------------------------------------------------------
-- Function to compute the adjusted cost using the formula:
--   C'() = C() + C(h)
CREATE OR REPLACE FUNCTION get_adjusted_cost (
    p_base_cost IN NUMBER,
    p_cost_delta IN NUMBER
) RETURN NUMBER IS
BEGIN
    RETURN p_base_cost + p_cost_delta;
END;
/


--------------------------------------------------------------------------
-- Procedure to simulate the effect of optimizer hints:
-- It calculates the adjusted cost and the performance improvement
↪  ratio:
--   P = P_optimized / P_baseline
CREATE OR REPLACE PROCEDURE simulate_hint_effect IS
    v_base_cost          NUMBER;
    v_cost_delta         NUMBER;
    v_adjusted_cost      NUMBER;
    v_base_perf          NUMBER;
    v_optimized_perf     NUMBER;
    v_improvement_ratio  NUMBER;
BEGIN
    -- Retrieve metrics for the analytical query
    SELECT BASE_COST, COST_DELTA, BASE_PERFORMANCE,
    ↪  OPTIMIZED_PERFORMANCE
      INTO v_base_cost, v_cost_delta, v_base_perf, v_optimized_perf
      FROM QUERY_COST_EVALUATION
     WHERE QUERY_ID = 1;

    -- Calculate adjusted cost using the cost function model
    v_adjusted_cost := get_adjusted_cost(v_base_cost, v_cost_delta);
```

```
    -- Calculate performance improvement ratio: P = P_optimized /
    ↪  P_baseline
    v_improvement_ratio := v_optimized_perf / v_base_perf;

    -- Update the table with the computed values
    UPDATE QUERY_COST_EVALUATION
       SET ADJUSTED_COST = v_adjusted_cost,
           IMPROVEMENT_RATIO = v_improvement_ratio
     WHERE QUERY_ID = 1;

    COMMIT;

    DBMS_OUTPUT.PUT_LINE('Adjusted Cost C''(): ' ||
    ↪  v_adjusted_cost);
    DBMS_OUTPUT.PUT_LINE('Performance Improvement Ratio P: ' ||
    ↪  v_improvement_ratio);
EXCEPTION
    WHEN NO_DATA_FOUND THEN
        DBMS_OUTPUT.PUT_LINE('No data found for the given
        ↪  QUERY_ID.');
    WHEN OTHERS THEN
        DBMS_OUTPUT.PUT_LINE('Error: ' || SQLERRM);
END;
/

-- Execute the simulation procedure to show calculated results.
BEGIN
    simulate_hint_effect;
END;
/


-------------------------------------------------------------------
-- Create a sample table for analytic demonstration.
-- This table represents a typical data set where optimizer hints
↪  are applied.
-------------------------------------------------------------------
CREATE TABLE SALES_ANALYTICS (
    SALE_ID    NUMBER GENERATED BY DEFAULT AS IDENTITY,
    REGION     VARCHAR2(50),
    SALE_DATE  DATE,
    AMOUNT     NUMBER,
    CONSTRAINT SALES_ANALYTICS_PK PRIMARY KEY (SALE_ID)
);
/


-------------------------------------------------------------------
-- Insert sample sales data into the SALES_ANALYTICS table.
INSERT ALL
    INTO SALES_ANALYTICS (REGION, SALE_DATE, AMOUNT)
        VALUES ('North', DATE '2023-09-01', 1000)
    INTO SALES_ANALYTICS (REGION, SALE_DATE, AMOUNT)
        VALUES ('South', DATE '2023-09-02', 1500)
    INTO SALES_ANALYTICS (REGION, SALE_DATE, AMOUNT)
```

```
           VALUES ('East', DATE '2023-09-03', 1200)
SELECT * FROM DUAL;
COMMIT;

------------------------------------------------------------------------
-- Perform an analytical query with embedded optimizer hints.
-- The hint directs the optimizer to push predicates and use nested
↪  loops.
-- This represents the practical application of modifying the cost
↪  function.
SELECT /*+ PUSH_PRED(SA) USE_NL(SA) */
       REGION,
       SUM(AMOUNT) AS TOTAL_SALES
FROM SALES_ANALYTICS SA
WHERE SALE_DATE BETWEEN DATE '2023-09-01' AND DATE '2023-09-30'
GROUP BY REGION;

------------------------------------------------------------------------
-- Dynamic SQL demonstration integrating optimizer hints.
-- This block uses DBMS_SQL to parse and execute a SQL statement
↪  with hints.
DECLARE
    v_cursor NUMBER;
    v_count  NUMBER;
    v_sql    VARCHAR2(4000);
BEGIN
    v_sql := 'SELECT /*+ PUSH_PRED(SA) INDEX_ASC(SA
    ↪  SALES_ANALYTICS_PK) */ ' ||
             'COUNT(*) FROM SALES_ANALYTICS SA WHERE SALE_DATE >=
             ↪  DATE ''2023-09-01''';
    v_cursor := DBMS_SQL.OPEN_CURSOR;
    DBMS_SQL.PARSE(v_cursor, v_sql, DBMS_SQL.NATIVE);
    DBMS_SQL.DEFINE_COLUMN(v_cursor, 1, v_count);
    IF DBMS_SQL.EXECUTE(v_cursor) > 0 THEN
        DBMS_SQL.FETCH_ROWS(v_cursor);
        DBMS_SQL.COLUMN_VALUE(v_cursor, 1, v_count);
        DBMS_OUTPUT.PUT_LINE('Row Count with Hint: ' || v_count);
    END IF;
    DBMS_SQL.CLOSE_CURSOR(v_cursor);
EXCEPTION
    WHEN OTHERS THEN
        IF DBMS_SQL.IS_OPEN(v_cursor) THEN
            DBMS_SQL.CLOSE_CURSOR(v_cursor);
        END IF;
        DBMS_OUTPUT.PUT_LINE('Dynamic SQL Error: ' || SQLERRM);
END;
/
```

Multiple Choice Questions

1. What is the primary role of optimizer hints in PL/SQL queries?

    (a) They revise the SQL syntax to conform to coding standards.

    (b) They modify the cost estimation process, biasing the selection of execution plans.

    (c) They enforce strict data integrity constraints.

    (d) They manage transaction control within the PL/SQL block.

2. In PL/SQL, where are optimizer hints typically embedded?

    (a) In the declaration section of the PL/SQL block.

    (b) As specially formatted comment directives within embedded SQL statements.

    (c) In the exception handling code.

    (d) Within the stored procedure header.

3. The modified cost function after applying an optimizer hint is best represented by:

    (a) $C'(\pi) = C(\pi) - C(h) C'(\pi) = C(h)$

(b) $C'(\pi) = C(\pi) + C(h) C'(\pi) = C(\pi) \ddot{O} C(h)$

(4) Which of the following aspects is NOT directly influenced by optimizer hints?

    (a) The choice of join algorithms.

    (b) The selection between index scans and table scans.

    (c) The specification of parallel execution parameters.

    (d) The enforcement of data integrity constraints.

5. The performance improvement effect of optimizer hints is quantified by the ratio:

    (a) $P = P_{baseline}/P_{optimized} P = P_{optimized} - P_{baseline}$

(b) $P = P_{optimized}/P_{baseline} P = P_{baseline} - P_{optimized}$

(6) What is one key challenge when utilizing optimizer hints in PL/SQL?

(a) Ensuring hints universally improve performance regardless of data dynamics.

(b) Balancing the aggressive hint directives with the evolving statistical metadata and data distributions.

(c) Guaranteeing that hints will always override the optimizer's natural plan selection.

(d) Automating the embedding of hints within every SQL statement.

7. How is the marginal impact of an optimizer hint on the cost function mathematically represented?

(a) C/

(b) C/h

(c) C/

(d) C(h) alone, without reference to any derivative

Answers:

1. **B: They modify the cost estimation process, biasing the selection of execution plans**
This answer is correct because optimizer hints are designed to alter the cost model used by the query optimizer. By adjusting the estimated cost (as shown by the relation

$$C'(\pi) = C(\pi) + \Delta C(h)$$

), they influence the choice of execution plans.

2. **B: As specially formatted comment directives within embedded SQL statements**
Optimizer hints in PL/SQL are integrated directly into the SQL statements via specially formatted comments. These directives are interpreted by the query optimizer without affecting the executable logic of the code.

3. **C: $C'(\pi) = C(\pi) + \Delta C(h)$**
The theoretical model provided in the chapter clearly shows that applying a hint adjusts the original cost $C(\pi)$ by an additional term $\Delta C(h)$, resulting in a modified cost function

$$C'(\pi) = C(\pi) + \Delta C(h).$$

4. **D: The enforcement of data integrity constraints**
   While optimizer hints influence execution strategies (such as join algorithm selection, index usage, and parallel execution), they do not impact data integrity constraints, which are maintained by the database management system.

5. **C:** $\Delta P = \frac{P_{\text{optimized}}}{P_{\text{baseline}}}$
   The performance improvement ratio defined in the chapter is

$$\Delta P = \frac{P_{\text{optimized}}}{P_{\text{baseline}}},$$

   where a value significantly greater than 1 indicates that the use of optimizer hints has favorably impacted query performance.

6. **B: Balancing the aggressive hint directives with the evolving statistical metadata and data distributions**
   A key challenge with using optimizer hints is ensuring that the explicit guidance they offer to the optimizer does not conflict with or undermine the optimizer's natural cost estimations, which are driven by current data statistics and distributions.

7. **B:** $\frac{\partial C}{\partial h}$
   The chapter models the sensitivity of the cost function with respect to the applied hint using the derivative

$$\frac{\partial C}{\partial h},$$

   which quantifies the marginal impact of changes in the hint on the overall cost function.

Chapter 26

Data Cleansing Routines and Validations

Foundational Concepts in Data Quality and Integrity

In many analytical contexts, raw data is subject to a plethora of imperfections, ranging from missing values and systematic errors to random noise and duplication. The intrinsic quality of any dataset is quantified through dimensions such as completeness, accuracy, consistency, and reliability. Formally, data quality may be conceptualized as a function $Q : R \to [0, 1]$, where R denotes the set of raw data and the range expresses a normalized quality measure. The integrity of the data is maintained only when each element $x \in R$ adheres to a collection of pre-established constraints. These constraints, defined through logical predicates, ensure that spurious entries or corrupt observations are identified and either amended or excluded from subsequent analytical routines. The mathematical characterization of these predicates enables a rigorous framework for evaluating the fitness of data for statistical and computational processing.

The Analytical Model for Data Cleansing Routines

Data cleansing routines are formalized as functions that map a set of raw data R into a cleansed set C. This transformation is captured by the function

$$f_{\text{clean}} : R \to C,$$

where

$$C = \{x \in R \mid \phi(x) = 1\}.$$

Here, the predicate $\phi(x)$ represents an aggregate of validity checks that may include threshold evaluations, pattern matching, and inter-field dependencies. The design of f_{clean} is critical; it must judiciously balance the elimination of aberrant data with the preservation of informative signals. The cleansing process often entails the standardization of data format, normalization of numerical values, and the resolution of semantic ambiguities. By rigorously applying these transformations, the routine reduces the dataset to elements that are consistent with the underlying assumptions of downstream analytical models.

Formal Techniques in Data Validation for Analytical Purposes

The process of data validation involves the systematic verification of each datum against a series of formal criteria that encapsulate domain-specific rules. These validation techniques are represented mathematically by a collection of predicates $\{\psi_1, \psi_2, \ldots, \psi_n\}$ such that the aggregate validation function is defined as

$$\Psi(x) = \bigwedge_{i=1}^{n} \psi_i(x).$$

A datum x is considered valid if and only if $\Psi(x)$ evaluates to true. The predicates $\psi_i(x)$ may incorporate range checks (e.g., verifying that numerical values satisfy $L \leq x \leq U$), type conformity, structural consistency, and inter-data referential constraints. The formalism not only aids in guaranteeing that the cleansed dataset is free of inconsistencies but also facilitates the automated detection of anomalies within large-scale databases. Furthermore, the sequential and parallel composition of these validation predicates is crucial for implementing scalable routines that ensure high-quality data is available for analytical computation.

Statistical Methods for Outlier Detection and Robust Correction

Robust statistical methodologies play an essential role in the identification and correction of outlier data points, which may unduly influence the outcome of analytical processes. Given a random variable X representing a specific data attribute, the z-score is computed as

$$z_i = \frac{x_i - \mu_X}{\sigma_X},$$

where μ_X and σ_X denote the mean and standard deviation of X, respectively. Data points with absolute z-scores exceeding a predetermined threshold, typically $|z_i| > 3$, are flagged as potential outliers. Alternative techniques such as the median absolute deviation (MAD) offer increased robustness in the presence of non-Gaussian distributions. In such frameworks, a correction mechanism is often employed whereby anomalous values are either adjusted using robust estimators or excluded from the analysis. The interplay between detection algorithms and iterative cleansing routines is mathematically formalized via optimization criteria that minimize residual error while preserving the intrinsic distributional characteristics of the data. The result is a statistically sound dataset, wherein the influence of aberrant observations is mitigated, thereby ensuring the fidelity of subsequent analytical computations.

Oracle 19c SQL Code Snippet

```
-- Create RAW_DATA table to simulate raw data with potential quality
↪    issues
CREATE TABLE RAW_DATA (
    ID                 NUMBER GENERATED BY DEFAULT AS IDENTITY,
    MEASUREMENT        NUMBER,
    OBSERVATION_DATE   DATE,
    VALID_FLAG         CHAR(1) DEFAULT 'N'
);

-- Create CLEAN_DATA table to store cleansed data after applying
↪    validation rules
```

```
CREATE TABLE CLEAN_DATA (
    ID                NUMBER,
    MEASUREMENT       NUMBER,
    OBSERVATION_DATE  DATE,
    Z_SCORE           NUMBER,
    VALID_FLAG        CHAR(1)
);

-- Insert sample raw data into RAW_DATA, including valid, outlier,
↪ and missing values
INSERT ALL
    INTO RAW_DATA (MEASUREMENT, OBSERVATION_DATE) VALUES (100, DATE
    ↪ '2023-09-01')
    INTO RAW_DATA (MEASUREMENT, OBSERVATION_DATE) VALUES (105, DATE
    ↪ '2023-09-02')
    INTO RAW_DATA (MEASUREMENT, OBSERVATION_DATE) VALUES (98,  DATE
    ↪ '2023-09-03')
    INTO RAW_DATA (MEASUREMENT, OBSERVATION_DATE) VALUES (102, DATE
    ↪ '2023-09-04')
    INTO RAW_DATA (MEASUREMENT, OBSERVATION_DATE) VALUES (500, DATE
    ↪ '2023-09-05') -- Potential outlier
    INTO RAW_DATA (MEASUREMENT, OBSERVATION_DATE) VALUES (97,  DATE
    ↪ '2023-09-06')
    INTO RAW_DATA (MEASUREMENT, OBSERVATION_DATE) VALUES (NULL, DATE
    ↪ '2023-09-07') -- Missing value
SELECT * FROM DUAL;
COMMIT;


-------------------------------------------------------------------------
-- Procedure: cleanse_data
-- This procedure computes aggregate statistics and applies
↪ cleansing routines.
-- It calculates the z-score using the formula:
--     z = (x - mean) / stddev
-- where mean and stddev are computed over the valid measurements.
-- Rows with |z| <= 3 are considered valid and inserted into
↪ CLEAN_DATA with VALID_FLAG 'Y'.
-- Outliers or data with missing measurements are marked with
↪ VALID_FLAG 'N'.
-------------------------------------------------------------------------


CREATE OR REPLACE PROCEDURE cleanse_data IS
    v_mean    NUMBER;
    v_stddev  NUMBER;
    v_threshold CONSTANT NUMBER := 3;  -- z-score threshold for
    ↪ valid data
BEGIN
    -- Compute mean and standard deviation for MEASUREMENT, ignoring
    ↪ null values.
    SELECT AVG(MEASUREMENT), STDDEV(MEASUREMENT)
      INTO v_mean, v_stddev
      FROM RAW_DATA
     WHERE MEASUREMENT IS NOT NULL;
```

249

```
    DBMS_OUTPUT.PUT_LINE('Computed Mean: ' || v_mean || ' | StdDev:
    ↪  ' || v_stddev);

    -- Iterate over each row in RAW_DATA to perform data validation
    ↪  and cleansing.
    FOR rec IN (SELECT ID, MEASUREMENT, OBSERVATION_DATE FROM
    ↪  RAW_DATA) LOOP
        IF rec.MEASUREMENT IS NOT NULL THEN
            DECLARE
                v_zscore NUMBER;
            BEGIN
                -- Calculate z-score using: z = (measurement - mean)
                ↪  / standard deviation
                v_zscore := (rec.MEASUREMENT - v_mean) / v_stddev;

                -- Validate data: Accept if |z| is within the
                ↪  threshold, else mark as outlier.
                IF ABS(v_zscore) <= v_threshold THEN
                    INSERT INTO CLEAN_DATA (ID, MEASUREMENT,
                    ↪  OBSERVATION_DATE, Z_SCORE, VALID_FLAG)
                    VALUES (rec.ID, rec.MEASUREMENT,
                    ↪  rec.OBSERVATION_DATE, v_zscore, 'Y');
                ELSE
                    INSERT INTO CLEAN_DATA (ID, MEASUREMENT,
                    ↪  OBSERVATION_DATE, Z_SCORE, VALID_FLAG)
                    VALUES (rec.ID, rec.MEASUREMENT,
                    ↪  rec.OBSERVATION_DATE, v_zscore, 'N');
                END IF;
            EXCEPTION
                WHEN ZERO_DIVIDE THEN
                    DBMS_OUTPUT.PUT_LINE('Error: Standard deviation
                    ↪  is zero.');
            END;
        ELSE
            -- For rows with missing measurements, mark as invalid
            ↪  with NULL z_score.
            INSERT INTO CLEAN_DATA (ID, MEASUREMENT,
            ↪  OBSERVATION_DATE, Z_SCORE, VALID_FLAG)
            VALUES (rec.ID, rec.MEASUREMENT, rec.OBSERVATION_DATE,
            ↪  NULL, 'N');
        END IF;
    END LOOP;
    COMMIT;
EXCEPTION
    WHEN OTHERS THEN
        ROLLBACK;
        RAISE;
END cleanse_data;
/
```

```
-- Execute the cleansing procedure to transform RAW_DATA into
↪  CLEAN_DATA
--------------------------------------------------------------------------

BEGIN
    cleanse_data;
END;
/


--------------------------------------------------------------------------
-- Query the cleansed data to review validation results and computed
↪  z-scores
--------------------------------------------------------------------------

SELECT * FROM CLEAN_DATA;


--------------------------------------------------------------------------
-- Procedure: dynamic_validation
-- Demonstrates dynamic SQL execution to validate data quality.
-- This procedure accepts a table name and dynamically checks for
↪  records with NULL measurements.
--------------------------------------------------------------------------

CREATE OR REPLACE PROCEDURE dynamic_validation (p_table_name IN
↪  VARCHAR2) IS
    v_sql   VARCHAR2(1000);
    v_total NUMBER;
BEGIN
    v_sql := 'SELECT COUNT(*) FROM ' || p_table_name || ' WHERE
    ↪  MEASUREMENT IS NULL';
    EXECUTE IMMEDIATE v_sql INTO v_total;
    DBMS_OUTPUT.PUT_LINE('Total records with NULL MEASUREMENT in '
    ↪  || p_table_name || ': ' || v_total);
EXCEPTION
    WHEN OTHERS THEN
        DBMS_OUTPUT.PUT_LINE('Dynamic validation error: ' ||
        ↪  SQLERRM);
END dynamic_validation;
/


--------------------------------------------------------------------------
-- Execute dynamic validation for the RAW_DATA table
--------------------------------------------------------------------------

BEGIN
    dynamic_validation('RAW_DATA');
END;
/


--------------------------------------------------------------------------
-- Aggregation Query: Summarize cleansed data based on validation
↪  flag.
```

```
-- This query provides a count of valid versus invalid records and
↪   the average measurement.
-----------------------------------------------------------------------
SELECT
    VALID_FLAG,
    COUNT(*)          AS TOTAL_RECORDS,
    AVG(MEASUREMENT)  AS AVG_MEASUREMENT
FROM
    CLEAN_DATA
GROUP BY
    VALID_FLAG;
```

Multiple Choice Questions

1. Which of the following best represents the formal definition of data quality as described in the chapter?

    (a) Q: $[0,1] \to$ R

    (b) Q: R $\to$

    (c) Q: R $\to [0,1]$

    (d) Q: $[0,1] \to [0,1]$

2. In the analytical model for data cleansing routines, the function

$$f_{\text{clean}} : R \to C$$

    is defined such that

$$C = \{x \in R \mid \phi(x) = 1\}.$$

    Which of the following best describes the role of the predicate $\phi(x)$?

    (a) It transforms raw data into numerical summaries.

    (b) It represents an aggregate of validity checks applied to each datum.

    (c) It scales data values into a normalized range.

    (d) It randomly selects data points for further analysis.

3. The aggregated validation function is given by

$$\Psi(x) = \bigwedge_{i=1}^{n} \psi_i(x).$$

252

What does this expression imply about the criteria for data validity?

(a) A datum is valid if at least one of the predicates $\psi_i(x)$ is true.

(b) A datum is valid only if all the predicates $\psi_i(x)$ are true.

(c) A datum is valid if an odd number of the predicates $\psi_i(x)$ hold.

(d) A datum is valid if any two of the predicates $\psi_i(x)$ hold.

4. The design of the data cleansing routine f_{clean} must carefully balance:

(a) Maximizing computational speed and minimizing memory usage.

(b) Eliminating aberrant data while preserving informative signals.

(c) Increasing the size of the dataset and reducing redundancy.

(d) Standardizing data formats without altering data semantics.

5. Which statistical method is employed in the chapter for outlier detection?

(a) Data points are flagged if they do not conform to a pre-specified schema.

(b) Data points with z-scores computed as

$$z_i = \frac{x_i - \mu_X}{\sigma_X}$$

are flagged when $|z_i| > 3$.

(c) Outlier detection is based on the interquartile range (IQR) without normalization.

(d) Outlier data are identified using a simple threshold on raw values.

6. To address non-Gaussian distributions in outlier detection, the chapter recommends which of the following alternatives to the traditional z-score method?

(a) Mean absolute deviation (MAD)

(b) Coefficient of variation (CV)

(c) Median absolute deviation (MAD)

(d) Standard error of the mean (SEM)

7. In the context of formal data validation routines, which logical operation is primarily used to aggregate multiple validation predicates $\{\psi_1, \psi_2, \ldots, \psi_n\}$?

(a) Logical disjunction (OR)

(b) Logical implication

(c) Logical conjunction (AND)

(d) Logical negation (NOT)

Answers:

1. **C: Q: R $\rightarrow$ [0,1]**
   Explanation: The chapter defines data quality as a normalized measure that maps raw data elements from the set R to a quality score in the interval $[0, 1]$, indicating the overall fitness of data for analytic purposes.

2. **B: It represents an aggregate of validity checks applied to each datum.**
   Explanation: In the cleansing model, $\phi(x)$ encapsulates the collection of tests (such as threshold evaluations and pattern matching) that determine whether a given data element should be retained in the cleansed set C.

3. **B: A datum is valid only if all the predicates $\psi_i(x)$ are true.**
   Explanation: The validation function $\Psi(x)$ uses logical conjunction (AND) across all predicates, meaning every single condition must be met for the data item x to be considered valid.

4. **B: Eliminating aberrant data while preserving informative signals.**
   Explanation: The rationale behind f_{clean} is to remove noise and errors while still retaining the underlying trends and signals in the data, ensuring that valuable information is not inadvertently lost.

5. **B: Data points with z-scores computed as** $z_i = \frac{x_i - \mu_X}{\sigma_X}$ **are flagged when** $|z_i| > 3$.
   Explanation: The chapter details a standard statistical method using z-scores to identify outliers, flagging those observations that exceed the typical threshold of 3 standard deviations from the mean.

6. **C: Median absolute deviation (MAD)**
   Explanation: For distributions that are not well approximated by a Gaussian model, the median absolute deviation (MAD) is recommended owing to its robustness against the influence of extreme values.

7. **C: Logical conjunction (AND)**
   Explanation: Aggregating multiple validation predicates through a logical AND ensures that every criterion is satisfied for a datum to be considered valid, forming the backbone of the formal data validation routine.

Chapter 27

Data Transformation and Normalization in PL/SQL

Conceptual Foundations of Data Transformation

Data transformation constitutes the rigorous process of converting heterogeneous, raw data into a uniform format amenable to analytical processing. In many settings, data are acquired from multiple sources that differ in units, structure, and semantics. To address these disparities, a transformation function, typically represented by

$$f : R \to T,$$

is employed, where R denotes the domain of raw data and T represents the transformed space. The function f is often composed of a sequence of operations, including scaling, shifting, and non-linear modifications, which collectively ensure that the salient features of the data are preserved while eliminating inconsistencies. Such composite transformations may be expressed as

$$T(x) = g(h(x)),$$

where $h : R \to S$ performs an initial adjustment to a preliminary domain S, and $g : S \to T$ completes the mapping into the final target space. The design of these functions requires careful consideration of statistical properties and domain-specific constraints to avoid inadvertent distortion of the underlying data distributions.

Normalization Techniques for Consistent Data Analysis

Normalization is an essential procedure that standardizes the range and distribution of data values, thereby facilitating meaningful comparisons and robust analytical modeling. A common normalization approach is z-score standardization, which transforms a data element x by computing

$$x' = \frac{x - \mu}{\sigma},$$

where μ and σ denote the mean and standard deviation computed from the relevant subset of data. This technique repositions the data into a standard normal distribution with zero mean and unit variance, effectively mitigating the influence of scale differences. An alternative normalization strategy is the min-max scaling method, where each data value is rescaled according to the formula

$$x' = \frac{x - x_{\min}}{x_{\max} - x_{\min}},$$

with $x_{\min}$ and $x_{\max}$ representing the minimum and maximum observed values, respectively. Both methods serve to align the disparate ranges of data attributes, ensuring that each contributes proportionately to subsequent analytical algorithms. Robust normalization procedures may also invoke non-parametric techniques, such as transformations based on the median absolute deviation, to reduce the sensitivity to extreme values and non-Gaussian distributions.

Implementation in PL/SQL Environments

Within the PL/SQL ecosystem, transformation and normalization routines are encapsulated in procedural constructs that enforce data consistency and computational efficiency. The implementation typically begins with the extraction of summary statistics, such as the mean μ and standard deviation σ, from the input dataset.

These statistics then inform the parameterization of the normalization function, yielding a mapping

$$f_{\text{norm}} : R \to N,$$

where N designates the normalized data domain. In this framework, each datum $x \in R$ is processed through a deterministic pipeline, ensuring that its normalized counterpart x_{norm} retains the relevant structural and statistical characteristics of the original measurement. The integrity of this transformation is crucial, as it underpins the reliability of further computational analyses and statistical models. Furthermore, the procedural nature of PL/SQL facilitates the automation of these operations, allowing for dynamic recalibration of transformation parameters based on the evolving properties of incoming data.

An integral aspect of the methodology is the calibration of transformation functions to minimize error relative to predefined quality metrics. This often involves optimizing a loss function of the form

$$L = \sum_{i=1}^{m} (x_i - f_{\text{norm}}(x_i))^2,$$

where m denotes the cardinality of the dataset and the optimization objective is to achieve minimal residual error, thereby preserving the fidelity of the transformed data. Such an optimization framework guarantees that the transformation not only standardizes the data but also maintains a high degree of consistency across varied data sources.

Through the integration of advanced transformation paradigms and normalization techniques, the PL/SQL environment is capable of reconciling and preparing disparate datasets for comprehensive and reliable analysis.

Oracle 19c SQL Code Snippet

```
-- Create the RAW_DATA table to store heterogeneous, untransformed
↪   input data
CREATE TABLE RAW_DATA (
    DATA_ID    NUMBER GENERATED BY DEFAULT AS IDENTITY,
    RAW_VALUE  NUMBER,
    ENTRY_DATE DATE DEFAULT SYSDATE,
    CONSTRAINT RAW_DATA_PK PRIMARY KEY (DATA_ID)
);
```

```
-- Insert sample raw data values into RAW_DATA
INSERT ALL
    INTO RAW_DATA (RAW_VALUE) VALUES (120)
    INTO RAW_DATA (RAW_VALUE) VALUES (200)
    INTO RAW_DATA (RAW_VALUE) VALUES (150)
    INTO RAW_DATA (RAW_VALUE) VALUES (300)
    INTO RAW_DATA (RAW_VALUE) VALUES (250)
SELECT * FROM DUAL;
COMMIT;

-- Create the TRANSFORMED_DATA table to store the transformed
-- and normalized outputs computed from RAW_DATA
CREATE TABLE TRANSFORMED_DATA (
    DATA_ID              NUMBER,
    RAW_VALUE            NUMBER,
    TRANSFORMED_VALUE    NUMBER,
    Z_SCORE_NORMALIZED   NUMBER,
    MIN_MAX_NORMALIZED   NUMBER,
    CONSTRAINT TRANSFORMED_DATA_FK FOREIGN KEY (DATA_ID) REFERENCES
    ↪   RAW_DATA(DATA_ID)
);


-------------------------------------------------------------------------
-- Procedure: TRANSFORM_NORMALIZE_DATA
-- This procedure implements key formulas from the chapter:
--   1. Composite transformation: T(x) = g(h(x)) e.g., T(x) = (x +
↪ 50) / 2
--   2. Z-score normalization: x' = (x - ) /
--   3. Min-max normalization: x' = (x - x_min) / (x_max - x_min)
--   4. Loss function evaluation: L =  (x_i - T(x_i)) ^2
-------------------------------------------------------------------------


CREATE OR REPLACE PROCEDURE TRANSFORM_NORMALIZE_DATA IS
    -- Variables to hold summary statistics computed from RAW_DATA
    v_mean    NUMBER;
    v_stddev  NUMBER;
    v_min     NUMBER;
    v_max     NUMBER;

    -- Cursor to iterate through each row in RAW_DATA
    CURSOR c_raw IS
        SELECT DATA_ID, RAW_VALUE FROM RAW_DATA;

    v_data_id      RAW_DATA.DATA_ID%TYPE;
    v_raw_value    RAW_DATA.RAW_VALUE%TYPE;
    v_trans_value  NUMBER;
    v_znorm        NUMBER;
    v_mmnorm       NUMBER;
BEGIN
    -- Compute summary statistics: mean, standard deviation, min,
    ↪  and max values
```

259

```
    SELECT AVG(RAW_VALUE), STDDEV(RAW_VALUE), MIN(RAW_VALUE),
    ↪   MAX(RAW_VALUE)
      INTO v_mean, v_stddev, v_min, v_max
      FROM RAW_DATA;

    -- Process each raw data record
    FOR r IN c_raw LOOP
        v_data_id   := r.DATA_ID;
        v_raw_value := r.RAW_VALUE;

        -- Composite Transformation: Example function T(x) = (x +
        ↪   50) / 2
        v_trans_value := (v_raw_value + 50) / 2;

        -- Z-Score Normalization: z = (x - ) /
        IF v_stddev IS NOT NULL AND v_stddev <> 0 THEN
            v_znorm := (v_raw_value - v_mean) / v_stddev;
        ELSE
            v_znorm := 0;
        END IF;

        -- Min-Max Normalization: norm = (x - min) / (max - min)
        IF (v_max - v_min) IS NOT NULL AND (v_max - v_min) <> 0 THEN
            v_mmnorm := (v_raw_value - v_min) / (v_max - v_min);
        ELSE
            v_mmnorm := 0;
        END IF;

        -- Insert computed values into TRANSFORMED_DATA table
        INSERT INTO TRANSFORMED_DATA (DATA_ID, RAW_VALUE,
        ↪   TRANSFORMED_VALUE, Z_SCORE_NORMALIZED,
        ↪   MIN_MAX_NORMALIZED)
        VALUES (v_data_id, v_raw_value, v_trans_value, v_znorm,
        ↪   v_mmnorm);
    END LOOP;

    COMMIT;
EXCEPTION
    WHEN OTHERS THEN
        ROLLBACK;
        RAISE;
END TRANSFORM_NORMALIZE_DATA;
/

-- Execute the transformation and normalization procedure
BEGIN
    TRANSFORM_NORMALIZE_DATA;
END;
/

------------------------------------------------------------------------
-- Loss Function Calculation:
-- Evaluate error of transformation using the loss function:
```

```
--    L =  (RAW_VALUE - TRANSFORMED_VALUE)^2
-- This metric can be used to calibrate the transformation pipeline
------------------------------------------------------------------

SELECT SUM(POWER(RAW_VALUE - TRANSFORMED_VALUE, 2)) AS LOSS_FUNCTION
FROM TRANSFORMED_DATA;


-- Create a materialized view to precompute and cache the
↪    transformed and normalized data,
-- boosting query performance for analytic routines.
------------------------------------------------------------------

CREATE MATERIALIZED VIEW MV_NORMALIZED_DATA
BUILD IMMEDIATE
REFRESH FAST ON COMMIT
AS
SELECT  T.DATA_ID,
        T.RAW_VALUE,
        T.TRANSFORMED_VALUE,
        T.Z_SCORE_NORMALIZED,
        T.MIN_MAX_NORMALIZED
FROM TRANSFORMED_DATA T;

-- Query the materialized view to inspect the transformed and
↪    normalized dataset
SELECT * FROM MV_NORMALIZED_DATA;
```

Multiple Choice Questions

1. Which of the following expressions best characterizes a composite data transformation function as described in the chapter?

   (a) $T(x) = h\big(g(x)\big)$

   (b) $f(x) = x \times h\big(g(x)\big)$

   (c) $T(x) = g\big(h(x)\big)$

   (d) $f(x) = h(x) + g(x)$

2. What is the main objective of normalization in analytical processes as outlined in the chapter?

   (a) To enhance data security by encrypting data values.

   (b) To standardize the range and distribution of data values for meaningful comparisons.

(c) To increase the dimensionality of data for advanced modeling.

(d) To minimize storage space by compressing data.

3. In the context of z-score normalization, how is a data element x transformed?

(a) $x' = \dfrac{x - x_{\min}}{x_{\max} - x_{\min}}$

(b) $x' = \dfrac{x - \mu}{\sigma}$

(c) $x' = \dfrac{x - \sigma}{\mu}$

(d) $x' = \dfrac{\mu}{x - \sigma}$

4. Which normalization technique transforms data values to lie within the range $[0, 1]$?

(a) Z-score standardization

(b) Min-max scaling

(c) Median absolute deviation scaling

(d) Logarithmic normalization

5. When implementing transformation routines in PL/SQL, what is typically the first step?

(a) Executing complex join operations to combine datasets.

(b) Extracting summary statistics, such as the mean and standard deviation, from the input data.

(c) Performing bulk data insertions for transformation.

(d) Applying optimizer hints to improve SQL performance.

6. What role does the optimization of a loss function play in the calibration of transformation functions?

(a) It serves to maximize the variance in the transformed dataset.

(b) It ensures compression of the data range to a predetermined interval.

(c) It minimizes the residual error, thereby preserving the fidelity of the transformed data.

(d) It automates the management of transactional integrity.

7. How does the PL/SQL environment enhance the implementation of data transformation and normalization processes?

   (a) By allowing ad-hoc querying without the need for encapsulated procedures.

   (b) Through procedural encapsulation and automation that facilitate dynamic recalibration of transformation parameters.

   (c) By relying exclusively on external statistical packages for computation.

   (d) By restricting data operations to a purely declarative SQL paradigm.

Answers:

1. **C:** The chapter defines a composite transformation as one that is composed of sequential operations, where an initial mapping $h : R \to S$ is followed by a secondary mapping $g : S \to T$, succinctly expressed as $T(x) = g(h(x))$.

2. **B:** Normalization is implemented to standardize the range and distribution of data values, thereby enabling consistent and meaningful comparisons across heterogeneous datasets.

3. **B:** Z-score normalization transforms a data element by subtracting the mean μ and then dividing by the standard deviation σ, as represented by $x' = \frac{x-\mu}{\sigma}$.

4. **B:** Min-max scaling rescales data to a defined range, typically $[0, 1]$, using the formula $x' = \frac{x-x_{min}}{x_{max}-x_{min}}$.

5. **B:** The procedural approach in PL/SQL typically starts with the extraction of summary statistics (e.g., mean and standard deviation) from the dataset, which are essential for parameterizing the subsequent transformation or normalization functions.

6. **C:** Calibration of transformation routines involves formulating and minimizing a loss function (e.g., the sum of squared errors) to ensure that the transformed data faithfully represent the original values, thereby preserving data fidelity.

7. **B:** The strength of the PL/SQL environment lies in its support for procedural encapsulation, which enables the automation and dynamic recalibration of transformation routines, ensuring consistency and efficiency in data analytics workflows.

Chapter 28

Date and Time Manipulation for Temporal Analytics

Representation and Storage of Temporal Data

Temporal data is intrinsically multifaceted, encompassing a spectrum of calendrical and clock-based components that facilitate accurate indexing and retrieval. The underlying representation is often modeled by a composite tuple (d, t), where d denotes the discrete calendrical element (year, month, day) and t represents the continuous component of time (hour, minute, second, and subseconds). Such a numerical abstraction permits the uniform storage and retrieval of varied temporal records. In academic discourse, the granularity of these representations is achieved through normalization procedures that render disparate date and time formats into canonical forms. This standardization is paramount for system interoperability and the rigorous application of temporal queries.

Temporal Arithmetic and Interval Analysis

The arithmetic manipulation of temporal data constitutes a critical component in the analysis of sequential events and trends. Operations such as temporal subtraction yield intervals defined by the difference

$$\Delta t = t_2 - t_1,$$

which quantifies the duration between distinct time points t_1 and t_2. These computations often require adjustments that account for non-linear calendar conventions and variations in month lengths or leap year occurrences. Interval arithmetic further extends to summations and multiplications by scalars, enabling the precise modeling of time-based phenomena. Conceptually, the addition of an interval Δt to a temporal datum t is formalized as

$$t' = t + \Delta t,$$

thereby facilitating the projection of future or the retroactive analysis of past events. Such operations necessitate careful consideration of overflow conditions and the cyclical nature of clock time, ensuring that the computed intervals align with established calendrical systems.

Temporal Aggregations and Trend Analysis

Aggregating temporal data is indispensable for uncovering patterns and trends over predetermined periods. This process is often implemented through grouping and averaging techniques over time windows, which are defined either by fixed-length intervals or dynamically adjusted span sizes. For a sequence of observations $x(t)$, where t indexes specific time instants within a window W, the aggregate measure A is computed by

$$A = \frac{1}{|W|} \sum_{t \in W} x(t),$$

with $|W|$ representing the number of temporal data points contained within W. This formula underpins many statistical analyses, including the calculation of moving averages and other indicators that capture the central tendencies of time series data. The aggregation process not only aids in summarizing extensive datasets but also serves as a precursor to more sophisticated temporal statistical models. Trend detection and anomaly identification are routinely achieved by comparing aggregated measures across distinct periods, thereby enabling periodicity assessments and the forecasting of future trends.

Calendar Conventions and Adjustments in Data Processing

The processing of temporal data necessitates acute awareness of the heterogeneity inherent in calendrical conventions across different geographic and cultural contexts. Adjustments for time zone variations, daylight saving time transitions, and leap seconds are critical to ensuring that temporal comparisons remain valid and consistent. Formally, these considerations are integrated by introducing a zone correction variable Z, resulting in transformations of the form

$$T_{\text{adj}}(t) = t + Z,$$

where Z encapsulates the local offset relative to a global standard such as Coordinated Universal Time (UTC). The application of such corrections must account for periodic shifts induced by legislated changes in timekeeping policies as well as the astronomical phenomena that dictate leap year and leap second adjustments. Consequently, the calibration of temporal data involves algorithmic treatments that reconcile these variations, thereby preserving the chronological integrity necessary for robust period comparisons and analytics.

Oracle 19c SQL Code Snippet

```
-- Create a table to represent temporal data with separate date and
   time components.

CREATE TABLE TEMPORAL_DATA (
    EVENT_ID    NUMBER GENERATED BY DEFAULT AS IDENTITY,
    EVENT_DATE  DATE,
    EVENT_TIME  TIMESTAMP,
    CONSTRAINT TEMPORAL_DATA_PK PRIMARY KEY (EVENT_ID)
```

```
);

-- Insert sample data illustrating a composite (d, t)
↳  representation.
INSERT ALL
    INTO TEMPORAL_DATA (EVENT_DATE, EVENT_TIME)
        VALUES (DATE '2023-10-01', TIMESTAMP '2023-10-01 08:30:00')
    INTO TEMPORAL_DATA (EVENT_DATE, EVENT_TIME)
        VALUES (DATE '2023-10-02', TIMESTAMP '2023-10-02 12:45:00')
    INTO TEMPORAL_DATA (EVENT_DATE, EVENT_TIME)
        VALUES (DATE '2023-10-03', TIMESTAMP '2023-10-03 16:20:00')
SELECT * FROM DUAL;
COMMIT;

-------------------------------------------------------------------------
-- Temporal Arithmetic and Interval Analysis:
-- Compute the interval between consecutive events.
-- Equation: t = t2 - t1
-- Also demonstrate adding an interval to a timestamp:
-- t' = t + t (here we add 1 day and 2 hours to a given timestamp).
-------------------------------------------------------------------------

-- Calculate the interval between the current and previous event
↳  timestamps.
SELECT
    EVENT_ID,
    EVENT_TIME,
    LAG(EVENT_TIME, 1) OVER (ORDER BY EVENT_TIME) AS
    ↳  PREV_EVENT_TIME,
    EVENT_TIME - LAG(EVENT_TIME, 1) OVER (ORDER BY EVENT_TIME) AS
    ↳  INTERVAL_DIFF
FROM TEMPORAL_DATA;

-- Example to add an explicit interval (1 day and 2 hours) to the
↳  timestamp of the first event.
SELECT
    EVENT_ID,
    EVENT_TIME,
    EVENT_TIME + INTERVAL '1' DAY + INTERVAL '2' HOUR AS
    ↳  ADJUSTED_TIME
FROM TEMPORAL_DATA
WHERE EVENT_ID = 1;

-------------------------------------------------------------------------
-- Temporal Aggregations and Trend Analysis:
-- For a time series of observations x(t), compute the aggregate
↳  measure:
-- A = (1/|W|) SUM_{t in W} x(t), implemented here as a moving
↳  average.
-------------------------------------------------------------------------

-- Create a table to store temporal observations.
CREATE TABLE TEMPORAL_OBSERVATIONS (
```

268

```sql
    OBS_ID      NUMBER GENERATED BY DEFAULT AS IDENTITY,
    OBS_TIME    TIMESTAMP,
    OBS_VALUE   NUMBER,
    CONSTRAINT TEMPORAL_OBSERVATIONS_PK PRIMARY KEY (OBS_ID)
);

-- Insert sample observations.
INSERT ALL
    INTO TEMPORAL_OBSERVATIONS (OBS_TIME, OBS_VALUE)
        VALUES (TIMESTAMP '2023-10-01 08:30:00', 10)
    INTO TEMPORAL_OBSERVATIONS (OBS_TIME, OBS_VALUE)
        VALUES (TIMESTAMP '2023-10-01 09:00:00', 15)
    INTO TEMPORAL_OBSERVATIONS (OBS_TIME, OBS_VALUE)
        VALUES (TIMESTAMP '2023-10-01 09:30:00', 20)
    INTO TEMPORAL_OBSERVATIONS (OBS_TIME, OBS_VALUE)
        VALUES (TIMESTAMP '2023-10-01 10:00:00', 25)
SELECT * FROM DUAL;
COMMIT;

-- Compute a moving average over a sliding 1-hour window using
↪   analytic functions.
SELECT
    OBS_ID,
    OBS_TIME,
    OBS_VALUE,
    AVG(OBS_VALUE) OVER (
        ORDER BY OBS_TIME
        RANGE INTERVAL '1' HOUR PRECEDING
    ) AS MOVING_AVG
FROM TEMPORAL_OBSERVATIONS;

-------------------------------------------------------------------------
-- Calendar Conventions and Time.Zone Adjustments:
-- Adjust local event times to a global standard (UTC) using a time
↪   zone offset.
-- Equation: T_adj(t) = t + Z, where Z is the time zone difference.
-------------------------------------------------------------------------

-- Create a table to store event times along with their associated
↪   time zones.
CREATE TABLE EVENT_TIMEZONE_DATA (
    EVENT_ID         NUMBER GENERATED BY DEFAULT AS IDENTITY,
    LOCAL_EVENT_TIME TIMESTAMP,
    TIMEZONE         VARCHAR2(50),
    CONSTRAINT EVENT_TIMEZONE_DATA_PK PRIMARY KEY (EVENT_ID)
);

-- Insert sample event data with designated local time zones.
INSERT ALL
    INTO EVENT_TIMEZONE_DATA (LOCAL_EVENT_TIME, TIMEZONE)
        VALUES (TIMESTAMP '2023-10-05 14:00:00',
            ↪   'America/New_York')
    INTO EVENT_TIMEZONE_DATA (LOCAL_EVENT_TIME, TIMEZONE)
```

```sql
        VALUES (TIMESTAMP '2023-10-05 14:00:00', 'Europe/London')
SELECT * FROM DUAL;
COMMIT;

-- Adjust the local event times to UTC.
SELECT
    EVENT_ID,
    LOCAL_EVENT_TIME,
    TIMEZONE,
    FROM_TZ(LOCAL_EVENT_TIME, TIMEZONE) AT TIME ZONE 'UTC' AS
    ↪  UTC_EVENT_TIME
FROM EVENT_TIMEZONE_DATA;


-------------------------------------------------------------------
-- Procedure to Compute Temporal Metrics:
-- Demonstrates interval arithmetic and aggregation to derive
↪  overall temporal metrics.
-------------------------------------------------------------------

CREATE OR REPLACE PROCEDURE calculate_temporal_metrics IS
    v_start_time TIMESTAMP;
    v_end_time   TIMESTAMP;
    v_interval   INTERVAL DAY TO SECOND;
    v_avg_value  NUMBER;
BEGIN
    -- Retrieve the earliest and latest observation times.
    SELECT MIN(OBS_TIME), MAX(OBS_TIME)
      INTO v_start_time, v_end_time
      FROM TEMPORAL_OBSERVATIONS;

    -- Compute the total duration between the first and last
    ↪  observation.
    v_interval := v_end_time - v_start_time;
    DBMS_OUTPUT.PUT_LINE('Total Duration: ' || v_interval);

    -- Calculate the overall average observation value.
    SELECT AVG(OBS_VALUE)
      INTO v_avg_value
      FROM TEMPORAL_OBSERVATIONS;

    DBMS_OUTPUT.PUT_LINE('Overall Average Observation Value: ' ||
    ↪  v_avg_value);
EXCEPTION
    WHEN OTHERS THEN
        DBMS_OUTPUT.PUT_LINE('Error computing temporal metrics: ' ||
        ↪  SQLERRM);
END calculate_temporal_metrics;
/

-- Execute the procedure to display temporal metrics.
BEGIN
    calculate_temporal_metrics;
END;
```

Multiple Choice Questions

1. In the context of temporal data representation, the composite tuple (d, t) is used to represent:

   (a) A normalized integer value for the time component.

   (b) The pairing of a discrete calendrical element and a continuous time component.

   (c) An encoded value combining both date and time into a single scalar.

   (d) A binary flag indicating whether the data is temporal or not.

2. Temporal subtraction in PL/SQL analytics is used to compute:

   (a) The product of two time values.

   (b) The ratio between two sequential dates.

   (c) An interval that quantifies the duration between two time points.

   (d) The normalization factor for converting time zones.

3. Which of the following formulas correctly formalizes the projection of a temporal datum into the future with an interval?

   (a) $t' = t \times \Delta t$

   (b) $t' = \Delta t - t$

   (c) $t' = t + \Delta t$

   (d) $t' = t / \Delta t$

4. In the aggregate measure defined by

$$A = \frac{1}{|W|} \sum_{t \in W} x(t),$$

   what does $|W|$ represent?

   (a) The total duration of the time window.

(b) The weight assigned to each observation.

(c) The number of temporal observations within the window.

(d) The maximum value observed in the window.

5. Normalization of temporal representations is crucial because it:

   (a) Eliminates subsecond precision to simplify arithmetic operations.

   (b) Consolidates diverse date and time formats into canonical forms, ensuring interoperability.

   (c) Converts continuous time values into discrete integer indices.

   (d) Automatically adjusts for leap seconds without additional computation.

6. In the context of calendar conventions and adjustments, the zone correction variable Z is primarily used to:

   (a) Convert a continuous time value into a discrete calendrical format.

   (b) Adjust the temporal data by incorporating local time offsets relative to a global standard (UTC).

   (c) Normalize the date component by accounting for leap year corrections.

   (d) Partition time intervals into fixed-length segments for performance optimization.

7. Considering practical temporal analytics, why is it essential to account for factors such as daylight saving transitions and leap seconds?

   (a) They enable the compression of large timestamp values for efficient storage.

   (b) They ensure that temporal computations closely reflect real-world timekeeping practices, maintaining chronological integrity.

   (c) They facilitate the conversion of date strings into numeric formats.

(d) They allow temporal data to be directly used in linear algebraic computations.

Answers:

1. **B: The pairing of a discrete calendrical element and a continuous time component**
   The composite tuple (d, t) is explicitly defined to separate the calendrical (year, month, day) and the continuous time (hour, minute, second, and subseconds) components, allowing for standardized storage and manipulation of temporal data.

2. **C: An interval that quantifies the duration between two time points**
   Temporal subtraction as described produces a time interval Δt, which is essential in quantifying the duration between two sequential time points, a core concept in temporal arithmetic.

3. **C: $t' = t + \Delta t$**
   Adding a time interval Δt to an existing time t is the standard operation used to project a temporal value forward (or backward, if Δt is negative), aligning with the formal representation provided.

4. **C: The number of temporal observations within the window**
   In the aggregation formula, $|W|$ denotes the cardinality of the window (i.e., how many data points or time instants are contained within it), which is critical for correctly averaging the observed values.

5. **B: Consolidates diverse date and time formats into canonical forms, ensuring interoperability**
   Normalization is a vital process that converts various representations of date and time into a standardized format, facilitating consistent storage, retrieval, and cross-system intercommunication.

6. **B: Adjust the temporal data by incorporating local time offsets relative to a global standard (UTC)**
   The zone correction variable Z plays a pivotal role in adjusting raw temporal data to reflect any local time differences, such as those caused by time zone variations or daylight saving changes, relative to UTC.

7. **B: They ensure that temporal computations closely reflect real-world timekeeping practices, maintaining chronological integrity**
   Accounting for factors like daylight saving and leap seconds is essential to preserve the accuracy and relevance of temporal analytics, as these adjustments mirror the actual, non-linear changes in real-world timekeeping.

Chapter 29

Generating Dynamic Reports via PL/SQL Procedures

Dynamic Report Architecture and System Requirements

Dynamic reports in PL/SQL procedures are designed to accommodate a wide spectrum of analytic requirements through adaptable query structures and flexible result sets. The architecture underlying these procedures is characterized by a clear separation between static query components and dynamically constructed fragments. A base query template serves as the foundation, upon which additional conditions, grouping elements, and sorting directives are appended in response to specific report parameters. In formal terms, let Q_{base} denote the static portion of the query and $Q_{dynamic}$ the variable elements; the final query can be expressed as

$$Q_{final} = Q_{base} \cup Q_{dynamic},$$

where both parts are combined to yield a report tailored to current analytic demands. The design mandates that every dynamically generated query maintains syntactical correctness, ensures efficient performance, and adheres to the security constraints inherent in multi-tenant analytic environments.

Parameterization and Query Customization

The process of parameterization plays a pivotal role in transforming a static query template into a customized report. Report configuration is achieved through a set of parameters $P = \{p_1, p_2, \ldots, p_n\}$ that determine filtering conditions, grouping logic, and ordering preferences. A mapping function f is defined such that

$$Q = f(P),$$

where Q represents the complete SQL query after assimilating the relevant parameters. This approach allows for modular inclusion of various clauses—such as dynamic **WHERE, GROUP BY,** and **ORDER BY** constructs—based on the specific analytic context. Emphasis is placed on constructing these modular clauses in a manner that prevents the inadvertent generation of invalid SQL syntax and ensures that performance is not compromised even when complex aggregation or pivoting operations are requested.

Run-Time SQL Assembly and Execution

The assembly of dynamic SQL at run time necessitates an intricate synthesis of query fragments that account for a range of potential constraints and data structures. In this paradigm, the procedure systematically concatenates predefined query segments with dynamically generated strings, ensuring that the structural integrity of the resulting command is preserved. The resulting statement is then submitted to the PL/SQL execution engine, where it is parsed, compiled, and executed within the established session context. The dynamic assembly process is heavily dependent on runtime conditions and input parameters, leading to a non-deterministic but rigorously managed query formation. In the context of performance optimization, the dynamic generation approach leverages native mechanisms for query plan generation that are attuned to the specifics of the query structure, thereby ensuring that even dynamically assembled queries benefit from the underlying cost-based optimization techniques.

Error Handling, Validation, and Optimization Techniques

Robust error handling and meticulous validation are integral to the successful implementation of dynamic reporting via PL/SQL procedures. Prior to execution, dynamically constructed queries undergo comprehensive validation phases to ensure that the syntax adheres to SQL standards and that the parameters provided are consistent with expected data types. Such validation routines mitigate the risks associated with SQL injection and other security vulnerabilities that may arise from improperly sanitized input. The optimization process is further enhanced by introducing optimizer hints and execution plan analysis as part of the dynamic procedure workflow. By monitoring key performance metrics and validating the efficiency of dynamically generated queries, the procedure is capable of adapting to varying levels of data complexity and user-driven analytic scenarios. These measures ensure that the generated reports not only meet customizable requirements but also perform optimally under diverse operational constraints.

Oracle 19c SQL Code Snippet

```
-- Create FACT_SALES table to simulate a sales fact table for
↪   dynamic reporting
CREATE TABLE FACT_SALES (
    SALE_ID       NUMBER GENERATED BY DEFAULT AS IDENTITY,
    REGION        VARCHAR2(50),
    PRODUCT       VARCHAR2(50),
    SALE_DATE     DATE,
    SALE_AMOUNT   NUMBER,
    CONSTRAINT FACT_SALES_PK PRIMARY KEY (SALE_ID)
);

-- Insert sample data into FACT_SALES
INSERT ALL
    INTO FACT_SALES (REGION, PRODUCT, SALE_DATE, SALE_AMOUNT)
        VALUES ('North', 'ProductA', DATE '2023-01-10', 1200)
    INTO FACT_SALES (REGION, PRODUCT, SALE_DATE, SALE_AMOUNT)
        VALUES ('South', 'ProductB', DATE '2023-01-15', 1500)
    INTO FACT_SALES (REGION, PRODUCT, SALE_DATE, SALE_AMOUNT)
        VALUES ('East', 'ProductC', DATE '2023-01-20', 1800)
    INTO FACT_SALES (REGION, PRODUCT, SALE_DATE, SALE_AMOUNT)
        VALUES ('West', 'ProductD', DATE '2023-01-25', 2100)
SELECT * FROM DUAL;
COMMIT;
```

```
-------------------------------------------------------------------------
-- Procedure: generate_dynamic_report
--
-- This procedure dynamically constructs and executes an SQL query
↪  for
-- generating reports based on runtime parameters. The underlying
↪  algorithm
-- demonstrates the equation:
--
--    Q_final = Q_base   Q_dynamic
--
-- where Q_base is the static part of the query and Q_dynamic is
↪  built via the
-- mapping function f(P) on input parameters P = {p1, p2, ..., pn}.
-------------------------------------------------------------------------

CREATE OR REPLACE PROCEDURE generate_dynamic_report (
    p_region    IN VARCHAR2 DEFAULT NULL,
    p_date_from IN DATE DEFAULT NULL,
    p_date_to   IN DATE DEFAULT NULL,
    p_group_by  IN VARCHAR2 DEFAULT 'REGION',
    p_order_by  IN VARCHAR2 DEFAULT 'TOTAL_SALES DESC'
) AS
    v_query         VARCHAR2(4000);
    v_where_clause  VARCHAR2(1000) := ' WHERE 1=1 ';
    v_base_query    CONSTANT VARCHAR2(1000) :=
                    'SELECT REGION, SUM(SALE_AMOUNT) AS
                    ↪  TOTAL_SALES FROM FACT_SALES ';
BEGIN
    -- Construct dynamic WHERE clause based on provided parameters
    ↪  (Q_dynamic)
    IF p_region IS NOT NULL THEN
        v_where_clause := v_where_clause || ' AND REGION = :region
        ↪  ';
    END IF;

    IF p_date_from IS NOT NULL THEN
        v_where_clause := v_where_clause || ' AND SALE_DATE >=
        ↪  :date_from ';
    END IF;

    IF p_date_to IS NOT NULL THEN
        v_where_clause := v_where_clause || ' AND SALE_DATE <=
        ↪  :date_to ';
    END IF;

    -- Combine static base query (Q_base) with dynamic conditions to
    ↪  form Q_final
    v_query := v_base_query || v_where_clause ||
              ' GROUP BY ' || p_group_by ||
              ' ORDER BY '  || p_order_by;
```

278

```
DBMS_OUTPUT.PUT_LINE('Dynamic SQL Query:');
DBMS_OUTPUT.PUT_LINE(v_query);


↪   ------------------------------------------------------------------
-- Run-Time SQL Assembly and Execution
--
-- The dynamically assembled SQL is executed via a ref cursor,
↪   with bind
-- variables ensuring that the input parameters are safely
↪   applied.


↪   ------------------------------------------------------------------

DECLARE
    TYPE ref_cursor IS REF CURSOR;
    cur_report ref_cursor;
    v_region    FACT_SALES.REGION%TYPE;
    v_total     NUMBER;
BEGIN
    OPEN cur_report FOR v_query
        USING p_region, p_date_from, p_date_to;

    DBMS_OUTPUT.PUT_LINE('Region | Total Sales');
    DBMS_OUTPUT.PUT_LINE('--------------------');

    LOOP
        FETCH cur_report INTO v_region, v_total;
        EXIT WHEN cur_report%NOTFOUND;
        DBMS_OUTPUT.PUT_LINE(v_region || ' | ' || v_total);
    END LOOP;
    CLOSE cur_report;
EXCEPTION
    WHEN OTHERS THEN
        DBMS_OUTPUT.PUT_LINE('Error executing dynamic query: '
        ↪   || SQLERRM);
        RAISE;
END;

EXCEPTION
    WHEN OTHERS THEN
        DBMS_OUTPUT.PUT_LINE('Error in generate_dynamic_report: ' ||
        ↪   SQLERRM);
        ROLLBACK;
        RAISE;
END generate_dynamic_report;
/

--------------------------------------------------------------------
-- Example Calls Demonstrating the Dynamic Report Procedure
--------------------------------------------------------------------
```

```
-- Example 1: Generate a report for region 'North' over a specified
↪    date range
BEGIN
    generate_dynamic_report(
        p_region    => 'North',
        p_date_from => DATE '2023-01-01',
        p_date_to   => DATE '2023-12-31',
        p_group_by  => 'REGION',
        p_order_by  => 'TOTAL_SALES DESC'
    );
END;
/

-- Example 2: Generate a comprehensive report for all regions
↪    without a specific regional filter
BEGIN
    generate_dynamic_report(
        p_date_from => DATE '2023-01-01',
        p_date_to   => DATE '2023-12-31'
    );
END;
/
```

───────────── The code snippet above demonstrates the core algorithm for dynamic query construction and execution in Oracle 19c, encapsulating the principles: • $Q\_final = Q\_base\ Q\_dynamic$ • $Q = f(P)$ Here, runtime parameters drive the creation of a tailored analytic report while ensuring robust SQL syntax, performance optimization, and secure error handling.

Multiple Choice Questions

1. In the dynamic report architecture described in this chapter, how is the final SQL query constructed?

   (a) Qfinal = Qbase Qdynamic

   (b) Qfinal = Qbase Qdynamic

   (c) Qfinal = Qdynamic Qbase

   (d) Qfinal = Qbase Qdynamic

2. The chapter represents parameterization in dynamic report generation with a mapping function. Which equation best captures this relationship?

   (a) $Q = f(P)$

(b) $f(Q) = P$

(c) $Q = f(Q, P)$

(d) $f(P) = Qbase + Qdynamic$

3. Robust error handling and validation are critical in dynamic SQL assembly. Which of the following reasons best explains their necessity?

   (a) To ensure that dynamically constructed queries adhere to SQL syntax.

   (b) To mitigate security risks such as SQL injection.

   (c) To facilitate performance optimization via execution plan analysis.

   (d) All of the above.

4. Which method is primarily used to integrate static and dynamic components during run-time SQL assembly?

   (a) Merging separate queries using UNION ALL.

   (b) Concatenating predefined static segments with dynamically generated strings.

   (c) Precompiling dynamic fragments into a fixed query.

   (d) Executing static and dynamic queries independently and merging their results post execution.

5. In the context of dynamic SQL execution, what is the principal role of optimizer hints according to the chapter?

   (a) To enforce security restrictions on dynamically generated queries.

   (b) To guide the cost-based optimizer in generating efficient execution plans.

   (c) To automate the syntax validation of assembled query components.

   (d) To combine static and dynamic query segments into a unified command.

6. Why is it important to validate input parameters against their expected data types in dynamic report procedures?

   (a) It ensures that the final dynamically constructed query is syntactically valid and executes correctly.

(b) It forces the query to rely exclusively on static query templates.

(c) It minimizes the need for dynamic SQL assembly.

(d) It primarily improves code readability and maintenance.

7. How does the dynamic SQL assembly approach leverage the underlying cost-based optimizer to enhance performance?

(a) By using hardcoded execution plans for all dynamic queries.

(b) By incorporating runtime conditions and optimizer hints to tailor the execution plan to the query structure.

(c) By eliminating runtime validations to reduce overhead.

(d) By merging all dynamic fragments into a single static query.

Answers:

1. **B: Qfinal = Qbase Qdynamic**
   This chapter defines the final dynamic SQL query as the combination of a static base query (Qbase) with dynamic query fragments (Qdynamic), ensuring that both elements are integrated to meet specific analytic requirements.

2. **A: Q = f(P)**
   The mapping function f is used to transform a set of report parameters P into the complete SQL query Q, encapsulating the inclusion of various filtering, grouping, and ordering clauses in the dynamic report generation process.

3. **D: All of the above.**
   Robust error handling and validation are essential not only to guarantee syntactical correctness but also to mitigate security risks such as SQL injection, and to support performance optimization through careful execution plan analysis.

4. **B: Concatenating predefined static segments with dynamically generated strings.**
   The chapter emphasizes that the dynamic assembly of SQL is achieved by methodically concatenating static query segments with those generated at runtime, ensuring the overall structural integrity of the SQL command.

5. **B: To guide the cost-based optimizer in generating efficient execution plans.**
   Optimizer hints are incorporated into dynamic SQL to influence how the Oracle cost-based optimizer generates execution plans, thereby improving query performance for complex dynamic queries.

6. **A: It ensures that the final dynamically constructed query is syntactically valid and executes correctly.**
   Validating input parameters against expected data types is crucial for constructing a syntactically correct query and preventing runtime errors or security vulnerabilities, thereby ensuring reliable execution.

7. **B: By incorporating runtime conditions and optimizer hints to tailor the execution plan to the query structure.**
   The dynamic SQL assembly process leverages runtime conditions along with optimizer hints to enable the Oracle optimizer to generate a cost-based execution plan that is well-suited to the specific structure of the dynamically assembled query, thus ensuring optimal performance.

Chapter 30

Managing High-Volume Data Processing in PL/SQL

Scalability Paradigms in PL/SQL

PL/SQL applications that operate on high-volume data streams are architected to mitigate the performance pitfalls of row-at-a-time processing. Central to this paradigm is the transition from iterative executions to set-based operations that leverage Oracle's intrinsic query optimization mechanisms. The design philosophy emphasizes the consolidation of multiple data transactions into collective processing units, thereby reducing the overhead attributed to frequent context switches between the PL/SQL and SQL engines. In this context, the efficiency of data processing is mathematically correlated with the ratio of aggregated work per execution cycle, such that a higher value of

$$\frac{\text{Volume of Data}}{\text{Number of Executions}}$$

translates into improved throughput. Consequently, the architectural models focus on maximizing this ratio via bulk processing strategies and careful resource partitioning.

Techniques for Optimized Bulk Data Operations

Optimized bulk data operations are instrumental in addressing the challenges inherent in processing large databases. The collective execution of data manipulation language (DML) statements minimizes the cumulative cost of individual operations by amalgamating multiple actions into a single logical unit of work. This is achieved by retrieving and updating data in batches, which effectively reduces the number of execution cycles required. Such techniques inherently decrease the per-record overhead and curtail the latency introduced by repetitive SQL parsing and network round trips. Exception handling within these bulk operations is implemented in a manner that isolates and logs anomalies without impeding the overall performance, thereby ensuring that the processing pipelines remain both resilient and performant under significant load conditions.

Architectural Considerations and Resource Management

The architectural design of high-volume PL/SQL applications necessitates a meticulous evaluation of resource allocation and system configuration. Memory management assumes critical importance as large in-memory collections are employed to store intermediate data during bulk operations. This mandates a tuning of the session parameters and the explicit allocation of buffer pools optimized for high throughput. The structural decomposition of data processing tasks allows the segregation of computational logic from data retrieval operations, enabling concurrent execution paths that fully exploit the available CPU and I/O resources. Furthermore, the integration of transaction control mechanisms, such as rigorous usage of commit and rollback protocols, ensures that the data integrity is preserved even in the event of transient processing failures. The systematic partitioning of workloads, combined with a detailed assessment of resource utilization, forms the backbone of scalable PL/SQL system design.

Monitoring, Tuning, and Concurrency Control

The operational efficiency of high-volume PL/SQL systems is sustained through the continuous monitoring and methodical tuning of active database sessions. Instrumentation techniques are employed to capture granular performance metrics, including I/O throughput, memory utilization, and CPU load. Analysis of these data points, often represented as functions

$$f(\text{I/O}), \ g(\text{Memory}), \ h(\text{CPU}),$$

facilitates the identification of performance bottlenecks that may impede the data processing pipeline. Concurrency control mechanisms, which regulate access to shared resources, are implemented to avert deadlocks and contention issues. This involves the strategic management of lock granularity and isolation levels to balance data consistency against processing efficiency. Moreover, periodic re-evaluation of execution plans, aided by the judicious use of optimizer hints, permits the adaptive tuning of the system in accordance with evolving workload profiles. Such rigorous monitoring and dynamic adjustment protocols are indispensable for maintaining optimal performance in environments characterized by massive data volumes and high transactional concurrency.

Oracle 19c SQL Code Snippet

```
-- Create table HIGH_VOLUME_DATA to simulate a high-volume data
↪  processing scenario
CREATE TABLE HIGH_VOLUME_DATA (
    DATA_ID      NUMBER GENERATED BY DEFAULT AS IDENTITY,
    DATA_VALUE   NUMBER,
    PROCESSED    VARCHAR2(1) DEFAULT 'N',
    CREATED_DATE DATE DEFAULT SYSDATE,
    CONSTRAINT HIGH_VOLUME_DATA_PK PRIMARY KEY (DATA_ID)
);
COMMIT;


-- Create staging table STAGING_HIGH_VOLUME for ETL bulk operations
CREATE TABLE STAGING_HIGH_VOLUME (
```

```
        STG_DATA_ID   NUMBER,
        DATA_VALUE    NUMBER,
        CREATED_DATE  DATE
    );
    COMMIT;


    ---------------------------------------------------------------------------
    -- Insert sample data into STAGING_HIGH_VOLUME (simulating
    ↪   high-volume input)
    ---------------------------------------------------------------------------
    INSERT ALL
        INTO STAGING_HIGH_VOLUME (STG_DATA_ID, DATA_VALUE, CREATED_DATE)
            VALUES (1,  100, SYSDATE)
        INTO STAGING_HIGH_VOLUME (STG_DATA_ID, DATA_VALUE, CREATED_DATE)
            VALUES (2,  200, SYSDATE)
        INTO STAGING_HIGH_VOLUME (STG_DATA_ID, DATA_VALUE, CREATED_DATE)
            VALUES (3,  300, SYSDATE)
        INTO STAGING_HIGH_VOLUME (STG_DATA_ID, DATA_VALUE, CREATED_DATE)
            VALUES (4,  400, SYSDATE)
        INTO STAGING_HIGH_VOLUME (STG_DATA_ID, DATA_VALUE, CREATED_DATE)
            VALUES (5,  500, SYSDATE)
    SELECT * FROM DUAL;
    COMMIT;


    ---------------------------------------------------------------------------
    -- Bulk Processing Procedure: Load data from STAGING_HIGH_VOLUME
    ↪   into HIGH_VOLUME_DATA
    -- This procedure uses BULK COLLECT and FORALL to optimize the data
    ↪   transfer.
    -- It embodies the principle that efficiency improves with a higher
    ↪   ratio of
    -- Volume of Data/Number of Executions.
    ---------------------------------------------------------------------------
    CREATE OR REPLACE PROCEDURE process_high_volume_data IS
        -- Define PL/SQL table types for bulk collection
        TYPE t_ids IS TABLE OF STAGING_HIGH_VOLUME.STG_DATA_ID%TYPE;
        TYPE t_values IS TABLE OF STAGING_HIGH_VOLUME.DATA_VALUE%TYPE;
        v_ids    t_ids;
        v_values t_values;

        batch_size CONSTANT NUMBER := 100; -- Batch size for bulk
        ↪   operation
        l_count NUMBER;
        total_processed NUMBER := 0;
    BEGIN
        LOOP
            -- Bulk fetch a batch of records from the staging table
            SELECT STG_DATA_ID, DATA_VALUE
              BULK COLLECT INTO v_ids, v_values
              FROM STAGING_HIGH_VOLUME
             WHERE ROWNUM <= batch_size;

            l_count := v_ids.COUNT;
```

287

```
        EXIT WHEN l_count = 0;

        -- Bulk insert retrieved data into the main table
        FORALL i IN 1..l_count
            INSERT INTO HIGH_VOLUME_DATA (DATA_ID, DATA_VALUE,
            ↪ CREATED_DATE)
            VALUES (v_ids(i), v_values(i), SYSDATE);

        -- Delete the processed records from staging to avoid
        ↪ reprocessing
        FORALL i IN 1..l_count
            DELETE FROM STAGING_HIGH_VOLUME
              WHERE STG_DATA_ID = v_ids(i);

        COMMIT;
        total_processed := total_processed + l_count;
    END LOOP;

    DBMS_OUTPUT.PUT_LINE('Bulk Processing Completed. Total Rows
    ↪ Processed: ' || total_processed);
EXCEPTION
    WHEN OTHERS THEN
        ROLLBACK;
        DBMS_OUTPUT.PUT_LINE('Error during bulk processing: ' ||
        ↪ SQLERRM);
        RAISE;
END process_high_volume_data;
/


--------------------------------------------------------------------
-- Execute the bulk processing procedure
--------------------------------------------------------------------
BEGIN
    process_high_volume_data;
END;
/


--------------------------------------------------------------------
-- Calculation of Throughput Ratio using the formula:
--     Throughput = Volume of Data / Number of Executions
--------------------------------------------------------------------
DECLARE
    v_volume      NUMBER;
    v_executions NUMBER := 5; -- Simulated number of execution
    ↪ cycles
    v_throughput NUMBER;
BEGIN
    SELECT COUNT(*) INTO v_volume FROM HIGH_VOLUME_DATA;
    v_throughput := v_volume / v_executions;
    DBMS_OUTPUT.PUT_LINE('Calculated Throughput Ratio
    ↪ (Volume/Executions): ' || v_throughput);
END;
/
```

-- Dynamic SQL with Optimizer Hint Example for Adaptive Tuning
-- Demonstrates the use of dynamic SQL to execute a query with
↪ *optimizer hints.*

```
DECLARE
    l_sql         VARCHAR2(4000);
    l_recent_cnt NUMBER;
BEGIN
    l_sql := 'SELECT /*+ PUSH_PRED(C) */ COUNT(*) FROM
    ↪  HIGH_VOLUME_DATA C ' ||
            'WHERE CREATED_DATE >= SYSDATE - 1';
    EXECUTE IMMEDIATE l_sql INTO l_recent_cnt;
    DBMS_OUTPUT.PUT_LINE('Records processed in the last day: ' ||
    ↪  l_recent_cnt);
END;
/
```

-- Simulate Performance Metric Functions: f(I/O), g(Memory), h(CPU)
-- These functions simulate the retrieval of system performance
↪ *metrics.*

```
CREATE OR REPLACE FUNCTION get_performance_metrics RETURN VARCHAR2
↪  IS
    l_io     NUMBER := 1200;   -- Example I/O throughput value
    l_memory NUMBER := 2048;   -- Example memory utilization in MB
    l_cpu    NUMBER := 85;     -- Example CPU usage percentage
BEGIN
    RETURN 'Performance Metrics - f(I/O) = ' || l_io ||
            ', g(Memory) = ' || l_memory ||
            ', h(CPU) = ' || l_cpu;
END get_performance_metrics;
/
```

```
-- Display the performance metrics
BEGIN
    DBMS_OUTPUT.PUT_LINE(get_performance_metrics);
END;
/
```

-- Concurrency Control Demonstration: Explicit Locking and Update
-- Illustrates the usage of row-level locking to ensure data
↪ *consistency*
-- during concurrent operational updates.

```
DECLARE
    l_current_value NUMBER;
BEGIN
    -- Acquire a lock on a specific row in HIGH_VOLUME_DATA
    SELECT DATA_VALUE INTO l_current_value
```

```
   FROM HIGH_VOLUME_DATA
   WHERE DATA_ID = 1
   FOR UPDATE;

   -- Update the locked row (simulate controlled increment)
   UPDATE HIGH_VOLUME_DATA
     SET DATA_VALUE = DATA_VALUE + 50
   WHERE DATA_ID = 1;

   COMMIT;
   DBMS_OUTPUT.PUT_LINE('Row updated. New Data Value: ' ||
   ↪  (l_current_value + 50));
EXCEPTION
   WHEN NO_DATA_FOUND THEN
       DBMS_OUTPUT.PUT_LINE('No record found with DATA_ID = 1.');
   WHEN OTHERS THEN
       ROLLBACK;
       DBMS_OUTPUT.PUT_LINE('Error during row update: ' ||
   ↪  SQLERRM);
END;
/

---------------------------------------------------------------------
-- Create a Materialized View for Precomputed Aggregates to Enhance
↪  Query Performance
---------------------------------------------------------------------
CREATE MATERIALIZED VIEW MV_HIGH_VOLUME_SUM
BUILD IMMEDIATE
REFRESH FAST ON COMMIT
AS
SELECT COUNT(*) AS TOTAL_COUNT, AVG(DATA_VALUE) AS AVG_VALUE
  FROM HIGH_VOLUME_DATA;

-- Query the materialized view to retrieve precomputed aggregate
↪  values
SELECT * FROM MV_HIGH_VOLUME_SUM;
```

Multiple Choice Questions

1. The chapter describes high-volume data processing in PL/SQL as being more efficient when the system maximizes the ratio:

    (a) Number of Executions / Volume of Data

    (b) Volume of Data / Number of Executions

    (c) Memory Utilization / CPU Load

    (d) Buffer Pool Size / I/O Throughput

2. Which of the following best explains the primary benefit of consolidating multiple DML operations into bulk processing units?

   (a) It increases the granularity of per-record processing.

   (b) It minimizes cumulative overhead by reducing the number of SQL context switches.

   (c) It improves the clarity of individual SQL statements.

   (d) It allows for completely asynchronous processing.

3. When designing the architecture for high-volume PL/SQL applications, which resource management strategy is emphasized in the chapter?

   (a) Relying exclusively on dynamic SQL to handle data operations.

   (b) Tuning session parameters and allocating optimized buffer pools for handling large in-memory collections.

   (c) Avoiding bulk operations to simplify memory management.

   (d) Using only row-at-a-time processing for better control.

4. In the context of optimized bulk data operations, how is exception handling implemented according to the chapter?

   (a) All exceptions halt the entire process immediately to prevent data corruption.

   (b) Exceptions are ignored to maintain processing speed.

   (c) Exceptions are isolated and logged so that anomalous records do not impede overall processing.

   (d) Exception handling is deferred until after all bulk operations are complete.

5. The chapter introduces functions such as

$$f(\text{I/O}), \ g(\text{Memory}), \ h(\text{CPU})$$

for monitoring purposes. What do these functions collectively represent?

   (a) They measure the efficiency of query parsing and compilation.

(b) They capture key performance metrics to monitor I/O throughput, memory utilization, and CPU load.

(c) They calculate the ratio of data volume to execution cycles.

(d) They provide a framework for load balancing among server nodes.

6. Concurrency control mechanisms in high-volume PL/SQL systems are implemented primarily to:

(a) Eliminate the need for complex transaction control.

(b) Manage access to shared resources and prevent deadlocks and contention.

(c) Force sequential execution of all SQL statements.

(d) Increase the number of context switches for each transaction.

7. What role do optimizer hints play in the context of tuning high-volume PL/SQL applications as discussed in this chapter?

(a) They permanently lock the execution plan to avoid unexpected changes.

(b) They guide the SQL optimizer to re-evaluate plans, allowing adaptive performance tuning in response to workload variations.

(c) They increase the time spent on SQL parsing and network round trips.

(d) They eliminate the need for monitoring performance metrics.

Answers:

1. **B: Volume of Data / Number of Executions**
The chapter highlights that throughput improves when a larger volume of data is processed per execution cycle, minimizing the overhead caused by frequent context switches.

2. **B: It minimizes cumulative overhead by reducing the number of SQL context switches**
By consolidating multiple DML operations into bulk processing, the system minimizes repetitive SQL parsing and network round trips, thereby enhancing overall performance.

3. **B: Tuning session parameters and allocating optimized buffer pools for handling large in-memory collections**
Efficient memory management is critical in high-volume data processing. The chapter underscores the importance of properly tuned session parameters and optimized buffer pool allocation to manage large in-memory collections for intermediate data.

4. **C: Exceptions are isolated and logged so that anomalous records do not impede overall processing**
The bulk processing strategy discussed involves robust exception handling where errors are captured and logged without compromising the performance of the entire processing pipeline.

5. **B: They capture key performance metrics to monitor I/O throughput, memory utilization, and CPU load**
The functions $f(I/O)$, $g(Memory)$, and $h(CPU)$ are introduced as tools for granular performance monitoring, ensuring that any bottlenecks can be quickly identified and addressed.

6. **B: Manage access to shared resources and prevent deadlocks and contention**
Concurrency control is essential in high-volume systems to balance data consistency and processing efficiency by strategically managing lock granularity and isolation levels.

7. **B: They guide the SQL optimizer to re-evaluate plans, allowing adaptive performance tuning in response to workload variations**
Optimizer hints are used to influence the execution plan dynamically, thereby helping the system adjust to changing workload profiles and maintain optimal performance.

Chapter 31

Optimizing Data Storage with Partitioning Strategies

Foundational Concepts of Data Partitioning

Within expansive analytic environments, data partitioning emerges as a critical methodology for decomposing monolithic datasets into logically segmented units. This decomposition is achieved by dividing a table or data repository into discrete partitions based on specific key attributes. The theoretical underpinnings of partitioning posit that if a dataset T is segmented according to a partitioning key K, then each partition T_i represents a subset where $T = \bigcup_{i=1}^{n} T_i$ and $T_i \cap T_j =$ for all $i \neq j$. Such segmentation not only facilitates focused query operations but also isolates data management tasks, thereby reducing the overhead associated with bulk operations on undivided repositories. The benefits of partitioning are two-fold: enhanced query performance through reduced search domains and improved administrative procedures that exploit data locality.

Methodologies for Logical Segmentation

A spectrum of partitioning methodologies is available, each tailored to the intrinsic characteristics of the dataset and the anticipated workload. Range partitioning divides data by numerical or temporal intervals, thereby allowing each partition to encapsulate a sequential segment of the data. In contrast, list partitioning categorizes data based on explicit discrete values of the partitioning key, ensuring that each partition reflects a distinct membership criterion. Hash partitioning utilizes a hash function applied to the key K, effectively distributing records uniformly across available partitions; mathematically, if $h(K)$ denotes the hash function, then a record is assigned to partition T_i where $i = h(K) \mod n$, with n being the total number of partitions. Composite partitioning combines two or more of these techniques, offering a layered approach that capitalizes on the advantages of each methodology. Such logical segmentation techniques support the principle of minimizing the dataset portion processed during query execution and administrative operations.

Enhancements in Query Performance through Partition Pruning

One of the most significant performance benefits of data partitioning is realized through the optimization technique known as partition pruning. When queries incorporate the partitioning key K within their predicates, the query execution engine can restrict its examination to only those partitions that satisfy the specified constraints. Formally, if a query predicate confines the domain to a subset $P_q \subseteq \{T_1, T_2, \ldots, T_n\}$, then the query execution cost is approximated by the ratio $\frac{|P_q|}{n}$ relative to a full table scan. In this formulation, minimizing $|P_q|$ relative to n directly contributes to a reduction in the volume of data loaded into memory during query processing. Such partition pruning leads to decreased disk I/O and fosters enhanced utilization of cache hierarchies. This deterministic relationship between partition selection and query execution cost reinforces the critical role of partitioning in performance-sensitive applications.

Manageability in Large Analytic Environments

In addition to performance gains, data partitioning substantially augments manageability in large-scale analytic architectures. Logical segmentation of data facilitates targeted administrative operations such as backup, restoration, and purging, which can be isolated to individual partitions without affecting the entire dataset. The ability to drop or truncate a single partition, for example, significantly reduces maintenance downtime and resource consumption. Moreover, partition-level indexing can be maintained independently, allowing for more granular control over statistics collection and index rebuilding procedures. The compartmentalization of data enables database administrators to allocate storage and memory resources in an optimized manner across partitions, aligning physical storage structures with data access patterns. This modular approach ensures that routine tasks such as data archiving and load balancing are executed with minimal disruption to overall system performance, thereby reinforcing the robustness of data storage architectures in environments characterized by high data velocity and volume.

Oracle 19c SQL Code Snippet

```
--------------------------------------------------------------------
-- Demonstration of Data Partitioning Strategies in Oracle 19c
-- This code snippet illustrates key partitioning concepts as
↪    described in the chapter.
-- The underlying theory is that for a dataset T partitioned on key
↪    K:
--     T = T1   T2   ...   Tn     and     Ti   Tj =  for all  i   j.
-- For hash partitioning, the algorithm is:
--     partition_id = MOD(hash_value, number_of_partitions)
--------------------------------------------------------------------


--------------------------------------------------------------------
-- 1. Range Partitioning Example:
-- Create a SALES_DATA table partitioned by RANGE on SALE_DATE.
--------------------------------------------------------------------
CREATE TABLE SALES_DATA (
    SALE_ID      NUMBER GENERATED BY DEFAULT AS IDENTITY,
    SALE_AMOUNT  NUMBER(10,2),
    SALE_DATE    DATE,
    REGION       VARCHAR2(50)
```

```
)
PARTITION BY RANGE (SALE_DATE)
(
    PARTITION P_Q1_2023 VALUES LESS THAN (DATE '2023-04-01'),
    PARTITION P_Q2_2023 VALUES LESS THAN (DATE '2023-07-01'),
    PARTITION P_Q3_2023 VALUES LESS THAN (DATE '2023-10-01'),
    PARTITION P_Q4_2023 VALUES LESS THAN (DATE '2024-01-01'),
    PARTITION P_FUTURE  VALUES LESS THAN (MAXVALUE)
);

-- Insert sample data into SALES_DATA
INSERT ALL
    INTO SALES_DATA (SALE_AMOUNT, SALE_DATE, REGION) VALUES (1500,
    ↪  DATE '2023-03-15', 'North')
    INTO SALES_DATA (SALE_AMOUNT, SALE_DATE, REGION) VALUES (2200,
    ↪  DATE '2023-05-20', 'South')
    INTO SALES_DATA (SALE_AMOUNT, SALE_DATE, REGION) VALUES (1800,
    ↪  DATE '2023-08-10', 'East')
    INTO SALES_DATA (SALE_AMOUNT, SALE_DATE, REGION) VALUES (2500,
    ↪  DATE '2023-11-05', 'West')
SELECT * FROM DUAL;
COMMIT;


----------------------------------------------------------------------
-- 2. Hash Partitioning Example:
-- Create a CUSTOMER_TRANSACTIONS table partitioned by HASH on
↪  CUSTOMER_ID.
----------------------------------------------------------------------
CREATE TABLE CUSTOMER_TRANSACTIONS (
    CUSTOMER_ID          NUMBER,
    TRANSACTION_AMOUNT   NUMBER(10,2),
    TRANSACTION_DATE     DATE,
    DESCRIPTION          VARCHAR2(100)
)
PARTITION BY HASH (CUSTOMER_ID)
PARTITIONS 4;

-- Insert sample data into CUSTOMER_TRANSACTIONS
INSERT ALL
    INTO CUSTOMER_TRANSACTIONS (CUSTOMER_ID, TRANSACTION_AMOUNT,
    ↪  TRANSACTION_DATE, DESCRIPTION)
        VALUES (101, 500, DATE '2023-06-15', 'Payment Received')
    INTO CUSTOMER_TRANSACTIONS (CUSTOMER_ID, TRANSACTION_AMOUNT,
    ↪  TRANSACTION_DATE, DESCRIPTION)
        VALUES (102, 750, DATE '2023-06-16', 'Order Payment')
    INTO CUSTOMER_TRANSACTIONS (CUSTOMER_ID, TRANSACTION_AMOUNT,
    ↪  TRANSACTION_DATE, DESCRIPTION)
        VALUES (103, 300, DATE '2023-06-17', 'Refund Issued')
SELECT * FROM DUAL;
COMMIT;


----------------------------------------------------------------------
-- 3. Composite Partitioning Example:
```

```
-- Create an ORDERS table partitioned by RANGE on ORDER_DATE and
↪   subpartitioned by HASH on REGION.
--------------------------------------------------------------------------
CREATE TABLE ORDERS (
    ORDER_ID     NUMBER GENERATED BY DEFAULT AS IDENTITY,
    ORDER_TOTAL NUMBER(10,2),
    ORDER_DATE   DATE,
    REGION       VARCHAR2(50)
)
PARTITION BY RANGE (ORDER_DATE)
SUBPARTITION BY HASH (REGION)
SUBPARTITIONS 2
(
    PARTITION ORDERS_Q1_2023 VALUES LESS THAN (DATE '2023-04-01'),
    PARTITION ORDERS_Q2_2023 VALUES LESS THAN (DATE '2023-07-01'),
    PARTITION ORDERS_Q3_2023 VALUES LESS THAN (DATE '2023-10-01'),
    PARTITION ORDERS_Q4_2023 VALUES LESS THAN (DATE '2024-01-01'),
    PARTITION ORDERS_FUTURE   VALUES LESS THAN (MAXVALUE)
);

-- Insert sample orders data
INSERT ALL
    INTO ORDERS (ORDER_TOTAL, ORDER_DATE, REGION) VALUES (1200, DATE
    ↪   '2023-03-20', 'North')
    INTO ORDERS (ORDER_TOTAL, ORDER_DATE, REGION) VALUES (1600, DATE
    ↪   '2023-05-10', 'South')
    INTO ORDERS (ORDER_TOTAL, ORDER_DATE, REGION) VALUES (2100, DATE
    ↪   '2023-08-25', 'East')
    INTO ORDERS (ORDER_TOTAL, ORDER_DATE, REGION) VALUES (1900, DATE
    ↪   '2023-11-30', 'West')
SELECT * FROM DUAL;
COMMIT;


--------------------------------------------------------------------------
-- 4. User-Defined Function for Hash Partition Calculation:
-- This function calculates the partition ID based on a given key
↪   and total partitions.
--------------------------------------------------------------------------
CREATE OR REPLACE FUNCTION get_partition_id (p_key IN NUMBER,
↪   p_partitions IN NUMBER)
RETURN NUMBER IS
BEGIN
    RETURN MOD(p_key, p_partitions);
END;
/

-- Example usage of get_partition_id function:
DECLARE
    v_partition_id NUMBER;
BEGIN
    v_partition_id := get_partition_id(12345, 4);  -- For a key
    ↪   value 12345 and 4 partitions
```

```
    DBMS_OUTPUT.PUT_LINE('Calculated Partition ID: ' ||
    ↪  v_partition_id);
END;
/
COMMIT;


-- 5. Query Demonstrating Partition Pruning:
-- When filtering on the partitioning key, Oracle can prune
↪  partitions to optimize query performance.

SELECT *
FROM SALES_DATA
WHERE SALE_DATE BETWEEN DATE '2023-05-01' AND DATE '2023-05-31';


-- 6. Optimizer Hint for Enhanced Query Performance:
-- Using the PUSH_PRED hint to encourage partition pruning in
↪  analytical queries.

SELECT /*+ PUSH_PRED(SD) */
       REGION,
       SUM(SALE_AMOUNT) AS TOTAL_SALES
FROM SALES_DATA SD
WHERE SALE_DATE BETWEEN DATE '2023-01-01' AND DATE '2023-03-31'
GROUP BY REGION;


-- 7. Administrative Operation: Dropping a Specific Partition
-- This demonstrates targeted maintenance by dropping the 'P_FUTURE'
↪  partition.

ALTER TABLE SALES_DATA DROP PARTITION P_FUTURE;
COMMIT;


-- 8. Creating a Local Index on the Partitioned Table:
-- Local indexes can be maintained independently for each partition.

CREATE INDEX IDX_SALES_REGION ON SALES_DATA (REGION)
LOCAL;
```

Multiple Choice Questions

1. What is the primary purpose of data partitioning in expansive analytic environments?

   (a) To improve query performance by reducing the search domain and isolating administrative tasks.

(b) To store data redundantly across multiple partitions.

(c) To merge multiple datasets into a single monolith.

(d) To guarantee uniform data distribution solely for load balancing.

2. Which property best characterizes the partitions created by data partitioning?

(a) Partitions may overlap in order to share related records.

(b) Partitions are mutually exclusive and collectively exhaustive subsets of the dataset.

(c) Partitions are created randomly without any systematic boundaries.

(d) Partitions are organized based solely on physical storage requirements.

3. How does range partitioning differ from list partitioning in terms of logical segmentation?

(a) Range partitioning divides data by sequential intervals, while list partitioning segments data based on explicit discrete values.

(b) Range partitioning groups data based on discrete values, whereas list partitioning uses continuous intervals.

(c) Both methods utilize hash functions to distribute records evenly.

(d) There is no significant difference; both methods yield identical partition schemes.

4. In the hash partitioning formula given as $i = h(K) \bmod n$, what do $h(K)$ and n represent, respectively?

(a) $h(K)$ is the original key value; n is the total number of records.

(b) $h(K)$ is a randomized value; n is the overall size of the dataset.

(c) $h(K)$ is the hash value derived from the key K; n is the total number of partitions.

(d) $h(K)$ denotes a partition index directly; n is an arbitrary scaling factor.

5. What best describes the concept of partition pruning in query optimization?

   (a) Combining multiple partitions to create a larger, efficient block for data consolidation.

   (b) An optimization technique that restricts query execution to only the relevant partitions based on predicate constraints.

   (c) Periodically removing older partitions to free up system resources.

   (d) Continuously re-indexing each partition to maintain data consistency.

6. How does data partitioning enhance manageability in large analytic environments?

   (a) By enabling targeted administrative operations—such as backup, restoration, and purging—on individual partitions without impacting the entire dataset.

   (b) By ensuring that all partitions are processed simultaneously during maintenance tasks.

   (c) By removing the need for dedicated indexing on each partition.

   (d) By guaranteeing that every administrative task is applied uniformly across all partitions.

7. What is the primary feature of composite partitioning?

   (a) It employs a single partitioning strategy, typically hash partitioning, for all data.

   (b) It utilizes multiple partitioning techniques (e.g., range and hash) in a layered approach to segment data.

   (c) It partitions data exclusively based on temporal attributes.

   (d) It merges all previously partitioned data into one partition for simplified query processing.

Answers:

1. **A: To improve query performance by reducing the search domain and isolating administrative tasks.**
   Partitioning breaks a monolithic dataset into logically segmented units, which not only minimizes the search domain

during query operations (leading to reduced disk I/O and faster retrieval) but also allows administrators to perform maintenance tasks on specific partitions with minimal system disruption.

2. **B: Partitions are mutually exclusive and collectively exhaustive subsets of the dataset.**
   The fundamental property of data partitioning is that each partition contains a distinct subset of records without any overlap, and the union of all partitions completely represents the original dataset.

3. **A: Range partitioning divides data by sequential intervals, while list partitioning segments data based on explicit discrete values.**
   Range partitioning assigns records to partitions based on intervals (e.g., date ranges, numeric intervals), whereas list partitioning groups records by matching them to a predefined set of discrete values.

4. **C: h(K) is the hash value derived from the key K; n is the total number of partitions.**
   In hash partitioning, a hash function (denoted by $h(K)$) is applied to the partitioning key K to produce a numerical value. The modulus operation with n, the total number of partitions, determines the specific partition to which a record belongs.

5. **B: An optimization technique that restricts query execution to only the relevant partitions based on predicate constraints.**
   Partition pruning optimizes query performance by allowing the database engine to scan only those partitions that satisfy the query's WHERE clause, thereby reducing the volume of data processed.

6. **A: By enabling targeted administrative operations—such as backup, restoration, and purging—on individual partitions without impacting the entire dataset.**
   Data partitioning enhances manageability by localizing administrative tasks to specific segments of data. This isolation minimizes downtime and resource consumption, as operations can be executed on partitions independently.

7. **B: It utilizes multiple partitioning techniques (e.g., range and hash) in a layered approach to segment data.**

Composite partitioning combines two or more partitioning strategies, leveraging the strengths of each to handle complex data segmentation requirements. This layered approach provides flexibility in how data is organized and accessed.

Chapter 32

Automating Data Load and ETL Processes in PL/SQL

Architectural Foundations of ETL Automation

ETL processes constitute a critical pipeline in data-centric systems, whereby data is systematically extracted from disparate sources, transformed to adhere to analytical schemas, and loaded into target repositories for subsequent analysis. Within the context of PL/SQL, these processes are architected as a series of interdependent operations that, when automated, yield a resilient and scalable data integration framework. This architecture capitalizes on the intrinsic capabilities of PL/SQL to orchestrate complex transaction control, error handling, and batch processing, thereby facilitating the seamless transition of data across heterogeneous environments. In formal terms, if the overall ETL operation is regarded as a function $\mathcal{E}$, then the composite process can be defined as

$$\mathcal{E}(D) = L(T(E(D))),$$

where D represents the source dataset, E denotes the extraction phase, T symbolizes transformation procedures, and L corresponds to the loading mechanics.

Automated Data Extraction from Heterogeneous Sources

Data extraction involves the methodical retrieval of data from multiple origins, which may include relational databases, flat files, or external web services. The extraction phase is designed to standardize diverse data formats into a cohesive structure that facilitates subsequent transformation efforts. In PL/SQL-driven environments, automated extraction leverages declarative SQL constructs and PL/SQL procedural logic to establish connections with external repositories and execute extraction routines at predetermined intervals. This systematic approach ensures that data inflow is both consistent and concurrent with the overall data integration strategy.

Automated Data Transformation in PL/SQL

Transformation processes apply a series of operations aimed at enhancing data consistency, quality, and compatibility with the target analytical schema. Within PL/SQL, data transformation is realized through a combination of procedural constructs, control flow mechanisms, and built-in functions that perform tasks such as data cleansing, normalization, and type conversion. The transformation phase is characterized by the application of conditional logic and iterative procedures that collectively convert raw data into refined datasets. This stage may be mathematically encapsulated as the function

$$T : D_{\text{raw}} \to D_{\text{transf}},$$

where D_{raw} denotes the initial data state and D_{transf} is the resultant, cleaned dataset, thereby ensuring that the data adheres to the expected analytical and schema constraints.

Automated Data Loading and Ingestion

The data loading phase is the final stage in the ETL continuum wherein transformed data is ingested into the target database. PL/SQL facilitates this process by capitalizing on bulk insertion techniques and transactional control, which collectively reduce the overhead associated with high-volume data transfers. Loading operations are optimized through the use of procedural loops and array processing capabilities inherent in PL/SQL, thereby ensuring that data is accurately and efficiently integrated into the repository. The loading function may be expressed as

$$L : D_{\text{transf}} \to D_{\text{target}},$$

in which the function L systematically maps the transformed data to its corresponding structure in the target database, observing referential integrity and other consistency constraints crucial for subsequent analytical queries.

Automation, Scheduling, and Process Orchestration

Automation within ETL implementations is achieved through the integration of scheduling mechanisms that coordinate the execution of extraction, transformation, and loading tasks. PL/SQL supports the creation of recurring job definitions and the orchestration of dependent tasks via built-in scheduling capabilities. This orchestration ensures that ETL processes occur in a predefined sequence, with each phase triggered upon the successful completion of its predecessor. The scheduling system may be conceptualized as a directed acyclic graph (DAG), in which nodes represent individual ETL operations and directed edges enforce execution order. The formal structure inherent to this arrangement guarantees consistency and predictability in data processing workflows, thereby enhancing both system reliability and performance.

Reliability and Error Handling Mechanisms

Robust automation of ETL processes necessitates careful design of error handling and logging frameworks that capture anomalies and ensure data integrity. In PL/SQL, exception handling is meticulously integrated into the procedural logic to catch and manage errors at each stage of the ETL pipeline. This includes strategies such as rolling back transactions upon detection of inconsistencies and logging detailed error information for subsequent analysis. By embedding error resolution protocols within the ETL framework, the overall system maintains a high degree of reliability and is able to resume operations in a consistent state following any transient failures. This systematic approach to error management is essential in environments where data quality and operational continuity are paramount.

Performance Optimization in Automated ETL Processes

Efficiency in automated ETL pipelines is paramount, particularly when handling large-scale data transfers. Optimization techniques in PL/SQL involve the strategic use of bulk processing constructs, parallel execution facilities, and advanced memory management routines. Each of these techniques is designed to minimize latency, reduce input/output (I/O) overhead, and allow the system to manage high volumes of data without compromising transactional integrity. Analytical models of performance, such as throughput and latency metrics, are employed to guide the tuning of individual components within the ETL process. In many instances, performance optimization may be mathematically modeled as minimizing a cost function $C(\theta)$, where θ represents the set of tunable parameters, with the objective being to achieve the minimal operational cost while satisfying all processing constraints.

Oracle 19c SQL Code Snippet

```
-- The following comprehensive Oracle 19c SQL code snippet
↪   demonstrates an ETL process
-- that follows the conceptual formula:
--      (D) = L( T( E(D) ) )
-- where:
--   E(D) represents the Extraction phase from the raw data source,
--   T(...) represents the Transformation phase that cleanses and
↪   normalizes the data,
--   L(...) represents the Loading phase to persist the data into
↪   the target table.


-- Step 1: Create a raw data table to simulate the source dataset
↪   (D_raw)
```

```
CREATE TABLE RAW_CUSTOMER_DATA (
    CUSTOMER_ID   NUMBER,
    CUSTOMER_NAME VARCHAR2(100),
    EMAIL         VARCHAR2(100),
    SIGNUP_DATE   DATE
);

-- Insert sample raw data into RAW_CUSTOMER_DATA
INSERT ALL
    INTO RAW_CUSTOMER_DATA (CUSTOMER_ID, CUSTOMER_NAME, EMAIL,
    ↪   SIGNUP_DATE)
        VALUES (101, ' alice johnson ', 'alice@example.com', DATE
        ↪   '2023-10-01')
    INTO RAW_CUSTOMER_DATA (CUSTOMER_ID, CUSTOMER_NAME, EMAIL,
    ↪   SIGNUP_DATE)
        VALUES (102, ' BOB SMITH ', 'bob@example.com', DATE
        ↪   '2023-10-02')
    INTO RAW_CUSTOMER_DATA (CUSTOMER_ID, CUSTOMER_NAME, EMAIL,
    ↪   SIGNUP_DATE)
        VALUES (103, 'carol white', 'carol@example.com', DATE
        ↪   '2023-10-03')
SELECT * FROM DUAL;
COMMIT;

-------------------------------------------------------------------------
-- Step 2: Extraction Phase E: Copy raw data into a staging table
↪   for ETL processing
-------------------------------------------------------------------------

CREATE TABLE STG_CUSTOMER_DATA AS
SELECT * FROM RAW_CUSTOMER_DATA;
COMMIT;

-------------------------------------------------------------------------
-- Step 3: Transformation Phase T: Cleanse, normalize, and transform
↪   the data (T(D_raw))
-------------------------------------------------------------------------

-- Create a function to perform transformation: trim spaces and
↪   convert the name to proper case.
CREATE OR REPLACE FUNCTION transform_customer (
    p_id    NUMBER,
    p_name  VARCHAR2,
    p_email VARCHAR2,
    p_date  DATE
) RETURN VARCHAR2
IS
    v_transformed_name VARCHAR2(100);
BEGIN
    -- Remove extra spaces and convert to proper case using INITCAP
    v_transformed_name := INITCAP(TRIM(p_name));
    RETURN v_transformed_name;
END transform_customer;
```

```
/

-- Create a transformed data table to hold cleansed data (D_transf)
CREATE TABLE TRANSFORMED_CUSTOMER_DATA (
    CUSTOMER_ID   NUMBER,
    CUSTOMER_NAME VARCHAR2(100),
    EMAIL         VARCHAR2(100),
    SIGNUP_DATE   DATE
);
COMMIT;

-- Perform bulk transformation using PL/SQL collections, BULK
↪  COLLECT and FORALL
DECLARE
    TYPE t_raw_data IS TABLE OF RAW_CUSTOMER_DATA%ROWTYPE;
    raw_data t_raw_data;
BEGIN
    -- Extract data from the staging table into a PL/SQL collection
    SELECT * BULK COLLECT INTO raw_data FROM STG_CUSTOMER_DATA;

    -- Execute transformation and insert cleansed data into
    ↪  TRANSFORMED_CUSTOMER_DATA
    FORALL i IN INDICES OF raw_data
        INSERT INTO TRANSFORMED_CUSTOMER_DATA (
            CUSTOMER_ID,
            CUSTOMER_NAME,
            EMAIL,
            SIGNUP_DATE
        )
        VALUES (
            raw_data(i).CUSTOMER_ID,
            transform_customer(
                raw_data(i).CUSTOMER_ID,
                raw_data(i).CUSTOMER_NAME,
                raw_data(i).EMAIL,
                raw_data(i).SIGNUP_DATE
            ),
            raw_data(i).EMAIL,
            raw_data(i).SIGNUP_DATE
        );

    COMMIT;
EXCEPTION
    WHEN OTHERS THEN
        ROLLBACK;
        RAISE;
END;
/

-----------------------------------------------------------------------
-- Step 4: Loading Phase L: Load the transformed data into the
↪  target table (D_target)
-----------------------------------------------------------------------
```

```
CREATE TABLE CUSTOMER_MASTER (
    CUSTOMER_ID   NUMBER PRIMARY KEY,
    CUSTOMER_NAME VARCHAR2(100),
    EMAIL         VARCHAR2(100),
    SIGNUP_DATE   DATE
);

-- Insert data from TRANSFORMED_CUSTOMER_DATA into CUSTOMER_MASTER
↪  with error handling
DECLARE
BEGIN
    INSERT INTO CUSTOMER_MASTER (CUSTOMER_ID, CUSTOMER_NAME, EMAIL,
    ↪  SIGNUP_DATE)
    SELECT CUSTOMER_ID, CUSTOMER_NAME, EMAIL, SIGNUP_DATE
      FROM TRANSFORMED_CUSTOMER_DATA;

    COMMIT;
EXCEPTION
    WHEN OTHERS THEN
        ROLLBACK;
        RAISE;
END;
/


----------------------------------------------------------------------
-- Additional Component: Performance Optimization Simulation
-- Here, we simulate the evaluation of a cost function C() used to
↪  gauge ETL performance.
----------------------------------------------------------------------


CREATE OR REPLACE PROCEDURE optimize_etl_performance IS
    v_current_cost NUMBER;
BEGIN
    -- A hypothetical cost function is simulated by counting total
    ↪  raw records
    SELECT COUNT(*)
      INTO v_current_cost
      FROM RAW_CUSTOMER_DATA;

    DBMS_OUTPUT.PUT_LINE('Current ETL process cost (simulated): ' ||
    ↪  v_current_cost);
    -- Real-world logic would adjust parameters to minimize C()
END optimize_etl_performance;
/


----------------------------------------------------------------------
-- Automation and Scheduling: Create a repetitive ETL job using
↪  DBMS_SCHEDULER
----------------------------------------------------------------------


BEGIN
    DBMS_SCHEDULER.CREATE_JOB (
```

```
    job_name       => 'ETL_CUSTOMER_JOB',
    job_type       => 'PLSQL_BLOCK',
    job_action     => 'BEGIN
                        -- This block would call procedures
                        ↪  for extraction, transformation,
                        ↪  and loading.
                        NULL; -- Placeholder for complete
                        ↪  ETL process call
                       END;',
    start_date      => SYSTIMESTAMP,
    repeat_interval => 'FREQ=MINUTELY; INTERVAL=10',
    enabled         => TRUE,
    comments        => 'Automated ETL job for customer data
    ↪  processing following (D) = L(T(E(D)))'
  );
END;
/
```

Multiple Choice Questions

1. Which of the following equations correctly represents the composite ETL process as described in the chapter?

   (a) $\mathcal{E}(D) = E(T(L(D)))$
   (b) $\mathcal{E}(D) = L(T(E(D)))$
   (c) $\mathcal{E}(D) = T(L(E(D)))$
   (d) $\mathcal{E}(D) = L(E(T(D)))$

2. In the context of PL/SQL-based ETL automation, what is the primary purpose of the automated data extraction phase?

   (a) To transform raw data into a refined format.
   (b) To retrieve and standardize data from diverse sources.
   (c) To load transformed data into the target repository.
   (d) To schedule the execution of ETL tasks.

3. Which PL/SQL components are chiefly utilized during the data transformation phase to ensure data quality and schema conformity?

   (a) Declarative SQL constructs
   (b) Conditional logic, iterative procedures, and built-in functions
   (c) Bulk insertion techniques

(d) External web service integrations

4. To optimize performance during high-volume data loading, PL/SQL leverages which of the following techniques?

   (a) Row-by-row cursor processing

   (b) Bulk processing techniques such as FORALL and array loops

   (c) Frequent COMMIT operations after each row insertion

   (d) Dynamic SQL for each individual record insertion

5. The orchestration of interdependent ETL tasks in PL/SQL is conceptually modeled as which of the following?

   (a) A relational database schema

   (b) A directed acyclic graph (DAG)

   (c) A cyclic dependency network

   (d) A hierarchical tree with redundant branches

6. Within an automated PL/SQL ETL pipeline, what is the primary role of integrated exception handling mechanisms?

   (a) To initiate bulk data load operations

   (b) To capture and manage errors, ensuring system reliability and transactional integrity

   (c) To schedule recurring execution of ETL jobs

   (d) To transform raw data into analytic formats

7. Minimizing the performance cost function $C(\theta)$ in automated ETL processes primarily aims to:

   (a) Maximize the number of transformation procedures applied

   (b) Reduce latency and I/O overhead while maintaining data integrity

   (c) Increase the frequency of data extraction routines

   (d) Expand the complexity of scheduling interdependencies

Answers:

1. **B:** $\mathcal{E}(D) = L(T(E(D)))$

   This representation correctly models the sequential nature of the ETL process, where data is first extracted (E), then transformed (T), and finally loaded (L) into the target system.

2. **B: To retrieve and standardize data from diverse sources**

   The extraction phase is focused on gathering data from various, often heterogeneous, origins and standardizing it for further processing in the transformation phase.

3. **B: Conditional logic, iterative procedures, and built-in functions**

   In PL/SQL, these programming constructs are essential for applying data cleansing, normalization, and other transformation operations to convert raw data into a refined dataset.

4. **B: Bulk processing techniques such as FORALL and array loops**

   For high-volume loading, PL/SQL utilizes bulk processing to minimize overhead and enhance performance by processing multiple records in batches rather than one at a time.

5. **B: A directed acyclic graph (DAG)**

   The orchestration of ETL tasks is modeled as a DAG to ensure that tasks are executed in a predetermined sequence, with dependencies that prevent cyclic execution and guarantee process integrity.

6. **B: To capture and manage errors, ensuring system reliability and transactional integrity**

   Exception handling within the ETL process detects anomalies, allows for transaction rollbacks if needed, and logs errors for analysis, all of which are critical for maintaining reliable, consistent data processing.

7. **B: Reduce latency and I/O overhead while maintaining data integrity**

   Performance optimization in automated ETL processes is driven by the need to handle large-scale data efficiently, which involves minimizing operational costs represented by the cost function $C(\theta)$, thereby ensuring faster processing without compromising data quality.

Chapter 33

Implementing Security and Access Control in PL/SQL Analytics

Foundations of Security in PL/SQL Environments

The design of secure PL/SQL analytic systems necessitates the rigorous application of principles that govern data confidentiality, integrity, and availability. The underlying architecture is informed by established models from computer security research, including concepts derived from the Bell-LaPadula and Biba models, which influence the delineation of privilege boundaries and the construction of audit mechanisms. Security in these environments is realized through the careful segregation of duties and the enforcement of the principle of least privilege. The mapping between user identities and corresponding access rights can be formalized as a function

$$\Phi : U \times R \to P,$$

where U represents the set of users, R denotes the roles assigned to these users, and P comprises the privileges attributed to each role. This formalism underpins a defense-in-depth strategy that systematically minimizes the risk of unauthorized data access and preserves the integrity of analytical operations.

Authentication Strategies in PL/SQL Analytics

Authentication constitutes the primary barrier against unauthorized access and is critical in ensuring that only legitimate entities may initiate operations on sensitive analytic resources. The process involves verifying the identity of users through mechanisms that may include password validation, token-based methods, and integration with external identity providers. A robust authentication scheme is conceptually analogous to a function that rigorously validates input credentials against a secure repository of known identities, thereby establishing a trusted communication channel with minimal latency. Multi-factor authentication, which corroborates user identity through a combination of something known, something possessed, and optionally a biometric factor, further strengthens the security posture. The systematic implementation of these authentication protocols is essential in preserving the integrity of subsequent authorization and access control measures.

Authorization Techniques and Role-Based Access Control

Following authentication, the assignment of privileges according to well-defined authorization protocols ensures that users operate exclusively within the bounds of their designated roles. The role-based access control (RBAC) paradigm abstracts privilege management by associating users with roles that encapsulate specific access rights. This association is captured by the assignment function

$$\alpha : U \to 2^R,$$

which maps each user to an appropriate subset of roles, while the permission function

$$\beta : R \to 2^P$$

assigns the privileges P corresponding to each role. This structured approach mitigates the risks of unauthorized privilege escalation and enforces the policy of least privilege. The incorporation of discretionary and mandatory access control mechanisms further refines the granularity of access restrictions. Schema-level controls, such as the definition of secure views and row-level security policies, play a crucial role in preventing unauthorized data exposure, thereby ensuring that analytic queries operate solely on data for which access has been explicitly granted.

Implementing Access Control for Sensitive Analytical Resources

Sensitive analytical resources demand a layered access control framework that blends static policies with dynamic, context-aware enforcement mechanisms. The protection of data objects is achieved via stringent schema isolation, logical partitioning of data, and the adoption of secure naming conventions that limit inadvertent exposure. Access control in these environments is reinforced by continuous auditing and monitoring methods that detect anomalies and flag unauthorized access attempts. The orchestration of access permissions is embedded in security policies that govern both user interactions and procedural routines, ensuring that only authenticated and duly authorized actors are permitted to execute analytical operations. The integration of security controls into the data access layer provides an additional barrier against both internal and external threats, thereby safeguarding critical datasets and maintaining overall system resilience.

Integration of Security Measures in PL/SQL Code

Embedding security within the procedural logic of PL/SQL necessitates a modular design where authentication, authorization, and audit logging become intrinsic components of the analytic workflow. The integration process mandates that security considerations are addressed at the early stages of system design, ensuring that every stored procedure, view, and trigger is constructed with security as a foundational element. A disciplined implementation strategy involves the segregation of security-critical operations from routine data manipulation tasks, thereby preserving clarity and maintainability in codebases. This modular framework supports the independent evolution of security policies and facilitates systematic enforcement of access controls through clearly defined interfaces. The use of centralized error handling and audit logging further enhances the system's capability to detect, report, and mitigate security incidents in real time.

Challenges and Considerations in Securing Data and Code

The implementation of robust security and access control measures in PL/SQL analytics presents a number of technical challenges that require careful consideration. One of the primary issues is the trade-off between deep security integration and the performance requirements of large-scale data analysis. Security measures, such as fine-grained access controls and real-time audit logging, can introduce additional computational overhead that must be managed to avoid degrading system performance. Furthermore, the dynamic nature of security threats necessitates an adaptable framework that can respond to emerging vulnerabilities and continuously evolving attack vectors. Periodic security audits and performance benchmarking are imperative to ensure that both data and code maintain their integrity without incurring prohibitive latency. Decisions regarding encryption protocols, key management systems, and the deployment of security policies must be informed by both theoretical analyses and empirical evaluations, thereby ensuring that the system remains resilient in the face of sophisticated threat landscapes.

Oracle 19c SQL Code Snippet

```
-- This code snippet demonstrates key security mappings and access
↪   control mechanisms
-- in a PL/SQL analytics environment based on Oracle 19c.
--
-- Important theoretical formulations used in this example:
--    The user-role-privilege function:  : U × R → P
--    The assignment function (User to Roles):  : U → 2^R
--    The permission function (Role to Privileges):  : R → 2^P
--
-- Step 1: Create tables for users, roles, and privileges

CREATE TABLE SEC_USERS (
    USER_ID        NUMBER GENERATED BY DEFAULT AS IDENTITY,
    USERNAME       VARCHAR2(50) UNIQUE,
    USER_PASSWORD  VARCHAR2(100),
    CONSTRAINT SEC_USERS_PK PRIMARY KEY (USER_ID)
```

```sql
);

CREATE TABLE SEC_ROLES (
    ROLE_ID   NUMBER GENERATED BY DEFAULT AS IDENTITY,
    ROLE_NAME VARCHAR2(50) UNIQUE,
    CONSTRAINT SEC_ROLES_PK PRIMARY KEY (ROLE_ID)
);

CREATE TABLE SEC_PRIVILEGES (
    PRIV_ID         NUMBER GENERATED BY DEFAULT AS IDENTITY,
    PRIVILEGE_NAME  VARCHAR2(50) UNIQUE,
    CONSTRAINT SEC_PRIVILEGES_PK PRIMARY KEY (PRIV_ID)
);

-- Step 2: Create mapping tables representing the functions  and
-- Mapping function:  (User to Roles)
CREATE TABLE USER_ROLES (
    USER_ID NUMBER,
    ROLE_ID NUMBER,
    CONSTRAINT USER_ROLES_FK_USER FOREIGN KEY (USER_ID) REFERENCES
    ↪  SEC_USERS(USER_ID),
    CONSTRAINT USER_ROLES_FK_ROLE FOREIGN KEY (ROLE_ID) REFERENCES
    ↪  SEC_ROLES(ROLE_ID)
);

-- Mapping function:  (Role to Privileges)
CREATE TABLE ROLE_PRIVILEGES (
    ROLE_ID NUMBER,
    PRIV_ID NUMBER,
    CONSTRAINT ROLE_PRIVILEGES_FK_ROLE FOREIGN KEY (ROLE_ID)
    ↪  REFERENCES SEC_ROLES(ROLE_ID),
    CONSTRAINT ROLE_PRIVILEGES_FK_PRIV FOREIGN KEY (PRIV_ID)
    ↪  REFERENCES SEC_PRIVILEGES(PRIV_ID)
);

-- Step 3: Insert sample data for users, roles, and privileges

-- Insert sample users into SEC_USERS
INSERT INTO SEC_USERS (USERNAME, USER_PASSWORD) VALUES ('alice',
↪  'password_alice');
INSERT INTO SEC_USERS (USERNAME, USER_PASSWORD) VALUES ('bob',
↪  'password_bob');
COMMIT;

-- Insert sample roles into SEC_ROLES
INSERT INTO SEC_ROLES (ROLE_NAME) VALUES ('ROLE_ANALYST');
INSERT INTO SEC_ROLES (ROLE_NAME) VALUES ('ROLE_ADMIN');
COMMIT;

-- Insert sample privileges into SEC_PRIVILEGES
INSERT INTO SEC_PRIVILEGES (PRIVILEGE_NAME) VALUES ('READ_DATA');
INSERT INTO SEC_PRIVILEGES (PRIVILEGE_NAME) VALUES ('WRITE_DATA');
```

```sql
INSERT INTO SEC_PRIVILEGES (PRIVILEGE_NAME) VALUES
↪  ('SECURITY_AUDIT');
COMMIT;

-- Step 4: Map users to roles (function : U → 2^R)
-- For instance:
--   ('alice') → { ROLE_ANALYST }
--   ('bob')   → { ROLE_ADMIN }
INSERT INTO USER_ROLES (USER_ID, ROLE_ID)
SELECT USER_ID, (SELECT ROLE_ID FROM SEC_ROLES WHERE ROLE_NAME =
↪  'ROLE_ANALYST')
FROM SEC_USERS
WHERE USERNAME = 'alice';

INSERT INTO USER_ROLES (USER_ID, ROLE_ID)
SELECT USER_ID, (SELECT ROLE_ID FROM SEC_ROLES WHERE ROLE_NAME =
↪  'ROLE_ADMIN')
FROM SEC_USERS
WHERE USERNAME = 'bob';
COMMIT;

-- Step 5: Map roles to privileges (function : R → 2^P)
-- For example:
--   ('ROLE_ANALYST') → { READ_DATA }
--   ('ROLE_ADMIN')   → { READ_DATA, WRITE_DATA, SECURITY_AUDIT }
INSERT INTO ROLE_PRIVILEGES (ROLE_ID, PRIV_ID)
SELECT (SELECT ROLE_ID FROM SEC_ROLES WHERE ROLE_NAME =
↪  'ROLE_ANALYST'),
       (SELECT PRIV_ID FROM SEC_PRIVILEGES WHERE PRIVILEGE_NAME =
       ↪  'READ_DATA')
FROM DUAL;

INSERT INTO ROLE_PRIVILEGES (ROLE_ID, PRIV_ID)
SELECT (SELECT ROLE_ID FROM SEC_ROLES WHERE ROLE_NAME =
↪  'ROLE_ADMIN'),
       (SELECT PRIV_ID FROM SEC_PRIVILEGES WHERE PRIVILEGE_NAME =
       ↪  'READ_DATA')
FROM DUAL;

INSERT INTO ROLE_PRIVILEGES (ROLE_ID, PRIV_ID)
SELECT (SELECT ROLE_ID FROM SEC_ROLES WHERE ROLE_NAME =
↪  'ROLE_ADMIN'),
       (SELECT PRIV_ID FROM SEC_PRIVILEGES WHERE PRIVILEGE_NAME =
       ↪  'WRITE_DATA')
FROM DUAL;

INSERT INTO ROLE_PRIVILEGES (ROLE_ID, PRIV_ID)
SELECT (SELECT ROLE_ID FROM SEC_ROLES WHERE ROLE_NAME =
↪  'ROLE_ADMIN'),
       (SELECT PRIV_ID FROM SEC_PRIVILEGES WHERE PRIVILEGE_NAME =
       ↪  'SECURITY_AUDIT')
FROM DUAL;
COMMIT;
```

319

```
-- Step 6: Create a procedure to verify if a user possesses a given
↪    privilege.
-- This procedure encapsulates dynamic security checking by joining
↪    the user-role
-- and role-privilege mappings, in line with the theoretical mapping
↪    : U × R → P.
CREATE OR REPLACE PROCEDURE check_user_privilege (
    p_username  IN SEC_USERS.USERNAME%TYPE,
    p_privilege IN SEC_PRIVILEGES.PRIVILEGE_NAME%TYPE
) IS
    v_count NUMBER;
BEGIN
    SELECT COUNT(*)
      INTO v_count
      FROM SEC_USERS U
      JOIN USER_ROLES UR ON U.USER_ID = UR.USER_ID
      JOIN SEC_ROLES R ON UR.ROLE_ID = R.ROLE_ID
      JOIN ROLE_PRIVILEGES RP ON R.ROLE_ID = RP.ROLE_ID
      JOIN SEC_PRIVILEGES P ON RP.PRIV_ID = P.PRIV_ID
     WHERE U.USERNAME = p_username
       AND P.PRIVILEGE_NAME = p_privilege;

    IF v_count > 0 THEN
        DBMS_OUTPUT.PUT_LINE('User "' || p_username ||
                             '" has the privilege "' || p_privilege
                             ↪ || '".');
    ELSE
        DBMS_OUTPUT.PUT_LINE('User "' || p_username ||
                             '" does NOT have the privilege "' ||
                             ↪ p_privilege || '".');
    END IF;
EXCEPTION
    WHEN OTHERS THEN
        DBMS_OUTPUT.PUT_LINE('Error in check_user_privilege: ' ||
        ↪ SQLERRM);
END check_user_privilege;
/

-- Step 7: Test the security check procedure
BEGIN
    -- Evaluate if 'alice' has privilege 'READ_DATA'
    check_user_privilege('alice', 'READ_DATA');

    -- Evaluate if 'bob' has privilege 'WRITE_DATA'
    check_user_privilege('bob', 'WRITE_DATA');
END;
/
```

Multiple Choice Questions

1. Which of the following functions correctly formalizes the mapping between users, roles, and privileges in a secure PL/SQL analytic system?

   (a) $\Phi : U \to R \times P$

   (b) $\Phi : U \times R \to P$

   (c) $\Phi : P \times U \to R$

   (d) $\Phi : R \to U \times P$

2. Which of the following best describes the multi-factor authentication method outlined in the chapter?

   (a) Utilizing a single password for user verification.

   (b) Combining factors such as something known, something possessed, and optionally a biometric factor.

   (c) Relying solely on token-based authentication.

   (d) Authenticating users based exclusively on their IP addresses.

3. Within the Role-Based Access Control (RBAC) paradigm presented, the function $\alpha : U \to 2^R$ is primarily used to:

   (a) Map users to their assigned roles.

   (b) Directly assign privileges to individual users.

   (c) Map roles to their corresponding privileges.

   (d) Determine the security classification for each analytic resource.

4. What does the principle of least privilege entail in the context of PL/SQL analytics?

   (a) Granting full access rights to all users by default.

   (b) Allowing users to autonomously modify their own privileges.

   (c) Restricting access strictly to the minimal set necessary for a user's designated role.

   (d) Automatically escalating privileges according to system load.

5. Which of the following practices is recommended for integrating security measures into PL/SQL code, as discussed in the chapter?

(a) Embedding security logic within every SQL statement without any modular separation.

(b) Segregating security-critical operations from routine data manipulation tasks, supplemented by centralized error handling and audit logging.

(c) Hardcoding user credentials and access rules within stored procedures.

(d) Disabling audit logging to maximize performance.

6. One of the primary challenges in implementing robust security in PL/SQL analytic systems is:

(a) Achieving deep security integration with zero performance overhead.

(b) Balancing the robustness of security measures with the high-performance requirements of large-scale data processing.

(c) Relying solely on static security policies with no dynamic adjustments.

(d) Eliminating the need for periodic security audits through comprehensive initial setup.

7. To effectively detect and respond to unauthorized data access in PL/SQL analytic environments, the chapter emphasizes:

(a) Deploying exclusively static access control policies.

(b) Continuous auditing and monitoring of user activities and system events.

(c) Relying solely on encryption mechanisms without additional oversight.

(d) Conducting infrequent manual reviews of access logs.

Answers:

1. **B:** $\Phi : U \times R \to P$
This function maps a combination of a user and a role to a set of privileges, aligning with the formalism presented for establishing security boundaries in PL/SQL analytic systems.

2. **B: Combining factors such as something known, something possessed, and optionally a biometric factor.**
Multi-factor authentication enhances security by requiring multiple, independent forms of verification, which significantly reduces the risk of unauthorized access.

3. **A: Map users to their assigned roles.**
The function $\alpha : U \to 2^R$ is used to assign to each user the appropriate subset of roles, a fundamental step in implementing Role-Based Access Control (RBAC).

4. **C: Restricting access strictly to the minimal set necessary for a user's designated role.**
The principle of least privilege ensures that users possess only those rights essential for their tasks, thereby limiting the risk of unnecessary exposure or misuse of privileges.

5. **B: Segregating security-critical operations from routine data manipulation tasks, supplemented by centralized error handling and audit logging.**
A modular integration of security measures, with clearly separated components for auditing and error handling, is recommended to maintain clarity, manageability, and robust defense mechanisms within the PL/SQL code.

6. **B: Balancing the robustness of security measures with the high-performance requirements of large-scale data processing.**
Deep security integration can introduce performance overhead. Therefore, the key challenge is to ensure that enhanced security does not unduly degrade the performance of large-scale analytic operations.

7. **B: Continuous auditing and monitoring of user activities and system events.**
Continuous auditing enables real-time detection and response to potential security breaches, ensuring that unauthorized access is promptly identified and mitigated.

www.ingramcontent.com/pod-product-compliance
Lightning Source LLC
LaVergne TN
LVHW022334060326
832902LV00022B/4037